THE AUTHOR

LEWIS B. MAYHEW is professor of education at Stanford University, and he also serves as director of institutional research for Stephens College. Mayhew is one of the leading spokesmen on American higher education, and his books and numerous articles are well known. His prominence in the field was recognized by his election as president of the American Association for Higher Education for 1967-1968.

Mayhew was awarded the Ph.D. in history in 1952 from Michigan State University.

COLLEGES
TODAY
AND
TOMORROW

COLLEGES
TODAY
AND
TOMORROW

Lewis B. Mayhew

COLLEGES TODAY AND TOMORROW

 Jossey-Bass Inc., Publishers

615 Montgomery Street • San Francisco • 1969

COLLEGES TODAY AND TOMORROW
by Lewis B. Mayhew

Copyright © 1969 by Jossey-Bass, Inc., Publishers

Copyright under Pan American and Universal
Copyright Conventions

Jossey-Bass, Inc., Publishers
615 Montgomery Street
San Francisco, California 94111

Library of Congress Catalog Card Number 74-75939

Standard Book Number SBN 87589-037-7

Manufactured in the United States of America
    Composed and printed by York Composition Company, Inc.
    Bound by Chas. H. Bohn & Co., Inc.
    Jacket design by Willi Baum, San Francisco

FIRST EDITION

Code 6907

THE JOSSEY-BASS SERIES IN HIGHER EDUCATION

General Editors

JOSEPH AXELROD *and* MERVIN B. FREEDMAN

San Francisco State College

Preface

‌

*C*olleges Today and *Tomorrow* is a result of some concentrated effort over the past decade to understand and interpret the evolution of American higher education into the critical institution that it is in today's rapidly changing society. This effort is based on the notion that American society has experienced since World War II a series of the most profound revolutions ever to visit mankind: the revolt of colonial peoples, the revolution in weaponry, the explosion of knowledge, the urbanization and technocratization of the society, and undreamed-of affluence. These sudden changes are continuing challenges to which the society must respond if it is to remain viable.

In some respects higher education has proven itself to be highly adaptable and has solved, at least for a time, some problems which at one time could justifiably have been regarded as insurmountable. It has accommodated large numbers of students, learned to live with the

federal government, produced effective professionals, and become more rigorous as demanded by the times. But failures have been marked as well and unless it can rectify these, its very promise may in the end prove false. Higher education has not been responsive to the just demands and needs of many minority group members. The academic revolution has resulted in higher education's becoming central to the life of the society; but higher education has not been responsive to undergraduate students, and the magnitude of its failure is reflected in the violence of student protests. It has been unable, in spite of highly visible imperatives, to address itself to the problems of an urban society in the effective way that nineteenth-century higher education contributed to agricultural and engineering sciences.

Many facets of higher education could be used to show the nature and magnitude of the challenges that face it, but none more effectively than relationships of students to their colleges. It is in these relationships that curricular failures are most accurately perceived. It is from the demands of post-Baccalaureate students that professional education has been forced to reform itself. It is in the sharp difference between student expectations and faculty expectations concerning relevance that the dilemma of the academy is etched most vividly. Hence these have been given a somewhat more extended treatment than, say, problems directly involving faculty interests. And it is in terms of the impact or lack of impact on students that the curriculum is viewed.

The full implications of these relationships will be realized only in an emerging future, and with considerable risk. Some attempt is made in this book to predict how things will be at least until 1980. These predictions are extrapolations from existing tendencies. While many of them seem likely to come about, the discussion is far from deterministic. If higher education and the American people do not like the directions in which the enterprise is moving, there is still time to make the necessary changes. Some of the predictions may seem stark and pessimistic; however, the ideas of the entire book are expressed in the faith that although man may not be perfectible, he nevertheless is improvable for an almost infinite distance.

Many persons have contributed in one way or another to the preparation of this book. The many institutions that have played host to me so that I could study them, the associations and organizations that have allowed me the chance to look broadly into the subject, and the colleagues all over the world who provided me with letters, reports, memoranda, and books about higher education all have helped. But especial obligation goes to three: Mrs. Evelyn S. Tahl, my secretary, who needled me into putting the book in shape; Joseph Axelrod, who helped edit the initial draft and encouraged me to finish the task; and above all my wife, Dorothy C. Mayhew. All have earned my gratitude. I hope the results are even in part worthy of their efforts. But an especial word should be said about my publisher. The Jossey-Bass Series in Higher Education is one of a very few efforts at making public significant research in an increasingly critical area of American society. The books in this series brighten a sometimes too bleak landscape. I take pride in knowing that this effort of mine is included in that growing list of important works.

LEWIS B. MAYHEW

Stanford, California
February 1969

Contents

xiii

COLLEGES TODAY AND TOMORROW

PART ONE

The Social Context

CHAPTER 1

In the Public Service

American higher education shares with higher education in the Western world a concern for several functions or purposes. It is a means by which people are screened and some are allowed to enter the higher prestige vocations and professions. Early New England colleges served as the device for filling ministerial and legal positions. Land-grant colleges permitted bright students of limited means to move from rural or small town life into the more prestigeful life of teacher, railroad official, engineer, doctor, or county agricultural agent. One theorist, Robert Havighurst, in commenting on the influx of students to college following World War II, predicted that the demand for collegiate education would soon decrease as the higher-level positions became filled. Clarence B. Randall, after a lifetime of selecting men for managerial positions in one of the largest steel companies, could remark, ". . . I would choose my candidates not because of what they knew, but rather because of their proven capacity to learn." The same point was made by an Eastern industrialist who recruited liberal arts graduates for his corporation—not that the liberal arts had intrinsic virtue or value for Wall Street, but that passing such courses was proof of persistence and self-discipline, which would make the applicant a good employment risk. Now the content that colleges teach has varied with changing styles and theories—one period emphasizes the liberal arts and sciences while another period stresses specialized courses in engineering, business, or journalism. The substance of what students study is of some importance. But the sheer variety of substantive means that are adopted for the same higher vocational ends suggests that the process of higher education must be perceived, in one essential dimension, as a rite.

Secondly, higher education has a custodial function. It is a means by which people in certain age or class groups are kept somewhat occupied until they can be assimilated by the labor force or retirement. A New England farmer, presumed to value education highly because he sent his son to college, remarked, "No, I don't see much value in education—I just don't like to have a boy that age around the house." Some may judge this custodial function to be an evil—necessary perhaps—but still an evil. Robert M. Hutchins, in presenting his utopian scheme for education, recognizes that America may require a custodial system; but if it does, it should so label that system and not confuse it with education. But others view the custodial role as one of the essential services. Higher education throughout the world has expanded since the 1940's. Those regions that underwent the greatest increase of interest in higher education were the ones that expanded most their capacity in secondary education; they produced a large number of individuals who had to move *some* place. College seemed appropriate, especially during periods when the labor force was relatively static. Currently in the United States, the interest in expanding higher education, especially in the form of junior colleges, correlates positively with a significant unemployment problem particularly among the eighteen- to twenty-one-year-old age group.

Aside from its screening and custodial functions, higher education is an archival institution. It has come to be a depository in which the collective memory of the race is preserved for future generations. The undergraduate curriculum is one means of preserving and transmitting knowledge. Regardless of whether an institution creates new general education courses, experiments with contemporary problems courses, or offers an array of traditional disciplinary courses, the same key elements of knowledge and the same transcendent ideas are identifiable.

But colleges do more. Libraries—which, if one were to judge them by actual use, could scarcely be justified—are regarded as the heart of the collegiate campus. And rightly so, for libraries preserve an important part of the collective wisdom. Museums and art galleries similarly are sanctioned not for essential educational purposes, but for their function as cultural depositories. College professors are traditionally relatively conservative in their educational ideas—especially as contrasted with college administrators. This phenomenon is most understandable as a manifestation of the university's archival function. Perhaps the majority of courses offered in a university are conservative or archival and the virtues of the past come to be personified in those who teach.

Higher education serves another purpose—one that is, in some respects, antithetical to its archival function. The American college or university is an agent for causing social change. What is not usually recognized is the connection between the university as change agent and the emphasis on research in the American university. Research did not become significant in American higher education until the nineteenth-century pressures of the industrial revolution made ordered change imperative. At that time, the American university, with its emphasis on research—so well exemplified by Chicago, Johns Hopkins, Michigan and Stanford—came into being. But the great crescendo of interest in research is a post-World-War-II event, sparked partly by military demands for changed techniques and partly by the needs of the by now almost self-perpetuating technology.

In 1958, the knowledge industry involved 136 billion dollars or 30 per cent of the national effort. This industry consists of research and development, education, printing, entertainment, information equipment, professional services, and communications. Of these, the fastest growing segment is research and development, which increased more than 90 per cent between 1954 and 1958, and almost as much between 1958 and 1963. The United States now spends some twenty billion dollars on research.[1] American universities are directly or indirectly involved in spending a large portion of that amount.

[1] Gilbert Burck, "Knowledge: The Biggest Growth Industry of Them All," *Fortune,* November 1964.

Lastly, higher education is a means by which people are helped to find meaning for their lives, or to develop a sense of personal identity. Within the United States, going to college has historically read "going *away* to college." It has been the traditional way for the young of a certain class to break away from home and become adults. Less advantaged young accomplished the same thing by exploiting a frontier. More recently, higher education has become a means of individual development. The amount of leisure time has increased, and consequently the role of work in an individual's self-realization has diminished. Education has permitted the individual to feel personally related to an important effort.

These, then, are the central purposes of higher education; under these headings fall many of the activities in which colleges and universities engage. But on American college campuses can be found considerable preoccupation with an enormous range of matters only indirectly or tangentially related to these central functions. American colleges and universities sponsor full colleges in other nations; they make their faculties available to government and industry; they provide contract services for the military; they offer lectures, concerts, and other cultural events to the general public, not to speak of athletic contests and the most visible of all public entertainments—big-time football. Further, they provide services for their alumni, solve practical problems experienced by farmers, aid in the renewal of blighted urban areas, and assist in the pre-college education of disadvantaged elements of the national population.

How American colleges and universities came to assume such a range of public services as a natural function and to pay for them as a legitimate use of institutional funds can be understood only by examining the intellectual tradition from which American higher education has evolved. Four strands seem paramount.

First among these strands is the religious impulse prominent in the formative years of the nation. Predominantly Protestant, this impulse taught the notion of self-improvement as central to human life. Such a conception was essential for membership in Calvin's elect. Highly valued were missionary activity as a means of carrying out God's will and stewardship, which implied improvement of property while one guarded it. Colonial clergy demanded a laity sophisticated enough to follow theological discussions; hence they urged secondary education and the creation of libraries to facilitate adult education.

A central concern of early Congregational and Presbyterian churches was evangelism, one form of which was the creation of religiously-oriented colleges on the American frontier and another, missionary activity in foreign regions. It probably is no accident that colleges that have undergone the longest development in non-Western studies stem directly from this missionary impulse. The founder of Mills College, for example, presided over a missionary school in Ceylon. Goucher College was named after the founder of another missionary school in India.[2] And from the Christian doctrine of an economy based on the sanctity of private property and the value of individual enterprise and profit emerged the notion that the rich were stewards of possessions to be used for the benefit of the needy.[3] The use of philanthropic dollars to support domestic and overseas educational efforts is a direct outgrowth of this concept. Andrew Carnegie and John D. Rockefeller shared a point of view that characterized our culture at that time; it is epitomized in Rockefeller's remark: "The good Lord gave me the money, and how could I withhold it from Chicago?"[4]

The second relevant strand is the democratic, or rather the egalitarian, ideal that runs through American history. Although tension has generally existed between the Hamiltonian aristocratic tendency and the Jeffersonian-Jacksonian faith in the people, the more democratic tendency has typically prevailed. Thus many landmarks in higher education exemplify a steady democratic evolution: the establishment of denominational colleges along the frontier, the creation of land-grant colleges for the agricultural and industrial classes, policy statements calling for larger numbers of high school youth to attend college, and the creation of community colleges to bring college close to where students live. The 1964 statement of the Educational Policies Commission has generally been accepted as the prevailing judgment when it urged virtual universal education through at least the fourteenth grade.[5]

The third of these principal traditions is more difficult to establish. American education, like American life, is pragmatic, practical,

---

[2] *Non-Western Studies in the Liberal Arts College* (Washington, D.C.: Association of American Colleges, 1964).

[3] Merle Curti, *The Growth of American Thought* (New York: Harper, 1943).

[4] *Ibid.,* p. 514.

[5] Educational Policies Commission, *Equal Educational Opportunity* (Washington, D.C.: National Education Association, 1964).

and applied. The earliest colleges were created to provide the leaders society needed. Land-grant colleges were needed to provide people to settle a continent-sized nation and to adapt the results of the industrial and scientific revolutions to the needs of an enormously expanding society. Research has been more preoccupied with application than with theoretical problems. Graduate school enrollments are largest in such professional and applied fields as education, physical sciences, and behavioral sciences; they are much smaller in mathematics, philosophy, religion, and the fine arts.[6] This pragmatism is even more pronounced for those who earn bachelor's degrees. Enrollment in education, business and commerce, engineering and social science far outstrips enrollment in other subjects.[7] And the principal educational philosopher the nation has produced emphasized pragmatism or instrumentalism. Although John Dewey is criticized from many quarters and by such diverse figures as Maxwell Rafferty and Robert Hutchins, his educational philosophy remains dominant.

Lastly, one must realize the strong element of nationalism and patriotic pride in the American ethos. Max Lerner remarks that "The People who came to the American shores felt intensely about the American experience because for each of them America was the wall broken down, door broken open."[8] Politically, of course, this nationalism is expressed in the two wars of revolution against England, the slogans of "Fifty-four forty or Fight," "Remember the Maine," and "Making the world safe for democracy." Intellectually, it is expressed in Emerson's views that we have "listened too long to the courtly muses of Europe. [The] confidence in the unsearched might of man belongs, by all motives, by all prophecy, by all preparation, to the American scholar." A similar feeling of pride is found in the desire of religious denominations to establish more and better colleges than the competing denominations. The creation of the University of Minnesota was accomplished in the hope and expectation that no Minnesota student would have to leave that state for an education. In the faith that American democracy has created ideas of supreme importance to other peoples, including the idea of America itself, colleges and universities have been willing sometimes even to weaken their own educational and re-

---

[6] OSIR, *A Fact Book on Higher Education* (Washington, D.C.: American Council on Education, 1960), p. 94.

[7] *Ibid.*, p. 92.

[8] Max Lerner, *America as a Civilization* (New York: Simon and Schuster, 1957).

search programs in order to expand their resources and activities off
the campus and outside the borders of the country. And they have
been willing to aid other agencies equally concerned with preserving
"Americanism."

There are obviously other factors in the American experience
that are also germane to the service efforts of American higher education. Guilt over slavery is undoubtedly somewhat involved in some
overseas efforts. Political capitalism plays its part in much that colleges
and universities attempt to do. And the ethnic and religious mixture
that is the American population has made off-campus enculturation
important. However, the four factors we have analyzed here—religious
Protestantism, the democratic ideal, pragmatism, and nationalism (or
perhaps better, ethnocentrism)—provide important keys to understanding why collegiate service to society has assumed such a variety of
forms.

The most obvious first example of the service-to-society orientation of American higher education is the land-grant college. Through
acts of Congress in 1862 and again in 1890, federal lands were granted
to the states to help support institutions that, without minimizing the
liberal arts and sciences, would provide agricultural and mechanical
training for the farming and working classes of the nation. These land-
grant institutions in their on-campus programs have sought, and generally successfully, "to adjust the relationship of the general and special, or liberal and technical, with the steadily increasing subject matter and rising standards in both realms."[9] But they have done more.
They have offered short courses for special groups of trainees such as
homemakers, farm managers, and mechanics. Through county agents
and home economics extension workers, they have helped improve
rural standards of living by sending these workers into local communities to deal directly with problems people faced. By providing military training to all young men who attended, the land-grant colleges
hoped to provide a nucleus of men with two years of military training,
who in event of war could become noncommissioned officers, and another nucleus of men with four years of instruction, who could become
the company grade and junior staff officers. In close collaboration with
United States Government Agricultural Experiment Stations, the land-

[9] Earle D. Ross, "Contributions of Land Grant Colleges and Universities
to Higher Education," in W. W. Brickman and S. Lehrer, *A Century of Higher
Education* (New York: Society for the Advancement of Education, 1962).

grant colleges have conducted research and disseminated results on methods of agronomy, animal husbandry, and methods of farm management. In addition, land-grant colleges have done some work in general extension projects; adult evening courses are offered wherever in the state people want them. The University of Wisconsin emphasizes that "the boundaries of the campus are the boundaries of the state" and puts this idea to practice through eight undergraduate campuses that double as adult education centers. At the University of California at Los Angeles over 10,000 adults are enrolled in evening courses ranging from liberal arts work to technical subjects needed by those in the electronics industry. Several institutions, in addition to providing off-campus adult education, have established centers for continuing education. Michigan State, Georgia, Nebraska, Minnesota, and Missouri all have created separate buildings in which courses are offered on virtually every subject the people in a complex society could want. Thus at Michigan State in a single week, courses will be offered for shop foremen, undertakers, insurance salesmen, hotel managers, secretaries, spot welders, and microbiologists.

With such a history of nonresidential service, it was natural that land-grant colleges led the nation in providing similar services to underdeveloped and newly emerging nations. It is but a logical extension of the land-grant idea that these American institutions have 26 per cent of all foreign students, 36 per cent of foreign faculty in the United States, 41 per cent of U. S. faculty serving abroad, 46 per cent of Agency for International Development contracts, and 70 per cent of AID contract funds.[10] Illustrative of this involvement in service abroad is the Michigan State University program which includes a Dean of International Programs, two agricultural colleges affiliated with the National University of Colombia, work in business administration at Brazilian universities, village aid programs in Pakistan, and a new university in Nigeria.

Possibly the twentieth-century expression of the nineteenth-century spirit which created land-grant colleges is the junior or community college. These institutions, which now number well over 700, seek to achieve several purposes. They provide as their normal, residential efforts the first two years of a four-year college program, technical-vocational education at a subprofessional level, and general education.

[10] Herman R. Allen, *Open Door to Learning* (Urbana: University of Illinois Press, 1963).

In addition, they offer adult evening courses and seek to serve as a cultural center for the community that supports them. Some idea of the magnitude of the adult evening program is illustrated by the fact that in California, which operates 10 per cent of all junior colleges, the typical evening enrollment is over twice the size of the typical day or residential enrollment. And the courses offered will range from beginning French, taken by adults about to go abroad, to recent real estate law, as well as printing, shorthand, flower arranging, computer science, and life drawing. The spirit of junior college adult evening work is expressed by one theorist who argued that the junior college should offer any subject for which there was sufficient public demand, a reasonably organized body of knowledge, and a qualified teacher.[11]

But junior colleges would attempt still more. As part of their community services, these institutions would like to make their faculties available as consultants and speakers for community problems. Some institutions provide radio and television programs, which range from straight music through public information to actual courses taught for credit. Many make their physical facilities, such as swimming pools, auditoriums, and classrooms, available to local groups of citizens at nominal or no cost. Others present a varied program of lectures, concerts, and dramatic events to which members of the community are invited.

In 1947, Harry Truman put before the country the idea of a different kind of service in his Point Four speech. In effect, this speech called upon the United States to employ part of its technical, scientific, and educational resources to aid nations and regions in need of such assistance. The Technical Cooperation Administration, which eventually became the Agency for International Development, thus came into existence and spawned a variety of attempts to render service. For one, American campuses welcomed an increasing number of foreign students each year. The 53,000 foreign students who each year enroll in American institutions arrive in this country singly or in groups. For example, from 1956 to 1958, Wayne State University conducted a special training program in public administration for Indonesian public officials. The University of Minnesota accepts a number of Koreans to work for advanced degrees in this country while at the same time it sends faculty members to assist the Seoul National University.

[11] James W. Thornton, Jr., *The Community Junior College* (New York: Wiley, 1960).

Another derivative, much larger in scope, has been the technical assistance project abroad, financed either by the federal government or by large philanthropic foundations and staffed by faculties from American universities. Thus, the University of California has helped modernize the Djakarta medical school and kept a team of ten American professors at Djakarta each year. The Spring Garden Institute of Philadelphia sent eight instructors to bolster Turkey's automotive repair and maintenance schools. North Carolina State sends research and teaching faculty to Peru to help broaden and improve the curriculum in textile engineering. And the University of California sent professors to teach teachers at the agricultural school in Chile; they even taught farmers directly. There is no doubt that American universities engage in more programs and send more professors abroad than universities of any other nation.[12] In 1962, for example, sixty-five American universities mounted, in thirty-seven countries, 107 projects, which embraced such fields as agriculture, engineering, business, education, labor affairs, medicine, public administration, home economics, community development, audio-visual and vocational industrial education.[13]

But American colleges and universities have not remained insensitive to the needs of their own society for service beyond the traditional ones of research and residential instruction. Adult education has come to represent a substantial portion of the effort of higher education. The land-grant colleges, of course, led in this development by offering service to the rural population through the Cooperative Extension Service. But other segments of the population now receive attention through, typically, a university extension division. By 1956, universities were offering twenty-one different kinds of programs, such as extension classes, correspondence courses, conferences, lecture series, traveling libraries, short courses, radio and television programs, community development programs, alumni programs, and publications for clubs, associations, and other special groups. These efforts have sought to focus on real life problems of adults and society rather than on theoretical or academic subjects. Universities have made a concerted effort to fit their programs to the psychological needs of adults rather than simply to offer adults material and methods contrived originally for late adolescent students. Further, during the past decade,

[12] Edward W. Weidner, *The World Role of Universities* (New York: McGraw-Hill, 1962).
[13] Allen, *op. cit.*

universities have begun to rethink the financial base upon which adult education programs rest. At one time, and still in perhaps the majority of situations, adult or extension programs were expected to be self-supporting—that is, through fees paid by consumers. Indeed a number of institutions expected the extension division to yield a profit. Gradually, however, extension work gained support from general institutional funds in the belief that tax-supported institutions owed service to adults as much as to undergraduate students. The proportion of extension programs receiving over 5 per cent of the total institutional budget rose from 35 per cent in 1930 to over 40 per cent during the 1950's.[14] Indicative of present practice: a counseling seminar of Michigan State, held in Grand Rapids, Michigan, to help technical workers decide whether or not to enter an extension program leading to a bachelor's degree in engineering; a summer seminar in the humanities offered by Stephens College for mature women; televised courses carrying college credit offered by Wright Junior College in Chicago; a short course involving the arts, held for shop foremen by Pennsylvania State University. Public institutions have carried the major burden of such service, but some private institutions have intensified adult education efforts, particularly when cooperation with a public university is possible. Earlham College, for example, a Quaker school, serves as the adult education center for Indiana University.

Of a completely different order of service to the society is the American university's involvement in the creative arts. For a long time creative or studio work was judged unacceptable as part of the curriculum of collegiate education.[15] That has changed, however, and with the change has come the belief that institutions of higher education ought properly to become a chief patron of the arts. Thus, universities appoint artists-in-residence—painters, musicians, writers, and dancers. They typically have no teaching responsibility but are brought to encourage excellence in the production of artistic statements. Some universities, notably the University of Wisconsin, have created centers for the performing arts in the hope that artistic impulses once initiated can spread to the farthest reaches of the state. In this regard some have seen the university as the salvation of serious drama in America

14 Malcolm S. Knowles, *The Adult Education Movement in the United States* (New York: Holt, 1962).
15 See Lawrence E. Dennis and Renate M. Jacob (Eds.), *The Arts in Higher Education* (San Francisco: Jossey-Bass, 1968).

because the traditional centers of drama, such as the Broadway stage, rely so heavily on investment capital and, consequently, on financial success. Harold Taylor represents the contemporary point of view:

> The institutions of education must make an effort to reach the aesthetic needs of the citizens without making the usual distinctions made by Europeans and by many others who are interested in the arts between culture for the masses and culture for the rest of us. It is not necessary to produce mass art and mass ideas merely because more and more people are interested. . . . The university is the exact place for the exploration of the new; and for the development of forms of art of the kind which can break down the distinctions of snobbery, along with the possibility of the inverse snobbery of the avant-garde.[16]

The American university sees an important role for itself not only in restoring the arts but in reconstructing important other parts of the society. The University of Chicago, Temple University, and the several institutions of higher education in Cleveland believe it quite appropriate to use institutional funds to renew major areas of urban deterioration. With foundation help, Negro universities in Nashville, Atlanta, and New Orleans are attempting to break the cycle of poor Negro motivation and poor achievement; they are working at altering parental ideas so that Negro children can be stimulated to see value in schooling. Universities are encouraging their students, sometimes for academic credit, but more often for sheer altruism, to tutor and to help disadvantaged youth overcome educational limitations.

Increasingly institutions of higher education see themselves as repositories for knowledge and talent that should properly be at the service of other institutions of society. Thus, universities offer courses for military personnel and during periods of national emergency provide the specialized training needed in the army or navy. Universities feel constrained to grant faculty members leaves of absence to consult with industry and the various levels of government. The influx of university professors to the federal government during the Kennedy administration was illustrative of a general tendency that has continued. Much of the research sponsored by the federal government is conducted by universities in further elaboration of the service ideal. Of course, contract research is supported financially by the government,

---

[16] Harold Taylor, "Art and the American Experience," *Arts and Society,* Fall–Winter 1962, 194.

but institutions make some outright contributions of space, staff arrangements, and administration as well. Overhead allowances are rarely sufficient. The social significance of this new image of higher education has of itself been well revealed in a statement of M. H. Trytten:

> More recently we have come to realize that the relationship between our supply of specially trained and qualified personnel and our welfare and security is a fundamental and primary one. We are living in an age in which the foundations of national power are shifting rapidly. Not long ago national power and prestige rested on such bases as colonial possessions, control of the seas, superior industrial and commercial strength, and great supplies of military manpower, suitably equipped with weaponry which again depended on industrial capacity. Many of these bases have now weakened or crumbled altogether. Most notably, colonial powers have seen their colonies disappear or become doubtful assets. Large scale military manpower resources are no longer a major or dominant factor. Air power has greatly modified the role of sea power.
>
> Perhaps the greatest change has been the emergence of intellectual matters as a basis of national strength. This finds its most immediate expression in the greatly enhanced role of education and research as prime factors in this context. It is not necessary at this juncture to emphasize the role of science and research in modern technological warfare of the conventional type. Nor indeed is it necessary to emphasize the role of these factors in the new dimension of space exploration. That there are other massive dimensions has recently been underscored by the report of the special committee on oceanography which sounded the need for a greatly expanded program of the study of the oceans. A similar sharp reminder of the need for more attention to the scientific investigation of our planet below the surface is, in the opinion of many, somewhat overdue.
>
> The general conclusion . . . is that we are living in an age when, because of the shifts of the bases of power, the whole power pattern of the world is in flux. When stability is achieved, as it will be some day, at least relatively, unquestionably the new pattern will have a basis of intellectual excellence.[17]

In addition to such assistance to society, American higher edu-

[17] M. H. Trytten, "Higher Education as an Instrument of National Policy," in *Current Issues in Higher Education 1959* (Washington, D.C.: American Association for Higher Education, 1959).

cation provides a range of services to its own students which are only indirectly related to the residential educational function. Health stations with attached psychiatric clinics, Placement Offices that care for graduates' employment needs until retirement, recreational facilities ranging from spectator activities such as football to stables of riding horses, and lending officers called "financial aids officers"—these are all relatively commonplace. And all draw support from institutional funds.

To show how these various activities fit into the American conception of higher education, imagine a hypothetical university of 10,-000 students located in midcontinent. It has a faculty of 600, which offers 1800 different courses mostly to undergraduate students. It offers evening courses in education, business, and engineering science in five centers scattered throughout the state, and twenty courses in the arts each night on the local campus. Twice a month it offers lectures or concerts open to the general public, which may also use its library by paying a modest fee. This university sends ten of its faculty each year to staff a South American business school and averages ten faculty each year on loan to state and federal government agencies. It has accepted $5,000,000 in research contracts; three-fourths of these are supported by the federal government while funds for the remaining fourth come from several of the large health foundations. It has a university press, which devotes most of its effort to printing research findings in agriculture, education, and engineering. To handle the problems of 500 foreign students, the university pays a director of foreign students who has offices in a newly built international building. The rare book collection of the library is regarded as one of the important cultural resources of the state. The president of the university serves on the state governor's biracial commission and on the advisory committee to the National Science Foundation. He spent eighteen months, on leave of absence from his campus, serving as an undersecretary of state.

Such is the service orientation of American higher education. But this effort is not without problems. First, there is the very real question of identity. Can an institution be a true university in the western European sense of the term and still offer such highly practical courses as cooking, key punch operating, or flower arranging? Will offering such practical courses prevent the proper focus on the abstract, the theoretical, the philosophical?

Related to the question of identity is the matter of finance. Should an institution that has limited resources spend money for an open circuit television station when it also needs a new science building? Should tuition money paid by students to a private university in Indiana be used in part to support research that will prove more useful to the peoples of India than to the people of Indiana?

Then, there is the matter of technique. The general extension division, the experimental station, the short course, and applied research were all well adapted to the problems of a rural, agricultural population. But the American nation is no longer rural. A serious question remains as to whether the university can devise techniques that are appropriate to an urban condition.

Finally, there is the matter of control. A strong service-to-society philosophy can set the stage for the disappearance of institutional autonomy. Yet the university is viable only if it can control its own destinies. This problem is most pronounced among public junior colleges which seek to serve the needs of their communities; and they find themselves subjected to rather severe community pressures regarding the substance of the curriculum and the content of lectures, of concerts, and even of collections of books in the library.

Generally, however, the American experience has suggested that these difficulties will be overcome and that the idea of higher education as a comprehensive servant of society will prevail.

CHAPTER 2

The City
and the University

Basic to a consideration of
the "town-gown" campus, or the relationship between the city and the
university, are two fundamental theses. The first is the increasing importance of urbanization. It is a fact that the United States of America has become an urban society and that the rapid urbanization is
certain to continue. The United States Bureau of the Census predicts
a population of 220 million by 1975. The Urban Land Institute of
Washington, D.C., predicts that by the year 2000, 85 per cent of the
country's 320 million people will be living in urban areas. Such
growth, it reports, would require a land area of 55,000 square miles
or seven times that of the state of New Jersey. It further predicts that
there will be ten super-cities containing one-third of our total population, with a 450-mile strip of continuous metropolitan flow from
Boston to Washington, containing a population of thirty-one million,
an industrial Riviera stretching from Gary, Indiana, around Chicago

and into Wisconsin, with a population of 8.5 million people, and a recreational and retirement belt stretching from Jacksonville to Miami containing three million. Two hundred and seventy-five million people living in our urban areas by the year 2000. This is indeed staggering.[1]

The second thesis is that an institution of higher education, like any social institution, is the creation of its supporting constituency, and is designed to accomplish socially desired ends. Although collegiate institutions may be mandated to criticize, lead, or instruct other segments of society, this mandate is, in a sense, a "delegated" responsibility, which may be withdrawn, circumscribed, or limited. But the university is not without an intrinsic dynamic, and it can engage in dialectic with representatives of the supporting society in establishing the perimeters of its function. Yet ultimately it is the supporting society that dictates what collegiate institutions generally must do, and it is the immediate constituency that determines the direction in which individual institutions shall move.

When collegiate institutions fail to respond to an expressed mandate, they tend to lose viability. The colonial college allowed its curriculum to solidify and its teaching to become arid at a time when the society was attempting to assimilate the fruits of the Industrial Revolution and to occupy and settle a continent. There was clearly a need for a scientific and applied education to provide the engineers, mechanics, and agriculturists the society demanded. When the existing institutions failed to respond, the society created a new kind of institution, the land-grant college. Gradually, private liberal colleges did modify themselves and disproved the prediction of President William R. Harper of the University of Chicago that such colleges would be extinct within fifty years after the end of the nineteenth century. At the end of World War II, the society reached a decision and expressed it through policy statements, such as that made by President Truman's Commission on Higher Education, that as many as 50 per cent of all high school graduates could profit from and should be provided formal education beyond the high school.[2] It is possible that existing institutions, especially private colleges, could have been expanded to meet this demand. What was done was that junior colleges were reoriented

[1] J. Martin Klotsche, *The Urban University and the Future of Our Cities* (New York: Harper, 1966).
[2] *Report of the President's Commission on Higher Education* (Washington, D.C.: U. S. Government Printing Office, 1947).

to offer not only transfer education but also technical vocational education, and the number of these institutions was increased. When the Soviet Union demonstrated its technological and scientific power by creating atomic weapons and launching rockets into space, the entire American society reacted with a demand for a new emphasis in higher education. Collegiate institutions apparently took this injunction seriously and for the last decade have stressed academic excellence, theoretical science, and mathematics to a degree never before attempted. In carrying out these new emphases, colleges and universities were aided by governmental subsidies, which were really an effort to help institutions to remain viable in the face of unforeseen requirements.

Putting these two theses together, then, we see institutions of higher education faced with an unprecedented set of needs and demands occasioned by the existence of an essentially urban America. These demands are legion; they include the need for training people to operate the emerging service and research industries, for educating the disadvantaged segments of the population which have drifted toward the inner city, for finding solutions through research on such vexing problems as transportation, air pollution, labor economics and urban ecology, and for teaching an urban population to use creatively ever-increasing amounts of leisure and to enrich the longer life that modern medicine has insured. The response of institutions of higher education to such demands have been mixed. There are notable examples of institutions not merely accepting but welcoming the imperatives of urbanization and adjusting to them. But with respect to the most vexing needs of an urban society, institutions of higher education have not been eminently responsive.

Most universities that can be considered as developing institutions—that is, those institutions that can expect to double or triple their enrollments during the next eight years—list urban studies as an important program into which they wish to invest resources. Administrators recognize in theory the existence of urban problems and the potential resources that an urban environment provides for educational use. Yet such programs have not been thoroughly planned, and for the most part are largely scissors-and-paste programs, consisting of bits and pieces of old curricular segments. These institutions seemingly are groping for ways by which the insights from the social and behavioral sciences can be combined with relevant parts of the natural sciences to focus on urban situations. But because the university has not been able to conceptualize the urban condition, it has done no research on the subject, and without cohesive research, the university can teach about the urban condition only at the descriptive level.

A second failure is the tendency to locate new institutions of higher education not in the inner city and closely related to other urban phenomena, but in the suburbs or semi-rural areas. It is almost as though those planning collegiate institutions are trying to recreate a stereotypic version of the colonial college; it was, understandably, located in an isolated rural situation, free from contact with the imagined temptations of cities. The creation of new college campuses in a suburban or semi-rural area undoubtedly has its charm, but it also cuts off from any real contact with the college important elements of the society which are intimately related to the inner city. Further, the bucolic tranquility of the isolated campus is unrealistic and misleading. The impetus for much of the creative life in the United States stems directly from the central city. The practice of medicine, for example, has made its most important contributions by having worked with a variety of health problems found in the central city. Much of the color of American life is found in the mixture of enterprises and ethnic groups found in our larger cities. It is this situation in which most college students will eventually live their lives, and one can argue that their education should prepare them more directly for what lies ahead.

An important aspect of decisions regarding the location of new campuses is the problem of bringing the services of American higher education to those populations that have, in the past, been most disadvantaged. The racial complexion of America's largest cities is shifting rapidly, and one can envision a time when the populations of San Francisco, Los Angeles, Chicago, Washington, New York, and Boston will be over 50 per cent nonwhite. Thus far, higher education has not successfully taken into consideration its responsibility to the nonwhite population. It is obvious that the location of new colleges is relevant here. For the Negro youth coming from a broken home that exists on an annual family income of $2,000 to $3,000, attending a college even four or five miles away from his home (and inadequately served by public transportation) becomes prohibitively expensive. For such a young person to be expected to own a car and to drive twenty or twenty-five miles along a toll road is completely unrealistic; yet one state university in Florida was created with just that expectation in mind. New state colleges being planned in California are also, according to present plans, to be located in suburban or semi-rural areas.

At the turn of the century, a number of developing American cities with considerable foresight created collegiate institutions within the city and supported them with municipal resources, and some of the Protestant denominations created universities specifically intended to serve municipal needs. Institutions such as Wayne, Cincinnati, Houston, Toledo, Boston University, Pittsburgh, and Louisville are illustrative of the type. These institutions quickly carved an important educational role for themselves within the city complex and stimulated a great deal of loyalty toward them on the part of the city dwellers. But as higher education became more and more expensive, municipalities and private donors reluctantly reached the conclusion that the institutions could no longer be maintained to serve primarily the needs of specific cities. Municipal institutions such as Houston, Wichita, Cincinnati, and Wayne have been absorbed by the state systems of higher education and reassigned missions consistent with the needs of the total state. Private institutions such as Pittsburgh and Temple have also been absorbed by state systems and reassigned educational tasks. Private institutions such as New York University and the University of Boston have found that they could no longer afford to serve their previous clientele, which generally came from the lower socioeconomic groups within the city, and have finally become more selective and appeal to a national clientele rather than a local one. This is not to argue, of course, that the needs of the nation or of a state should be neglected. The point is that institutions that once served the peculiar needs of an urban situation no longer find it possible to do so, and thus far no other educational institution has evolved to meet uniquely urban conditions and problems.

But the picture is not completely bleak. There have been some isolated examples of institutions of higher education truly relating to the urban situation and truly attempting to meet its problems. The University of Illinois, Chicago Circle Branch, is a distinguished effort. The University is located on a relatively small campus within five minutes of the Chicago Loop. Its buildings are vertical; the administration building, for example, is twenty-seven stories high. It is located at the confluence of the major traffic arteries for the city and, while it is intended to be a comprehensive university, it is clearly structuring its teaching and research efforts to meet the indigenous needs of Chicago. Thus the university will not compete with the Champaign-

Urbana campus by duplicating highly specialized, advanced courses
in certain of the natural sciences, but will stress the social and behavioral sciences, which have most relevance for urban conditions. Recognizing the important part that parks and recreational areas play in
Chicago's vitality, the University is developing its physical education
effort to provide park and recreational workers.

Among private universities, the University of Chicago has been
outstanding in recognizing its responsibility for the environs of the university. Over the past ten years, it has invested major university resources to help reestablish a balanced community surrounding the institution. The community had begun seriously to deteriorate and was
in process of becoming—in Kenneth Clark's term—"a dark ghetto."
The University, through judicious use of funds and through concerted
community action, seems to have been able to stem this tide; and for
several years now the community socioeconomic and racial composition
has been stabilized. Also in Chicago, the City College has resisted the
temptation to move its campuses out into the pleasant outlying areas
of the city and has resisted the temptation to expect or demand large
acreage. Rather, it has located its nine branches squarely in the centers
of populations it believed a city college ought to serve. One branch,
for example, was located in a renovated office building in which business activities and educational activities were allowed to function simultaneously. The Chicago City College also recognized that even
when it located campuses in population centers, it could not serve the
whole city. Hence it embarked on a major open-circuit educational
television effort which could bring degree-credit courses to people all
over the city. The only times a student would need to visit a campus
would be to matriculate and to take final examinations.

While Chicago seems to provide one of the best illustrations of
higher education sensing and meeting urban needs, it is by no means
the only city that is alert to the problem. Temple University and the
University of Pennsylvania, finding themselves with limited land and
surrounded by a rapidly deteriorating urban condition, were tempted
to move out of the city into more traditional collegiate environments.
However, the leadership elected to resist this temptation and instead
attempted to help renovate surrounding neighborhoods and to be of
immediate service to the people of Philadelphia.

In New York City, an even more intensive development has
taken place. Once the City University of New York was created and

provided with a reasonable source of state funds, it was able to develop a Master Plan of Higher Education for the City of New York which envisioned 100 per cent opportunity for all youth of the city by 1975. It anticipates accommodating 20 per cent of all high school graduates in the senior colleges and 40 per cent in community colleges. And it plans to provide specific needs for the culturally disadvantaged; it proposes accommodating 10 per cent in college discovery programs and 25 per cent in educational skills centers.

The University of Missouri at Kansas City struggled for years to be a privately supported institution serving the Kansas City area. When private resources proved insufficient, it became affiliated with the University of Missouri, but maintained for itself a primary mission of serving Kansas City. It developed a unique system of governance by which certain patterns of policy would be established by the University of Missouri Board of Curators, but certain matters of long-range planning and emphasis would be decided by the old Board of Trustees, which still maintained its corporate charter. The plans for this university call for major development in the life and health sciences, partly in order to exploit the existence of a large science library and the immediate availability of a number of outstanding hospitals.

A few distinguished private universities not lodged in an urban area have accepted social responsibility to contribute to the problems of an urban civilization. Princeton University is a good case in point. It has created the Woodrow Wilson School of Public Service and International Affairs, which attempts to train people to the master's level in problems of public policy, most of which involve urban problems. The University has also expanded its effort in architecture and has established a School of Architecture and Environmental Design, having as one of its emphases the training of people to make sense out of the urban condition from the point of view of architectural design. Most thesis work, for example, now focuses on urban problems. These two schools, with complete university backing, are attempting to create an interdisciplinary center for urban studies, which will bring policy and design into juxtaposition.

Cities have occasionally assumed a responsibility for new educational ventures in spite of objections on the part of the other state institutions. For example, the citizens of Mobile, Alabama, exerted sufficient pressure on the legislature so that the University of South Alabama was established. Then, to insure that the university began immediately to serve a region in which there had never been a tax-supported institution, the citizens of Mobile donated a tract of approximately 600 acres and the funds with which to build the first building. The University, for its part, is tailoring its curriculum, particularly in the professional areas, to meet the expressed demands of the Mobile region. Thus, while the tendency in more established universities is for engineering education increasingly to be confined to the upper or graduate level, the University of South Alabama proposes to stress undergraduate engineering, for that is what industry in the Mobile area feels it needs.

These isolated examples are heartening, but they are unfortunately still too isolated. If higher education in America is, as a total enterprise, to cope with urban conditions, it must shed itself of a number of vestiges of its colonial and agrarian past. Universities in Europe, from the founding of the University of Paris on to the evolution of German universities as the key cultural institutions of the nineteenth century, were urban institutions closely meshed with city environment and interacting with the many forces and counterforces found in the city. The American version of higher education, however, did not pattern itself after continental models. Rather, early colonial colleges sought to model themselves after the undergraduate colleges of Oxford and Cambridge, somewhat modified in view of frontier conditions and a very real Protestant fear of the evils and temptations of the city. Thus, American institutions, both along the Eastern seaboard during the colonial period on into the trans-Allegheny region after the United States became a nation, were located in small villages, hamlets, and out-of-the-way places. Even as cities developed and it was possible for institutions to be located in them, the majority of Protestant colleges, as well as a number of the state institutions, selected rural regions. There clearly was the fear that if colleges were located in cities, young people would succumb to the temptations of city life. This is nothing more than the educational manifestation of the agrarian myth which is so strong in American life—country life is good and healthy, city life is evil; country folk are honest, the city slicker not so. Thus, American institutions of higher education developed their characteristic forms and processes under agrarian and small-town conditions.

Part of the overall problem that colleges and universities currently face stems from an attempt to use techniques developed in a rural context to meet the problems of an urban situation. Consider, for instance, these points: The ideal colonial college was a walled quadrangle isolated from the rest of the world. Frequently it was placed on a hill making the college even more difficult for outsiders to enter. Walls and gates helped keep students in and threatening ideas and forces out. Now, as colleges have been overrun by cities, or as new colleges are created close to cities, in this older colonial form, the very "armed camp" concept has served to deny the college the benefits of the contrasting ideas and intellectual currents found in an urban culture. The point can be made by considering what life just outside a college wall is really like. Jane Jacobs, in her *Death and Life of Great American Cities*,[3] remarks that one of the most dangerous places in New York City is in the region just outside the walls of Barnard College. The dead space between the wall of the college and the region where normal city life again takes over, not subject to the constant eyes of the city, becomes a field of maneuver for delinquent and dangerous elements of the city. The deterioration that has taken place outside the walls of Columbia University or the University of Chicago is another illustration of the heritage of campus isolation from the world around it. This phenomenon has led to some speculation that the urban campus should be so designed as to penetrate the city rather than to hold the city at a distance. The University of Paris has for centuries been a dynamic element in a rich cultural life, yet it occupies no single space. Rather, its buildings, the places where students live, intermingle with other elements of the city. New York University, particularly its Washington Square campus, has always seemed an important part of its neighborhood, partly because it penetrates, through its various facilities, the rest of the life of that part of Manhattan Island.

Another vestige from the agrarian past is the academic calendar, which reflects the importance that rural society placed on the seasons. Another strong tradition that no longer fits contemporary conditions is the notion that going to college means going *away* to college. Actually, well over half of all American college students attend college as commuters from urban areas. Yet so powerful is the tradition of going *away* to college that parents and children are apologetic if they select a nearby institution. Going away to college does, of course, meet important psychological needs of late adolescents who are

[3] Jane Jacobs, *Death and Life of Great American Cities* (New York: Random House, 1961).

striving to break away, physically and psychologically, from parental influence. The residential college, by isolating students from other influences, can bring to bear a number of forces that accomplish this shift. The urban institution serving a commuting population has a similar responsibility, but it must devise new techniques to achieve this purpose.

American colleges and universities have historically assumed a custodial role regarding students. After all, students in the past came away from home and were physically under the jurisdiction of the college; and the college, in attempting to serve this parent-surrogate role, developed a number of regulations that it believed appropriate. Definite hours by which women had to be in residence halls, compulsory chapel, rules regarding dress and rules regarding class attendance— these all seemed part-and-parcel of a residential college charged by upper middle-class families with safeguarding late adolescent students for a few years. This custodial role, however, is inconsistent with the personal freedoms that urban families allow their young. Yet much of the effort expended by a student personnel staff, even in quite enlightened urban universities, is reminiscent of the custodial outlook characteristic of the rural residential college. Surely, much of the student reaction in the past several years is, in part, directed against a custodial role that is clearly incompatible with contemporary urban society.

Governance of academic institutions, too, has its roots in the rural scene. Colleges in the early nineteenth century were typically created by religious denominations, which appointed boards and provided some financial resources. The board typically appointed a president, who very likely had to make the trip West with wagonloads of books, supplies, produce, and some money to get the new institution started. The president solicited funds, recruited students, planned the first building, admitted students and taught them their most important courses—which generally had to do with character formation. Since the president *was* the institution, he came to view himself as the holder of complete power, and that tradition of presidential authority continues today.

But the president of a large, complex institution located in an urban setting can no longer function as his presidential forebears did. A few presidents have sensed the difference in mission, as did President Clark Kerr in analyzing the role of the president of a complex uni-

versity system;[4] but more presidents have not, and they still attempt
to conduct their corporation as the presidents of Midwestern liberal
arts colleges used to conduct their enterprises.

The curriculum must also be analyzed in the light of its historical trends. The colonial college attempted to provide an education
for a limited number of people who would serve leadership roles in
the ministry, government, and, to a lesser extent, law. It attempted
to transmit to them the then two vital intellectual trends of the restored classical learning as it came out of the Renaissance and the
spirit of the Reformation. Thus the curriculum was prescribed, and it
consisted primarily of classical languages, moral philosophy, and political philosophy. It required the better part of a century—the nineteenth—for the sciences, agriculture, and engineering to gain respectability as components of the college or university curriculum. That they
did is certainly due to the creation of land-grant institutions, the development of the free elective system, and, of course, the major scientific advances that characterized the closing decades of the nineteenth century.

But now colleges and universities are faced with the need to
put new elements into the curriculum that are consonant with urban
circumstances. And the going is hard. Somehow, conservative American faculties can now accept the application of biological sciences to
agricultural or medical problems but cannot accept the application of
anthropology, economics, and psychology to problems of the ghetto.
Yet this acceptance must come if the urban universities are to meet
their responsibilities. Further, so many of the urban problems have
both social and natural scientific facets that the several intellectual
cultures must be brought closer together than they presently are.

Thus far, our emphasis has been on institutions of higher education and what *they* have done or should do in order to relate to the
urban environment. But the urban community also has important responsibilities, if this essential mix of town and gown is to be accomplished. Perhaps the first of these responsibilities is for a community
to develop an understanding of what a university is. A university is
many things. It is a community in which ideas, regardless of how extreme they might be, can and should be pursued and elaborated. It is

[4] Clark Kerr, *The Uses of the University* (Cambridge: Harvard University Press, 1963).

a place where young people may test their own notions of reality, and go through the painful process of moving into adulthood. Further, it is a place where new knowledge, regardless of how threatening, should be sought and discovered.

These activities can be threatening and disturbing, but a community that wants its urban institution to contribute a fair share to the richness of city life, must be able to understand and accept such processes as student demonstrations at Berkeley; student picketing of segregated drug stores in Columbia, Missouri; student discussion of sex and evolution in Tampa, Florida; the development of an atomic pile at the University of Chicago; research, including photography, on human sexual response at Washington University; and objective comparisons of Communist and non-Communist governments at Harvard. These processes must all be accepted as normal and expected parts of university life. No community that is unwilling to understand them can expect to be the home of an important intellectual center.

A second responsibility of the larger community is a concern with control. A community that wishes to exercise absolute control over an institution located within its boundaries cannot expect to find that institution the free sort of place that a university ought to be. It is no wonder that the constitutional state universities have developed their present greatness. Such universities as the University of California, the University of Minnesota, the University of Michigan, and Michigan State University all owe their existence to constitutional provision and hence are freed in important ways from direct control of the people through the legislature. Ultimately, of course, the people do possess control, and this is proper; but the healthier kind of control is that which is filtered through several levels of society. A community in which a vibrant university can exist is one in which direct control will be, if not completely eliminated, certainly minimized. Expressions of community need can be made, but they must be made through free exchange of ideas with people in the university rather than through coercion and the application of sanctions.

Institutions of higher education are costly and the cost is going to increase markedly during the next several decades. An urban community that truly values its college or university must find various means of supporting it financially. Those private institutions that have made such enormous contributions to the American business community must be supported much more heavily by private donations than they ever have been in the past. If private institutions are to continue to be the important source of diversity that they now are, major new sources of funds must be found, and the likely location of these new sources will be in the cities in which the institutions are located. For public institutions, several forms of tax revenue must be tapped, and the tax bill for local citizens can go only up. A city or region that will limit its support of higher education chiefly for the convenience of local taxpayers or the local power elite is being short-sighted in the extreme. The evidence of the economic contribution a dynamic university can bring to the community in which it is located is incontrovertible. Just as an example, Emory University in Atlanta has an annual operating budget of approximately fifty million dollars. Yet through the existence of that university, hospital and research installations having budgets of upwards of 200 million dollars have been attracted to that part of Atlanta; and this contribution, stated only in terms of dollars and cents, does not include the contributions of future leaders for the Atlanta community that the university will produce.

The urban community must be willing, even eager, for its institutions of higher education to serve all elements of the urban society. This means that a community must be eager, naturally, to have the children of its power elite educated; but it must at the same time develop viable ways to educate the children of its slums and lower classes. This is no easy point of view to accept. Too frequently, as new junior colleges have been created, they have been located to serve conveniently the children of the well-to-do, even at the expense of excluding growing nonwhite portions of the population.

Thus, the responsibilities of urban communities and urban institutions of higher education must be brought together. There is no time to lose.

> Our society is irretrievably urban. Since our cities are here to stay, the time is at hand to take a new look at them. It is urgent that a major effort be made to reshape them. This will require serious reflection and positive action. In all of these matters the urban university can play a central role. It can, in fact, become the single most important force in the recreation of our cities. Since our universities possess the broadly-based knowledge of many disciplines, have as their purpose the creation of an intellectual climate necessary to achieve objectivity and perspective, and have

experience in relating learning to the needs of society, they are equipped to perform a task that no other institution can do as well. Here, then, is a unique role for our urban universities, that of giving meaning to urban life and assisting in the creation of a new image for our cities.[5]

---

[5] Klotsche, *op. cit.*, p. 129.

CHAPTER 3

Sources of
Tension

A hasty review of news-
paper articles of the past few years reflects the present United States
collegiate situation. "The use of marijuana on college campuses is
causing grave concern. . . ." The University of Oregon faculty refused
to accept a legislative offer of $1000 awards for excellent teaching on
the ground that the awards constituted legislative interference with
academic affairs. Students in many colleges carried signs reading, "I
am a human being; do not fold, bend, or mutilate." Yale students
have created a magazine called *Political* which aims to present "the
most important national issues each month by the men who make
them." The Rutgers faculty supported the right of one of its members
to welcome a Viet Cong victory—in the face of demands from political
candidates that the professor be fired. At Yale, some students will be
allowed to help judge faculty members when such matters as tenure
and promotion are at stake. The University of Chicago has mounted

32

a three-year campaign to acquire 160 million dollars in gifts. The University of California expects to have an enrollment of 300,000 students by the year 2000. Research has actually harmed university education in the sciences by draining off teachers into full-time research activities. In California, with perhaps the largest and most complex system of education in the country, only 3 per cent of the twenty-to-twenty-four age group received the bachelor's degree; the figure for the rest of the country was 3½ per cent. Nine Negro students are suing the institution that expelled them. Students at Berkeley have attempted to form a union to engage in collective bargaining with the university. University professors have become mercenaries in quest of research dollars and have thus shifted the focus of their loyalty from campus to funding agency. John Gardner criticizes "the crassest opportunism, job hopping, and wheeling and dealing among young college faculty members."[1] The University of Pittsburgh almost went under in a valiant quest for excellence. Columbia University was brought to a standstill in student-police confrontation, an event nearly eclipsed by the conflicts at San Francisco State College at the end of 1968.

The crosscurrents, the conflicts and tensions thus revealed are of several sorts. First are those derivative of the nature of the university in Western civilization or of the nature of man himself. Faculty and administration seem to maintain a continuous cold war over financial matters, governance of the institution, the curriculum and interference with academic freedom. And, furthermore, they have always done so. Although actual controversy between administrative powers and professors in medieval universities was rare, it was rare chiefly because the principle of authority was so well accepted. When on occasion, as when Abelard defied authority to use logic in studying theology, professors did exert genuine freedom, the same sorts of charges and countercharges were made as are found in the present struggle between faculty and administration at St. John's University. Charles Kraitser's remark in the 1840's that "The Board of Visitors . . . were gentlemen whom it was hard to please. They had kicked Dr. Blaetterman out because he had whipped his wife, and they have kicked me out because I have been whipped by my wife. What did they really want?"[2] is not in essence different from the feelings that Professor

[1] John W. Gardner, *The Flight from Teaching* (New York: Carnegie Corporation, 1964).
[2] Frederick Rudolph, *The American College and University* (New York: Knopf, 1962).

Koch must have had when he was discharged from the University of Illinois for airing his views about sexual behavior in the *Daily Illini*.

Faculty members are preoccupied with their own subjects often to the exclusion of family problems, social amenities, and even their own personal well-being. They are, in a very real sense, conservative, for they value most highly the small segment of culture that they have mastered. While in social, political, economic, or even personal conduct, individual professors may exhibit either liberal or conservative tendencies, yet on educational matters they are inclined to the status quo. Faculty views about academic innovation are reflected in the final speech of the retiring professor who remarked that he had seen many changes in his forty years as teacher and had been against all of them. W. H. Cowley identifies thirteen significant decisions regarding higher education in America; in only one could he find clear faculty initiative, and in one other, faculty initiative with student assistance. The others were engineered either by administration, outside groups, students or were sheer historical accidents.[3] The same point can be made by examining recent curricular developments. General education as a reform movement is most closely associated with the names of Hutchins, Carman, McGrath, Hannah and Woods—all administrators. The trimester was sparked by Litchfield at Pittsburgh, cooperative work-study by a dean of engineering and a president (Arthur Morgan), and tutorial study by President Aydelotte at Swarthmore.

Administration thus seems educationally more liberal and dynamic than faculty. It is the president who is responsible for the survival and continued growth of the institution and it is he and his subordinates who constantly search for the fresh ideas and innovations that enable an institution to remain viable in a rapidly changing environment. It is the president who challenges the faculty to make time-consuming self-studies, who imports the educational consultant, who circulates conference reports emphasizing educational reform, and who suggests that the financial well-being of faculty and curricular or educational reform are interrelated. Thus, a conservative faculty and a dynamic administration must exist in a perpetual state of tension and, very likely, conflict.

Then there are further tensions that stem from the existence of

[3] W. H. Cowley, "Critical Decisions in American Higher Education," in *Current Issues in Higher Education 1963* (Washington, D.C.: American Association for Higher Education, 1963).

many subcultures sharing a broader but ill-defined larger culture. Martin Trow suggests that there are at least four student subcultures each with quite discrete values and aspirations. The academic group values courses, ideas, and the ideal of scholarship. The vocational group exchanges effort for specific job preparation and job placement. The play subculture views life in college as a pleasant interlude before adulthood, and the bohemians use the collegiate setting as a locale for protesting prevailing social values. To these must be added the ingredients of several faculty subcultures. Burton Clark has elaborated the concept of locals and cosmopolitans to include four somewhat discrete types. These are, first, the teacher who is committed to students, the local campus, and to general education. Second is the scholar-researcher, a cosmopolitan who cares little for the local scene and gains his satisfactions from his discipline and his own play on ideas. Another cosmopolitan is the consultant who has and values a broad national reputation and high mobility. And, fourth, the teacher has another local counterpart who is the demonstrator. He may well be a local doctor or dentist who teaches part time or a professor who is devoted to serving his college. He is frequently the speaker local groups want.[4] Now these eight subcultures exist in varying proportions on various campuses, but seem generally represented on virtually all. The possibilities for conflict thus presented are enormous. Consider, just as an example, the tensions that would come to a faculty in which the teacher subculture predominated when it experienced a student body well represented by bohemians. John Bushnell has insightfully likened student subcultures to American colonies in foreign lands. Members of the group will sample foreign food and buy a few foreign objects but gain their security by returning to the enclave at night. Students similarly may sample the wares of the faculty, may purchase a few of their ideas, but in the end return to the safer values of other students. Only a few "go native," becoming the future graduate students and ultimately professors.

Related to these sources of conflict is the long-time dilemma as to whether the purpose of collegiate education was cultural or utilitarian. Medieval universities seem to have faced the issue in the form of these alternatives: whether the chief purpose of the university was to prepare officials for the growing centralized governments in France

---

[4] Burton R. Clark, *Faculty Culture: The Study of Campus Culture* (Boulder, Colo.: Western Interstate Commission for Higher Education, 1963).

and England or the more local state in Italy, or to elaborate, for its own sake, the reacquired Greek learning. Within the American tradition the issue has been faced and resolved in different ways at different times. In the late nineteenth century, the utilitarian and research points of view seem to have captured the American academic stage in the form of land-grant colleges and the German concept of the research university, but it was challenged by colleges and college professors, particularly along the Eastern seaboard. Hugo Munsterberg reflected this reaction when he pointed out that those in the university, ". . . miss in the technique of that new university method, the liberalizing culture which was the leading trait of Oxford and Cambridge. This longing for the gentleman's scholarship after the English pattern has entered many a heart."[5] Currently the issue is reflected in such matters as whether the liberal arts college is dead or dying, whether the junior college should emphasize technical-vocational or general and liberal studies, whether preprofessional work should or should not be closely articulated with graduate and professional specialization, and in the disputes over the nature of graduate studies. One can even see the conflict reflected in the constant war between the faculties of the arts and sciences and those of education. Russell Kirk currently reflects the cultural point of view when he argues, "The study of literature, I repeat, is the primary instrument of college education,"[6] and the opposing voice is that of the junior college spokesman who suggests that it should offer courses in whatever a community wants.

Then there is the town-and-gown tension, which seems to have existed as long as the college or university has. Medieval townspeople found university students as bothersome as did the people of Oakland when students wanted to protest the movement of troops to Viet Nam. The events at Berkeley, which galvanized the educational establishment to rectifying action, started over a piece of property the proper use of which was determined by whether it belonged to the town or the university, and the ideological issue was whether students could organize on campus forays against parts of the city. Some Midwestern colleges still restrict some forms of student behavior, for example, parietal rights, because inter-residence visitation would offend the sensi-

[5] Hugo Munsterberg, *American Patriotism and Other Social Studies* (New York: 1913).

[6] Russell Kirk, *The Intemperate Professor* (Baton Rouge: Louisiana State University Press, 1966).

bilities of townspeople. One can speculate that most of the contested cases involving academic freedom have been brought about because of the difference between lay and academic conceptions as to the proper nature and functioning of the university.

Another constant source of tension is the conflict between generations. Older and younger people exist in a somewhat artificial suspension on the college campus and are bound to misunderstand each other. The contemporary cry that students should trust no one over thirty years of age involves the same element as the story of a French youth and his father. In anger one day, the young man knocked his father down and dragged him into the orchard. Finally the father cried, "Stop! I only dragged my father as far as that tree."

But there are contemporary conflicts as well, which confound the traditional ones. The most visible is the student protest movement in its several manifestations. The dimensions of the protest could be described in the polemics of the Free Speech Movement or in the recoil statements of college presidents. Perhaps a more thoughtful analysis is provided by one of the students at a joint faculty-student conference held in 1965.

> Our position has grown paradoxically out of a new commitment to traditional liberal values. The traditional liberal accorded the individual the highest status in society; the individual is the end toward which all else was merely a means. But in serving this ideal, the traditional liberal invented the seeping bureaucracies he thought necessary to reach systematically every citizen. The problem of how to maintain the identity of the individual in this process, however, has become our inheritance. The civil rights movement has most clearly pointed up this problem. The American Negro represented one of the most passive elements in our society. One of the reasons for his plight was "organized America," which kept him in his place by the sheer weight of its structures. It became the task of the civil rights worker to convince Negroes that by standing up and asserting their individual identities, they could have some impact on their communities.
>
> On the campus, a student who understands this is outraged by the industrial values that have been applied to the educational process and by the bureaucratic models that the university follows in its organizational patterns. We find these things anathema to the realization of our objective, *i.e.*, the resurrection of the individual. The structural-functional approach is itself irrelevant or, worse, destructive. It's this reliance on bureaucracy,

the manipulation of structures, and the analysis of functions that makes some of us say, "Don't trust anyone over 30."

Our solution is to inject into the system more human qualities, the most obvious of which is emotion. Perhaps the combination of the McCarthy era and the departmental approach to knowledge have sterilized the academic process. It has certainly made it irrelevant to activist students because they have seen what a commitment to ideals can do for a group of people if it is fearlessly defended in front of the cameras of human conscience. No wonder the educational experience bugs us with its shallowness when professors aren't willing to lay their competence on the line publicly. Why load us with principles and ideals that obviously are less important than a $14,000.00 a year job and tenure?

The educational experience must be made relevant through a new solution. Just another new structure won't liberate the thinking of the student and open him up to the real learning experience—the one that goes on inside when we really try to examine ourselves. We need relationships with teachers who will help us face the big tough hang-ups: Am I a moral pacifist or a coward? Is abortion a humane answer to the problems of unwed motherhood, and what has the pill got to do with my answer? Who am I, where am I headed, and do I really want to go there? Is an academic career any less sterile than one in business? What are the things that make a society really worth fighting for?

No structure will ever open up the professor and the student to problems like these. Instead, we have to reshape the educational experience so the professor is more than a mechanism for dispensing information that enables the student to get the *symbols* of success.[7]

A further contemporary source of conflict is the growth of militant faculty demands for greater financial rewards, for greater voice in governance, and for greater personal and professional autonomy. The manifestations are clear and well known. In California, junior college and state college faculties demanded, and most have received, academic senates, which give to the faculty a direct voice in academic policy. At St. John's and Georgetown, faculty entered into open revolt against the administration; and some St. John's faculty, aided by the faculties of city-supported institutions, justified and encouraged strikes in the best trade union tradition. The AAUP, as one weapon in a war to gain reasonable salaries for its members, devised the salary grade report which, one suspects, has done as much as any

[7] Edward Joseph Shoben, Jr., *Students, Stress, and the College Experience* (Washington, D.C.: National Student Association, 1966).

other single thing to bring about the steady increases in faculty salaries that have characterized higher education in the last six or seven years. And the recent teach-ins in which faculty and students have protested about not only the educational but the political establishment as well is also illustrative of faculty unrest.

Faculty seem to be saying that for too long they have subsidized the education of youth by receiving marginal salaries; for too long they have been controlled and manipulated by the power of boards of trustees and presidents; for too long have they occupied a position of genteel poverty—trained to enjoy a rich cultural life, but too poor to afford it. Taking advantage of a general social demand for more education and the intersection of the high birthrate population of the forties and fifties with the low birthrate of the thirties, faculty now press their demands. Of course, there are regional differences. In the South and Southeast, faculty reaction to board contention that faculty members are after all employees, whom administration must closely supervise, is slower and less conclusively violent than in the East. But even there the idea that the faculty should really control the curriculum, its own membership, the conditions of student entrance and exit, and educational policy are growing. And administrative and board reaction to such claims can be expected on occasion to be severe.

A third current involves the changing role of colleges and universities and the uncertainties of status, effort, and procedure, which change occasionally. Until roughly 1955, even the presently highly selective institutions accepted most of the applicants who sought admission. It should be recalled that Harvard College, which now finds itself in the position to accept only the top 1 per cent of high school graduates, as recently as the early 1950's accepted one out of every two and a half students who applied. This phenomenon has its origin in the demand for college education, the national demand for excellence and rigor in education after the fright of Sputnik, and the increased awareness of the class relatedness of degrees held from certain institutions. The pressures flowing from this development are varied and enormous. The problems of admission offices with multiple applications and the problems of students wanting an assured berth, the stresses on students of living in a highly competitive system where the demand for grades may preclude an education, the sometimes foolish efforts of a mediocre faculty seeking to recruit a highly selective student body, the worries of parents that their children should go to a "good" college, the reliance on artificial and imprecise numerical indexes to determine whether students should be admitted (Brooklyn College raised its cutoff point from 85 to 87 and its arbitrary power has been upheld by the courts) are all well exemplified. From among many examples one will suffice.

> . . . these boys take the attitude that since Penn is presumed to be the bottom of the Ivy League the courses cannot be difficult, and that they can sit back and breeze through on the basis of no work. So they let their work pile up, or slide by, until they are in real academic difficulty. Whereupon, they either quit, or flunk out of a school they hadn't really wanted to attend in the first place and which they erroneously regarded as being beneath them.[8]

Then there is the effect of the agrarian myth. Originally, American colleges were located in small villages, partly because there were not many cities and partly through design to keep youth away from the temptations of the city. Concepts of what a college was thus developed in this rural or small town setting, as did the notion of going away to school. Residence hall living with a strong custodial emphasis, college life (including the long football weekend), small size with great reliance on intimate interpersonal relationships to carry a significant educational load, and even the shape of campus itself (a walled city shutting out the life outside), derive from the agrarian style. But colleges and universities are now typically large and equally typically located in large urban areas. The ethos of the modern city has broken into the college and causes a variety of reactions. Why should not students—men and women—share apartments, when others of their age group, who are not students, can? How does a student accomplish the psychological break from home, when he must return there each night? How can the idealized vision of the college as a community evolve when faculty members commute forty miles each day they work? How can a college insist upon the sole validity of the values of a single religious persuasion when it exists among a swirling pool of pluralistic values, many of which seem to work and to be quite valid?

Then another myth also prevails: the doctrine of "publish or perish." In the nineteenth century a number of universities were created or evolved in emulation of German research universities. The names of

[8] John Keats, *The Sheepskin Psychosis* (New York: Delta Books, 1963).

Johns Hopkins, Clark, Chicago, Stanford, Michigan, and then, gradually, Harvard, Yale, and Princeton are illustrative. Presidents of these universities stated that the highest value was to be placed upon the production of knowledge—and considerable research was actually done. But the true emphasis upon research has come about since World War II, an event that demonstrated that enormous good could come to the society through governmental and industrial subsidy of university research. The ideal then became a reality—in a few institutions. Probably not more than 150 could, even at present, be classified as true research institutions. But these became the glamour institutions, and research and related consulting became the most desirable professional roles. Now, young professors plot their careers to land in the research institution. Predominantly teaching institutions try to approximate the research institution in order to attract faculty, and the criteria for professional advance, even in the hundreds of colleges where they were inappropriate, became the doing and the publishing of research—or at least the publishing of *something*. The test of value for the professor became the number of items his bibliography contained just as the worth of the student was reflected by his SAT score. The emphasis on research has caused a number of distortions. It has tempted universities to orient their efforts in the directions dictated by available support. It has fostered false values in most of America's colleges and universities, which still must attend to the education of youth.

And size itself vexes and may cause tension. Most American college students are now receiving their education in vast complexes of schools, departments, and even smaller subunits. By the end of the century the average size for an American college will likely be 20,000 students. This very size demands a high degree of organization and a reliance on impersonal rules and procedures. The IBM card has already become indispensable and the magnetic tape is about to become so. A faculty member who once could enter the president's office whenever he wished now finds himself separated from the front office by four, five, or six tiers of administration. The psychology department at the University of Michigan now has over 140 full-time faculty members. Think how insignificant a young instructor could feel in that situation.

Students and faculty alike respond negatively to institutions that take on the characteristics of a multiversity. Most students and faculty would agree with this description: "The salient characteristic of the multiversity is massive production of specialized excellence. The multiversity is actually not an educational center but a highly efficient industry engaged in producing skilled individuals to meet the immediate needs of business or government."[9]

To these currents and crosscurrents could be added many more. Changing parental expectations, the notion of lifelong education, shifts in curricular balance of power, and changing doctrines regarding student relationships with the college are also operative. But sheer elaboration of such a list would only belabor the obvious to anyone who has spent much time on American college campuses. Eventually the origins of crosscurrents must be understood and ways devised for, if not controlling them, at least adapting creatively to them.

The visible currents are not unlike local weather conditions, even of a rather violent sort. These are generated by such intermediate forces as the flow of the jet stream and perhaps ultimately modified by shifting conditions in the upper atmosphere. Similarly the dislocations among campus subcultures, the struggles between town and gown, the insistent demands of the new breed of students, and the aspirations of militant faculty derive from more fundamental changes in the society.

Perhaps the first and most important of these basic, one might even say primeval, forces is the existence of what Kenneth Boulding has called a developed society.[10] While there are obvious malfunctionings, the present society in the United States seems to have reached mature realization of its basic goals. It is an affluent society having a productive enterprise no longer needing the work energies of most of its citizens. Indeed, were it not for the momentary dislocation of the war effort in Viet Nam and the defense spending occasioned by the national paranoia regarding Communism, unemployment would likely be at an all-time high. It is a psychologically sophisticated society, and at least many of the present college generation came from homes in which parents tried to understand their children and sought to provide whatever incentives and conditions were needed for healthy growth. The validity of this point is made by one of the militant students at Berkeley.

"We grew up as well believing that we lived in a great nation which had harnessed itself to the will of its people, pro-

---

[9] Seymour M. Lipset and Sheldon S. Wolin (Eds.), *The Berkeley Student Revolt* (New York: Doubleday, 1965).
[10] Kenneth Boulding, *The Impact of the Social Sciences* (New Brunswick, N.J.: Rutgers University Press, 1966).

viding them with education, the highest standard of living in the world, equality of opportunity, democracy, and the great middle class. We believed ours a humble nation that awkwardly and reluctantly shouldered the responsibilities a much more corrupt world forced upon her, but dispatched those responsibilities, once shouldered, with integrity, honor and the most peaceful intentions.

"We were in short, the first post-depression, post-war generation to emerge into the world with all the assists of the mildly permissive (in some cases almost progressive) family culture of upper middle class America. If our parents sometimes despaired at our inability to understand the austerity and struggle that made possible their achievements, they were nonetheless pleased with the generally enthusiastic and alert products of their work."[11]

It is, further, a surfeited society—surfeited in the sense that new needs must constantly be created in order to use the products that an increasingly cybernated system can produce. It is also surfeited in the sense that the waste from all this increased production and use is in danger of strangling man. To air and water pollution must now be added the danger of pollution in space. And this society, through its creation of techniques of mass overkill, may have ended the likelihood of the mass wars that began in the age of Napoleon and ended with Hiroshima.

The various educational implications stemming from the fact of the developed society are many and important. But perhaps the most important is the shift in survival values that the society must inculcate in the young. At various times in our history these values have involved hunting skills, skills to do manual work, and skills to do complex tasks. Now, however, these may well be obsolete and the use of leisure and the ability to communicate may be most important for survival. And this pill is a hard one to swallow for a generation still venerating the gospel of work.

The second force is the sheer rate of change the society is currently experiencing. Says Charles Frankel:

We come at this point to perhaps the profoundest consequence of the present revolution in human affairs. It is the simple change in the tempo of change. For nothing cuts more quickly or

[11] Paul Potter, "Student Discontent and Campus Reform," in *Order and Freedom on the Campus* (Boulder, Colo.: Western Interstate Commission for Higher Education, 1966).

deeply into a society's way of doing things than changes in its technology.

This quickened tempo represents an unprecedented challenge to the human ability to adjust to social change. It took man roughly 475,000 years to come to the Industrial Revolution. We have arrived at the "Space Age" in a hundred and fifty years— and while we do not know where we go from here, we can be sure that we shall go there fast. Our expectations of change, and the ability of our nervous systems or our social systems to withstand the shock of change, have been formed in the long experience of the race. And this experience, even in the nineteenth century, has not prepared us for the pace of events that lie ahead.

Such an extraordinary change in the basic tempo of human history means that new and deliberate efforts will be needed to control the processes of social change. As the last hundred years of Western history demonstrate, men can learn to change at a much quicker pace than before. But as these same years also suggest, there are limits, and it is difficult to imagine a day when it will not take time for men to adjust to new conditions, to learn new skills and habits, and to get over the nostalgia and resentments that come when old and familiar things are destroyed. There is a conservative in every man and, in the world into which we are moving, he is going to get a harder workout than ever before.

Accordingly, if the things we cherish from the past are not going to be carelessly destroyed, and if the best possibilities of the future are going to be realized, it seems probable that we shall have to have institutions that have been deliberately set up to exercise long-range social forethought. A steady process of technological innovation, for example, can mean recurrent crises of technological unemployment. If this is not to happen, institutions will have to exist to envisage the new skills that will be needed, to undertake the continuing task of retraining workers, and to control the pace at which new techniques are introduced so that we can make a sensible adjustment to them. Given the pace and magnitude of the technical changes that are in prospect, we cannot count on the market place and the price system to do this job alone. Technological innovation means social change; and there is no more reason to introduce such innovations, letting the chips fall where they may, than there is to introduce a new and powerful drug on the market without first making it meet the test of medical examination and control.[12]

[12] Charles Frankel, "The Third Great Revolution of Mankind," in A. Kerber and W. R. Smith (Eds.), *Educational Issues in a Changing Society* (Detroit: Wayne State University Press, 1964).

Then a weakening or a failure of Judeo-Christian theology must be assigned some force for determining the nature of campus crosscurrents and conflicts, even as it is involved in other paradoxes in American life. So many of the relevant factors on a college campus have been determined by religious or socioreligious conditions. The values assigned to work as a compulsive necessity can be traced to the Protestant concern with calling. Sex standards and proscription have in the past been determined by a religiously set equation: sex equals sin. Collegiate formalism from the first Sunday of the college year with suggested or required church attendance to weekly chapel is linked to religious values. A large number of colleges receive part of their support from church denominations and a few of these schools are viewed simply as arms of the church. Science courses in a few colleges are contrived to skirt issues that might bring science into conflict with religious tenets. And, of course, the entire development of the university idea and the concept of the college have been manifestations of a religious spirit.

But conditions have changed and adjustment to change has proven difficult. One can agree with Father Shea that, "Man is, as a thinker, incurably moralistic and metaphysical."[13] One can also agree that students, in their search for relevance, in their search for personal identity, and in their search for moral standards are asking theological or religious questions. One can also believe that professors, seeking to understand the nature of the university and seeking some integrating order, are also theologically inclined. But religion and theology in their traditional and orthodox idioms have failed. Father Shea reports a Thomist spinning a seamless proof of the impossibility of chemically creating living matter, while biologists on the same campus are establishing that very possibility. The advent of the pill has rendered harmless the church-inspired injunctions about sexual conduct, and the students' awareness of this has made them skeptical of other church moralisms. The fact that there is no relationship between students in denominational colleges and secular colleges with respect to amount of cheating is perhaps another example of a lack of contemporary relevance of religious teaching for campus life. Bryant M. Wedge, in a study of problems of college men, cites religion only once in the index,

[13] F. X. Shea, S.J., "Sectarian and Religious Pressures on the University," in *Current Issues in Higher Education 1965* (Washington, D.C.: American Association for Higher Education, 1965).

to refer the reader to the following sentence: "Most of them abandoned their religion, as had this one, even though in the depth of her
depression she talked about her illness as sin; she did not attend church
and, at least formally, she abandoned her religion."[14] And Sanford's
The American College reported shifts in student response to the question, "Do you personally feel that you need to believe in some sort of
religious faith?" Figures for men dropped from 88 to 51 per cent by
the end of the junior year, and for women from 91 down to 69 per
cent for the same period.[15] The critical problem is, of course, to find
new bases of conduct or to refurbish older ones.

Another possible cause of some of the current unrest on the
campus may be the experience of World War II. If it is, quite possibly
some of the more serious problems might be expected to lessen in the
next few years. The parents of the present generation of juniors, seniors, and younger graduate students are the generation of the eleven
million people who comprised the armed forces during World War II.
Thus, many of these war babies experienced broken homes for two,
three, and four years. And when parents were reunited the parental
struggle to reestablish civilian identity was severe. These parents were
included in the mass veteran enrollments in colleges and universities
who were determined never to experience the insecurities of the depression years during which they grew up, nor the insecurities of the
war years. And so far they have succeeded, but possibly at considerable
cost for their children.

The point cannot be elaborated far because little or no research
has been reported. But one can speculate regarding the dynamics involved.

It is a well known psychological fact that a person will misvalue
the significant people of his childhood to the extent to which his
early inter-personal tie-ups remain unresolved. If these early
inter-personal patterns stand uncorrected, people will distort the
image of various people whom they meet in the course of their
lives. They may or may not dimly sense that they do so, but they
will not recognize the inter-personal misconceptions of their early

---

[14] Bryant M. Wedge (Ed.), *Psychosocial Problems of College Men*
(New Haven: Yale University Press, 1958).
[15] Nevitt Sanford (Ed.), *The American College* (New York: Wiley,
1962), p. 826.

childhood as the root of the distortions of their inter-personal relationships.[16]

One can speculate from this that the Free Speech Movement warning to distrust everyone over thirty is a reflection of distrust developed when father or mother was not at home when the child needed them. Father or mother or both were off to war.

Fear of the bomb may be a related cause, but one must assume that if it is, it is a fear deeply embedded. Students, except for the militant minority, do not seem concerned about the bomb. But they are explicitly concerned about the pressures they experience in their academic work that stem directly from Sputnik. That event frightened the United States out of its complacent assumption that it was the most highly educated and technically competent nation in the world. Thus public support was galvanized to enable professors, teachers, and intellectuals to become enormously more vigorous and demanding. That little satellite, in effect, validated the demands of higher education for larger and larger financial support. It was responsible for the current victory of the enterprise of higher education—and the enterprise is finding it difficult to stand prosperity.

To the earlier noted rate of change must be added the pressures on colleges and universities of the so-called explosion of knowledge. Whether it be the matter of defining the curriculum, articulation between levels of education, the pressures on faculty to keep abreast of fields, or the demands made upon students to learn more of the tremendous and growing store of knowledge, the impact is well known and well documented. To suggest only a small example, consider the feelings of liberal arts college science faculties who are told they should no longer offer physics because the research is developing at such a rate that only research faculties can teach it. Such a judgment does require a revision of the professors' self-esteem.

Now, these currents and crosscurrents powered by such fundamental forces are going to perplex the academy for a long time to come. There can be no escaping them, but perhaps there are ways of alleviating them.

First, the fact of tension between faculty and administration

[16] Frieda Fromm-Reichmann, "Psychiatric Aspects of Anxiety," in M. R. Stein and others, *Identity and Anxiety* (Glencoe, Ill.: The Free Press, 1960).

can be expected and the structure so contrived that a creative tension, in a Hegelian sense, is achieved and maintained. Granting faculty some powers and administration others might achieve a system of checks and balances, which has worked well in the political sphere.

Then, students and institutions might help by reality testing as to the exact nature of higher education. One has the feeling that considerable tension is created on the basis of myths. Eliminate the myth and some resolution of conflict could result.

Further, communication seems as necessary to the health of institutions as it is to the mental health of individuals. This task requires the greatest energies of all in the academy, especially on the part of the administration.

And finally, conflict can be controlled by developing new and more consistent roles that are consonant with the changed nature of higher education.

PART TWO

Student Response

CHAPTER 4

Students

and Colleges

In a very real sense the relationships of students to their colleges or universities have changed little since the time of the earliest medieval institutions. So long as human nature, physical environment, and the broad purposes and functions of college education remain as they have been, the relationships of students to life and learning will also remain fairly constant.

Medieval students fought with each other, raised money at the end of the term by selling textbooks, and sought ways of circumventing such university regulations as those governing the subjects of conversation (an early four-letter word affair), assigning penalties for throwing things at professors, and indicating appropriate colors for caps and gowns (a no-Bermuda-shorts sort). Priests and professors believed that students' hearts were in the mire, that they spent most of their time fighting, and that they bothered passersby. There were poor medieval students who, although too broke to buy books, frequently earned

honors; and there were the children of the wealthy, who dressed well
and who followed the sun rather than their books. There were also
students who slept late, missed classes, slept in class, then spent most of
the evening in taverns. Then, when vacation time came, they worried
about how to show their parents what they had learned.

When students arrived at school they were hazed, provided
with manuals that pointed out places of interest in the city, and shown
where to buy the best food. To help them with Latin, a kind of early
programmed text was available. This document, in eighteen chapters,
taught the basic terms needed to move from matriculation through
final orals. And gamesmanship was practiced even then, as is evidenced
by the ways students were told to invite their masters to dinner. If
students treated masters well and provided great feasts for them, they
needed not fear the outcome of examinations. But to be safer still, students could purchase specially prepared phrase books so that they could
copy, in proper form, the answers to most questions they would be
asked.

University students seemed always short of funds and their letters home were full of requests for more. They found college towns to
be expensive and would embellish on their hardships in order to con-
vince a tight-fisted father. And parents responded, as they have ever
since, with funds and urgings that students study harder. But with or
without funds, they found college life to be good and would frequently
postpone graduation for years (an early prototype of the permanent
graduate student)'. Sometimes the transfer problem would appear as
students moved from one university to another, partly for educational,
but mostly for recreational reasons.

There were wild students who drank overmuch and who par-
odied all, from deity to professors. But there were also good students
who were colorless sorts, eager to learn, assiduous at lectures and bold
in debate. These good students kept complete notes, which now reveal
a great deal about the medieval curriculum and even more about student life. And some students even insisted upon getting their money's
worth from professors. University life could be intellectually stimulating and good students could profit from contact with professors.[1]

Five hundred years later, the picture had changed not appre-

---

[1] Based on Charles H. Haskins, *The Rise of Universities* (Ithaca, N.Y.:
Cornell University Press, 1957).

ciably. Students in American colleges studied the liberal arts and sciences, which had been transplanted from Europe. Students spent their study time translating from Greek and Latin on the theory that these exercises would sharpen their minds. Wealthy students could spend four years at college, but poor students, through perhaps an early version of advanced placement, could enter college as sophomores and thus complete the course earlier. In the senior year, students took a course in moral philosophy—which typically was dreary, but which in the hands of a great teacher could become in truth an integrating experience.

Teaching was routine and inclined toward drill and recitation, for teachers were overloaded with class hours, disciplinary chores, and other non-teaching duties (the present-day committee system). But fortunate students would have at least one good teacher and this would make the college years worthwhile.

Students, fed up with life at one college, would transfer to another but would find there the same sorts of teachers and the same courses of study. Even without state adoption of texts, there was a common core of work that all colleges sought to offer.

Not only was the curriculum standard, but so was the tempo of student life. Generally students lived in residence halls, were required to study at set times, hated the food and were regulated by a student code. These would forbid playing cards or dice, drinking and, of course, require daily church attendance. Professors were allowed— even encouraged—to enter student rooms to check on how well the students were keeping regulations.

And students resisted such a life through horseplay, sheer destructiveness, and even riots. Presidents would physically chase students into their rooms and haul them out of taverns. Punishment would be administered on the basis of hearsay evidence and without long hearings. One student caught ringing the church bell at three in the morning was expelled then and there. At another time, a college was almost wrecked when 125 out of a student body of 200 were expelled.

When life became too grim, the students themselves developed an extracurricular program, which included literary and debating societies, dramatic performances, intercollegiate athletics, and the fraternity system. The academic calendar was tied to conditions of early American life, with the long summer vacation the rule because American summers, for the most part, are hot. After commencement, college towns settled into summer somnolence, waiting for the cool breezes of October to bring the students and their wealth back to town.[2]

A hundred years later, American colleges had grown in size and complexity, the university ideal had been embraced, and higher learning became an instrument of big business. There were the same familiar elements of student relationship with his college and with the society. In the 1920's, students believed in a greater degree of sexual freedom—they read about sex, talked about sex, thought about sex, and defied anyone to say no. They rejected legislated morality and enforced propriety, which point of view made them passionate anti-prohibitionists. The more advanced thinkers believed that there were too many laws, that they were not really their brother's keepers, and that tolerance was one of the supreme virtues. They questioned religion and proclaimed their agnosticism and atheism, and rebelled against compulsory chapel. And while they used its fruits, they feared the effect upon themselves of the American mass-produced culture. The more idealistic took to the progressive education ideas as reflected in Antioch, Meiklejohn's Experimental College, and Swarthmore. In search of something better, students left college to seek their spiritual salvation in Europe, or if they could not actually go, at least they could go vicariously by reading Hemingway and F. Scott Fitzgerald.[3]

Such a brief résumé should suggest that as long as colleges deal with late adolescent students, a number of patterns of behavior are likely to be predictable, regardless of the generation. It should provide some comfort for those who are responsible for the collegiate enterprise that others, too, have experienced travail. A chancellor of a state university besieged by protesting students can gain some perspective from recalling the nineteenth-century student who, seeing the president sitting in the window, drew his pistol and fired at the too tempting target. Or the central administration worried about student drinking can reflect on this student poem of the twelfth century:

> In the public house to die
> Is my resolution
> Let wine to my lips be nigh
> At life's dissolution;

    [2] George P. Schmidt, *Princeton and Rutgers: The Two Colonial Colleges of New Jersey* (Princeton, N.J.: Van Nostrand, 1964).
    [3] Frederick Lewis Allen, *Only Yesterday* (New York: Bantam Books, 1946).

> That will make the angels cry,
> With glad elocution,
> Grant this taper, God on high,
> Grace and absolution.[4]

And perhaps the presidents recently forced from their offices by students can identify with the Dickinson College president. Students whispered outside his office of plans to raid a side-tracked railroad car and help themselves to its stock of oysters. They knew their president; it was not long before they had locked him in the railroad car.

But college presidents must attend not only to the perspective of history and the common pattern it reveals, but also to the uniqueness of each situation and of each generation. Students were complaining about something unique when they created libraries as part of nineteenth-century literary societies, which they could actually use. They did sense a unique lack in their education when they created, in the face of faculty opposition, the fraternity system. It becomes appropriate, therefore, to examine current relationships to determine both common and unique elements.

Perhaps the safest generalization to make is that student relationships with their colleges, like their relationships with other social institutions, are in flux. Very likely most students respond to changing conditions in somewhat similar ways. They will work at their subjects, but they do not take them too seriously. They are not really concerned about social, political, or community affairs; very probably most don't even read newspapers regularly. Most will violate campus rules, such as those governing use of alcohol, as a kind of adolescent protest, and most experience mild irritation at a piling up of rules and regulations. But most will tolerate whatever the college does or tells them to do. They seem to segregate academic tasks from the rest, and a more important rest, of their lives.

But others, a minority to be sure, sense dysfunctions in their relationships with college and with their society. They seem to see clearly, at least they believe it is clear, that times have changed and they react to this cultural lag. It is this small group of students that has precipitated a major crisis.

At the acme of success, American higher education stands on the verge of imminent impotency unless new ways of dealing with rest-

---

[4] Haskins, *op. cit.*, p. 84.

less students are discovered. The litany from 1964 to 1968 is well known. The movement begins when the University of California is brought to its knees. As aftermath a talented president is let go, a conservative governor elected, and a new term (Berkeley) added to the language. A liberal president of the University of Colorado, seeking to make his institution a bastion of academic freedom, is forced to recant and then is deposed. A university that has shown it could grow great by welcoming talented children of immigrants—Columbia—is forced to close its doors and is made to appear as an oppressor of minority groups. A sensitive psychologist, tuned to the liberal cause, is pilloried in the public press and by members of his own board of trustees because he was forced to extreme lengths in order to avoid bloodshed on the campus of San Francisco State College. And a wise, experienced administrator is told by a student at his inauguration that only time will tell whether he has the wisdom to preside over the University of Michigan.

In the midst of national material prosperity, relative psychological sophistication, and expanding frontiers of thought and opportunity is a student generation best characterized as restless and disenchanted. Its spokesmen, if not its leaders, reject the political and economic status quo and wish to change the entire social structure. They have rejected the values of their society and tradition and have retreated from an ethic of work, rationality, and responsibility. They have widened the historic gulf between generations and are irreverent, humorless, and relentless in their contempt for adults, especially their own parents. Although dissatisfied with the goals of their society and of their parents, they are generally unable to set goals for themselves or to sustain goal-directed activities. And they seem constantly on the brink of despair in spite of moments when they seem to be enjoying themselves. There is always a sense of foreboding about them so that depressed and suicidal feelings are not at all uncommon.

In a nation whose form, structure, and ideology are rationalistic, optimistic, and rooted in a belief in the perfectibility of man, pure nihilism has been elevated to one of the prevailing styles of thought. Much of student rhetoric echoes Nietzsche's belief that the will to power begets nihilism. If man becomes the master of his planet, then his universe, then galaxy, then what? Power for power's sake, no matter how far extended, leaves the dread of a void. Nihilism seems the only possible response to that void since God is dead, God in the sense of a supersensible reality.[5] Hear the overtones in excerpts from the Port Huron statement of the Students for a Democratic Society: "Our work is guided by the sense that we may be the last generation in the experiment with living. . . . Beneath . . . is the pervading feeling that there simply are no alternatives, that our times have witnessed the exhaustion not only of Utopias, but of any new departures as well. Feeling the press of complexity upon the emptiness of life, people are fearful of the thought that at any moment things might thrust out of control. . . ."[6]

At a time when more and more of the nation's youth are led to aspire to higher education, the most revered institutions are respected for limiting access and for encouraging professors to eliminate concern for students as a viable or desirable ethic. In prestige institutions undergraduate students are tolerated as a financial base, through tuition or full-time equivalent appropriations, for the support of professors' real work, and as a large source from which a few new recruits for the priesthood of scholarship may be chosen. The university, claimed to be the focus of the creative energies of the society, thus seeks to alienate itself from those whom society wishes served, and, in some of the most highly financed and selective institutions, it seems determined to alienate itself from all other professions and callings. The preparation of future scholars, whether they be in history, medicine, law, education, physics, or sociology, is judged of infinitely greater worth than producing those who would practice in the service of man.

Although apologists for higher education have canonized the role of higher education as properly a critic of society, free from the political restraints placed on other institutions and offices, it is increasingly being made an object of political concern partly through its own artlessness and partly through the efforts of nihilistic youth. States, private donors, and parents have been persuaded to support colleges and universities to do as they please. But the bills have become so large and the evidence of social utility so lacking that a rendering of accounts, long overdue, is likely to be demanded by political forces. These forces are strengthened in their resolve by the one tangible evidence of the outcomes of higher education blazoned on television

[5] William Barrett, *Irrational Man: A Study in Existential Philosophy* (New York: Doubleday, 1958).

[6] Mitchell Cohen and Dennis Hall, *The New Student Left* (Boston: Beacon Press, 1966).

screens and newspapers—the facts of student revolt, radicalism, and challenge of the conventional wisdom.

The combined influence of continued student protest and disorder in urban streets will at least bring greater political scrutiny of the operations of colleges and universities and could hasten a conservative or even fascist government to preserve order even—or especially—at the expense of law. Make no mistake about this. Students occupying administration buildings, conducting pagan happenings, or stressing the erotic in plays, poems, and publications are directly responsible for cuts in educational appropriations, investigations of academic operations, and overruling by political authorities of decisions and prerogatives of academic administrators.

The power of rampant nihilism encountering intrenched syndicalism of professors within a society of frightened and vengeful people could polarize the society in any of several directions. Youthful intellectuals allied with the poor could confront the establishment as did a similar alliance in France in 1789. One wonders what the twentieth-century version of the guillotine would be. Or, youthful intellectuals and their not-so-youthful mentors who decry growing up absurd could force themselves into a cul-de-sac rejecting society and denying it their very considerable talents. Or, the nihilism of youth could so spread to other segments of society that an atomic resolution of the bleak uncertainties of an age would seem a welcome respite. Of course there is always the counterrevolution standing in the wings with its powers of legitimacy and appeal to ordered convention.

But a more creative stance would be to seek a resolution of the conflict now confusing campuses, a resolution that would accommodate to realities and preserve educational energies for the benefit of society. Such a stance rests on the need for thorough diagnosis to determine whether the malaise of higher education is terminally malignant or benign. Since higher education is organically related to the rest of society, it, too, must eventually be scrutinized, but for a beginning some of the roots of dissent within education may be exposed.

Institutions are captives of their histories and nowhere is this more apparent than in dealings with students. The American college lodged considerable power in the hands of its president both to maintain the institution and to mold and shape students, exercising in the process the same prerogatives the law allowed a parent or the master of a slave. A president could dismiss a student from school the day of graduation, could search students' rooms, could punish by lowering grades for crimes against a community or make a matter of college concern acts of students committed while far distant from the campus and under even parental jurisdiction. Such powers were exercised in the belief that students were indulged, petted, and uncontrolled at home and allowed to trample upon all laws human and divine, that they came to college with undisciplined minds, uncultivated hearts but with exalted ideas of personal dignity. It is true that such a belief in the depravity of students gave way but not fast enough. Too many institutions, through their leaders, act as though they still really had the power of a colonial president and that students have no procedural rights nor rights to due process. Thus, one dean cancels, without consultation with students, their time-honored right to assemble in a space next to the campus. Still another official acts to suppress an article proposed for a student magazine, while another suspends a student for alleged violations of college rules—without a hearing. Now many such actions would make sense to outraged adults but are indefensible in the light of the American judicial tradition. Hence one angry reaction on the part of a university official to vexing problems of students provides the legitimate focus for many not so legitimate student protests. Virtually every major student uprising was made possible because at some point some college official made the institution vulnerable through denying generally recognized procedural rights. Behind every successful student outbreak stands some administrator who exercised discretion without legitimacy.

Institutions have been unable to take and maintain a strong moral stand against student destruction of property or violation of the rights of others partly because their own moral position was assailable —and bright militant students quickly recognize tarnished values. Thus, lurking in the background of presidential recanting in confrontations with students stand examples of arbitrary action, double standards, and even some examples of dishonesty. The dean of students who denies a white girl the right to bring a Negro date to a dance in the 1960's is not really in a position to face militant students sitting in an administration building in protest over Dow recruiters on the campus, even granted that the student technique and concern were inappropriate to the mission of the university. The institution that, through the unconcerned operation of its recruitment policies, allowed itself to become "lily white" is not really in a position to dispute charges that its athletic department had practiced racism. Or, the institution that acts out of anger or petulance in dealing with a difficult faculty member in violation of the spirit, if not the letter, of the law regarding tenure and the like, can scarcely confront students who similarly violate the spirit if not the letter of the law of a collegiate community.

Of a different order is the failure of institutions to recognize the fact that in many respects college students represent a new kind of adolescence, requiring a special kind of response. Of course, there is the counterpoint that students have not faced the fact that they are not yet full adults. Adolescence is that period between childhood and adult responsibility for oneself, one's mate, children, and society. It is as well a biological phenomenon involving the advent of puberty; but in an even more significant sense, it is a cultural phenomenon involving both status and function. Now within American middle-class society there has always been some dysfunction between various adult statuses and adult functions. One can drive at sixteen, kill at eighteen, drink at twenty-one, all adult statuses but not adult functions, in the sense of economic self-sufficiency, until one is twenty-five. In the past biological, status, and functioning adulthood were achieved within a relatively short span of time. Puberty would come at fourteen or sixteen, end of schooling at sixteen or eighteen, marriage at nineteen or twenty, franchise at twenty-one, and a full-time job at about the same time. During that five-year period, the characteristics of self-consciousness, exclusive allegiance to peer groups, irresponsible criticism of adults and adult values, and the hiatus status (neither children nor adults) could be tolerated; and ways could be worked out within the family to contain extreme manifestations.

At present, however, a number of forces have operated to extend the period of at least cultural adolescence to even before puberty. The early teen-ager has achieved economic power, yet by his late twenties he is not yet responsible for himself as an economic unit. Puberty may come slightly earlier and the opportunity for the killing or marrying prerogatives occur more frequently, but the *rite de passage* of formally ending education comes a great deal later. Thus, the time span of incomplete adulthood has been extended from perhaps five years to ten or fifteen years, and at the same time institutions other than the family, church, and high school are now required to deal with large

numbers of adolescents. Thus, the contemporary university is faced
with finding ways of dealing with large numbers of students who have
achieved biological adulthood and many, if not most, of the statuses
of adulthood, yet who cannot really be responsible for themselves,
mates, children, or society in any save limited ways. Until the present
the attempt was made to deal with these students in ways similar to
those appropriate for those adolescents with fewer of the attributes of
adulthood. And, of course, it doesn't work. Some of the struggles of
college students in their middle twenties to obtain a share in the governance of a college may in reality be an effort to simulate a part of
adulthood that their economic condition denies them. In earlier times
a twenty-five-year-old man was responsible for himself and family and
felt responsible for a part of society. The modern twenty-five-year-old
college student probably labors with considerable guilt because he is
not similarly placed, hence his drive to campus power sublimates guilt.

There are, of course, a number of other explanations or hypotheses as to why students, especially the restless or militant ones,
seek confrontations. One is that the permissiveness of liberal parents
has resulted in children who, wanting immediate gratification of desires
and not gaining their ends, protest violently, give up, or descend into
despair. Related is the theory that students have been so led to underlying psychological bases for behavior that they are unwilling to assume responsibility for their own conduct. If blame for problems can
be placed on parental conduct as recalled in an analytic session, the
student is thereby relieved of responsibility or guilt over lack of responsibility. Then, too, there is the belief that affluence has taken from
the young the need to earn things for themselves. Boredom and rest-
lessness come when the spirit of service goes. Some have thought, but
without much clinical evidence, that restless students are merely reflect-
ing family pathology and disorganization. It may be, however, that
in a highly charged society even minor family disturbances could be
operative. Then, a series of other explanations are advanced. The fact
of impersonality of life in a complex society is seen as a stimulus to
protest. The despair that comes when students see the difficulty of
acting in the political sphere is suggested as the reason radicals prefer
direct action. And feelings of powerlessness in the face of the inexorable advance of technology are said to be involved in feelings of de-
terminism tending toward nihilism. Then, there is the opposite force.

College youth have been bred on lessons of the power of science and
the perfectibility of man. When they experience the spotted reality,
they are shattered.

At least two other factors must be mentioned. The first is the
general affluence of middle-class white America existing as it does beside a tradition rooted in Calvinism and the rejection of pleasure.
Somehow both adults and students in American colleges display considerable guilt over "never having it so good," with restless students
opting for the poverty of dropping out and faculty opting for extending the work day and week into times once reserved for recreation as
a means of alleviating guilt. Somehow the student who can wear old
clothes, eat simple fare, and scorn the "fat cats" eases the guilt that
comes from knowing he has had a life of luxury. Equally the professor
who flies at night to avoid losing a day of work and who carries his
"own" work into the weekends is coping with the problems of affluence.

This problem of affluence is intensified by the twin issues of the
plight of minority groups in America and the war—now in Viet Nam,
but who can tell where next? With respect to the war, there is more
than a small suspicion that at least part of present affluence is war
based. Hence to enjoy affluence is to condone a war the justice of
which is in considerable doubt. In a very real sense the protesting college student may be covering the guilt he feels because he knows that
had his parents not been war-based affluent, he might be fighting the
war instead of going to college. Police billy clubs are still safer than
Viet grenades and he knows it and feels guilty about it. Of course, the
moral dilemma of affluent America over the plight of the Negro is the
most divisive force in the society. The guilt and grief that white America evidenced on the death of Martin Luther King is just illustrative
of the subterranean feeling there before his death. It is no accident
that the student protest derived from the civil rights movement. When
it ceased to attract, other protest activity could be used to sublimate
the guilt of over three hundred years of injustice.

If this analysis has even limited validity then some possible solutions to the problems dealing with restless students are suggested.
The first is really just a palliative, although a not insignificant one. It
is to put the problem in some kind of historical perspective. Students
have always been difficult to live with and have frequently assumed
postures that bothered adults and disturbed institutions. Medieval stu-

dents rioted, dumped garbage on passersby, wrote erotic or ribald poems and read them on church steps and in other sanctuaries of the establishment, coerced their professors, and, on occasion, killed one. Colonial college students rioted about food, stole, took pot shots at university presidents, protested infringement of their private lives, and gradually forced colleges to modify stringent rules regarding personal conduct. Nineteenth-century students took sides over the Civil War and demanded a voice in academic governance. Twentieth-century students signed the Oxford Peace Pledge, joined in the Spanish Civil War, rioted over food, violated the Eighteenth Amendment, and experimented with sex. There is probably good reason to believe that the present wave of student unrest may be qualitatively different from those earlier times. However, at least an important portion of student protest replicates those of the past simply because the process of growing up is after all a human process and human life has really not changed much in quite a few years. If somehow the embattled administrator could with some humor reflect on the past, and perhaps even learn from the past, his feelings, if not his plight, might be helped. Especially is learning from the past important. Students, when they have protested, have on occasion been trying to say something. Student riots over the quality of food in the commons and the subsequent organization of fraternities and eating clubs were real responses to bad conditions. A confrontation between Princeton students of different persuasions indicated that there were serious moral questions as to whether justice lay with the North or the South. Student agitation over strict rules of conduct was sparked by an overzealous desire on the part of faculty to impose a Puritan ideal of conduct that simply could not work in a changing society. Perhaps historical reflection might suggest that old standards can be changed and still the world turns.

But there are other, more direct ways that might be attempted. In virtually every major campus upset from 1964 on, involved was a lack of procedures and procedural rights that could have kept grievances within legitimate bounds. The technique of direct administrative handling of disciplinary matters has lost its legitimacy in the eyes of students and of many faculty and this loss should be recognized and appropriate changes made. The nature of these changes seems clear. First, there should be only a limited number of offenses over which the university should assume jurisdiction. These would include such academic offenses as cheating and plagiarism and such violations against persons and property as misusing equipment, damage to university property, or interference with the legitimate rights of others to use institutional facilities. These, codified, should then be the responsibility of a campus judicial system with procedures for indictment, hearings, and appeals made explicit. As a general rule no administrator should have the right to assess guilt or to assign punishment, nor should he have the right to make administrative rulings without the option of a review of both policy and specific substance. Also, generally, the campus judicial body should be elected from faculty, students, and administration, but administrative officers charged with administering regulations regarding conduct should be barred from membership and even from presence during deliberations. Very likely this campus judicial body might have original jurisdiction over offenses regarding the code of behavior and an appeals function for major controversy over other matters. For example, if a student editor and faculty advisor of a student publication disagreed over whether or not an item should be published and the campus editorial board could not resolve the matter, appeal to the campus judicial should be an option, with its ruling final, unless overturned by the institution's board of trustees. Within such a structure even the most vexing of campus issues could be resolved and the administration not placed in a vulnerable position. Student sit-ins of university property, obstruction of on-campus recruitment, and student destruction of university property all could be handled if the campus judicial body is allowed to act responsibly.

Then, too, institutions ought to be more parsimonious in their claimed objectives. Colleges and universities are not churches, clinics, nor even parents. They are devices by which a limited number of skills, insights, and points of view are communicated to the young in the belief that possession of these somehow aids the individual to become a better human being. It is true that the implements to achieve these limited goals are many and varied. Thus, residence halls and lectures, participation in faculty committees and discussions, symbols of institutional loyalty and libraries and laboratories are properly viewed as techniques of instruction and should be used in a professional manner much as the medical profession uses x-ray, medicine, or splints. University regulation of the professional uses of its technical resources seems quite appropriate and if regulations were so limited, few students could legitimately protest. Setting library or laboratory hours, establishing safety requirements for residence halls, or requiring conditions of quiet in classrooms or lecture halls do not seem to become issues in campus controversy except when drawn in the wake of a more central issue. It is when the institution claims too much that it becomes suspect. And it is when an institution attempts to regulate beyond what is necessary to achieve its limited educational goals that it becomes vulnerable. Whether or not a student burns a draft card, participates in a civil rights march, engages in premarital or extramarital sexual activity, becomes pregnant, attends church, sleeps all day, drinks all night is not really the concern of a collegiate institution as an educational institution. When colleges regulate such behavior, as many do, they are by implication taking responsibility for developing patriotism, one system of sexual standards, one system of health standards and one religious stance—activities that are more properly the province of other social institutions. This is not to say that such matters may not be of concern to an institution or that it cannot deal with them. But if they be of concern, it should be an educational—even a curricular one. Instruction in sex hygiene, ethics, law, or health is appropriate. Requiring a specific kind of behavior is no more appropriate than a requirement that all who finish a course in American government vote Democratic.

This is stark doctrine and will bother many. A religiously related school may feel that compulsory chapel is necessary. A girls' school may feel that pregnancy is something it cannot condone. But in each situation the college is acting the role of some other agency. Now many institutions are able to get away with appearing in these many different roles and to regulate a wide variety of conduct because of the kinds of students they attract, their traditions, and the like. But such institutions are always open to attack, whereas if they kept regulation limited to what is relevant for limited purposes, they would not be.

An even more significant reform involves the assertion or reassertion of administrative prerogative in relevant domains. For better or for worse, American higher education is and has been administrator centered. It is the president or central administration who brings about innovation when it does happen. It is the president or administrator whose goals are most close to those of students who want a better education. Actually the militant students who want to join with the faculty are in a sense allying themselves to the greatest danger, for it is the American college faculty that has so professionalized itself that it can disregard demands from its clients—the students. And it is the president who, if he errs, brings about confrontation and, on occasion, collapse. In each of the most widely publicized campus upheavals it was administrative failure that led to trouble—administrative failure in the sense that the chief executive or an associate used his powers on inappropriate problems.

The American college president should have control of the finances of the institution, certain veto powers, certain appointive powers, and, of course, the powers that attend possession of information. These he is expected to use in the exercise of educational leadership but in procedurally established ways and in the light of other powers belonging to other campus elements. The faculty quite properly should have control over the curriculum, its own membership, and the conditions of student entrance and exit. Students also should have the power of self-determination over their private lives and the conduct of their own group living, but with a number of procedural rights guaranteed. To illustrate how these powers might operate in potentially controversial situations, several examples are suggested. A president should have a voice in faculty appointment and tenure because of the financial commitment. A president should not be able to decree a new program, for that is the concern of the faculty, but he should be able to determine whether or not it will be financed. A president should not have the power to expel a student for misconduct but should have the power to veto a decision of the campus judicial body and the obligation to refer the matter to the board of trustees.

What all of this adds up to is a formulation involving delegation of powers and authority, the establishment of procedures and due process, and a concern for a limited number of purposes and objectives. It is a tight constructionist interpretation based on the belief that loose constructionism has really brought about the crises and the confrontations. If college officials concern themselves with defensible educational matters through the use of clearly defined powers and recognized procedures, leaving all other matters to individuals, order yet may be restored and accounts finally settled.

CHAPTER 5

Protest
and Resolution

Although the vast majority of American college students, regardless of the kind of institution they attend, are very likely to be content with their lives and with the society into which they will move, a minority has arisen—variously described as student protesters, militants, the Radical Left, or student activists—that is affecting every part of American life and American higher education. Although this group is proportionally small—not more than 5 per cent of all college students, according to some estimates—it is large enough, in a total student body of seven million, to number 350,000 students, enough to affect every single institution in the country, and to inundate quite a few. These students, whether the adult population wills it or not, will be heard, and with reason.

It is just possible that out of the extracurricular activities in which the militants engage, such things as a search for participatory democracy, experimentation with art forms, experimentation with

newer styles of interpersonal relationships, experimentation with newer
approaches to the solution of political problems, can be found the elements that will, several decades hence, comprise the collegiate curriculum. This has happened in the past. Fraternities, libraries, drama,
and intercollegiate athletics are all examples. Frederick Rudolph points
out that much of what is now standardly accepted orthodoxy within
higher education originated in the extracurricular life of students in
the nineteenth century who were resentful about the educational experience they received. Rudolph suggests that the library as it is now
known derived from libraries established in fraternities and literary societies, because the college library was archival rather than circula-
tory in function. Intercollegiate athletics evolved from student athletic
contests developed because the regimen of the gymnastic movement
was ill-suited to the physiological needs of late adolescents. The fraternity system, with both its strengths and its evils, emerged as a coun-
teraction to the dreary living conditions in college residence halls and
commons. Even drama and music as part of the collegiate curriculum
seem to be rooted in student experimentation with these activities as a
way to alleviate the boredom that a prescribed, recitation-centered curriculum imposed. One point of view suggests that if educators can but
understand what students are saying, they will be able to discover the
likely evolutionary pattern of the collegiate enterprise.[1]

Of even more immediate importance, it is now clear that this
small minority of students actually has the power to bring any collegiate institution to a halt, and quite possibly all of American higher education or the society itself to a halt. The various events from the student uprising at Berkeley in 1964 to the more recent controversies at
San Francisco State College, which resulted in the resignation of a
president, at Columbia University, which terminated the academic
term prematurely, and at Stanford, which hastened the granting of
prerogatives to students—all are indicative of what a militant minority
can accomplish. And, of course, the presidencies of France and of
the United States have been shaken by student power.

It also seems clear that these groups of students can divide a
society and alter the course of political and international events. There
still seems to be a polarization around liberal and conservative out-

[1] Frederick Rudolph, "Neglect of Students as a Historical Tradition,"
in L. E. Dennis and J. F. Kauffman (Eds.), *The College and the Student*
(Washington, D.C.: American Council on Education, 1966).

looks. It is quite possible that if the number of student revolts and protests increase, and if at the same time the cities of America experience a further series of riots, a backlash will be generated that may result in the election of extreme conservative candidates who believe in a restoration of "old-time values" and who are willing to become punitive and vindictive to achieve their ends. There is more than a little suspicion that the election of a conservative governor in California was related to student protests within the university and state college system. Somehow, the people of California, who had been so prideful of their magnificent educational enterprise, became frightened at student outbursts, believing somehow that the universities were creating a generation of revolutionaries; and they turned to whatever political figures presented hope for immediate and simple solutions to the problems of dealing with students on the campus. In this connection it should also be recalled that within a few years those under twenty-five years of age will be the absolute majority of the American population and that political power will reside in their hands.

But there are also moral and ethical reasons why this militant minority should be heard. They stand in direct continuation of the American protest movements of the past, which did result in the creation of a somewhat more open society than was found in other nations of the world. The Boston Tea Party was not appreciably different from the destruction at Columbia University, and the Declaration of Independence seems to reflect the same tone as the manifestos of the Students for Democratic Society. Then, too, there is a tenable conception that higher education is a professional enterprise organized to provide professional services to people who need them. As clients seeking these professional services, students would seem to have every right to indicate satisfaction and dissatisfaction. It is just possible that the young may be more acutely sensitive to the profound changes that have taken place in society and to the need for the creation of new social institutions with which to cope with those changes. The generation now occupying central positions within the established order may be listening so intently to the drummer who plays the tunes of the Great Depression and World War II that they miss the counterpoint of the post-World-War-II revolutions.

Although much has been written about student protest, no one can identify with any certainty the roots of the problem nor suggest remedies. However, it begins to appear that confrontations on college campuses probably occur through accretion of error and misjudgment by institutions, their officers, board members, and other constituencies, as well as by students. These accretions of error occur in a context of serious social and ethical malfunctionings. Since errors have been made in times past, it seems likely that the intensity of today's conflict is occasioned by the social context. For purposes of analysis, however, it is necessary to look at the sources of error first.

Although institutions of higher education have accomplished much since World War II—accommodation of veterans' enrollments with inadequate space and inadequate staff, acceptance of some seven million students seeking higher education, increased quality of faculties, and greatly enriched curriculum—still they have provoked student resentment through very real and very visible malfunctioning.

Despite a general relaxation of standards of personal conduct, colleges and universities have been overly concerned about managing and controlling the private lives of students. There have been too many incidents of students being denied procedural rights or due process because officers of an institution acted like Victorian parents. There are still too many institutions in the country in which officers still claim the right to search students' rooms, to employ the lie detector, or use academic penalties and sanctions for essentially nonacademic behaviors. The literature of the student protest movement suggests that if institutions would take a somewhat freer stance regarding the private lives of students, much of the trouble could be alleviated.

But there are other malfunctionings. In a very real sense, the American college or university, in spite of its professed liberal or democratic ideals, can be considered perhaps one of the most autocratic and authoritarian institutions in society. The society increasingly values the certification that comes from knowledge training, and yet places that certification in the unsupervised hands of college professors and college administrators. This seems particularly marked in graduate education, where the major professor does hold an almost life-and-death power over his students. If the professor decides that a thesis is inappropriate, the student's academic career is thus terminated. The American college professor, especially in large prestige institutions, seems finally to have achieved the position of independence that German professors were said to have achieved in the nineteenth century. The professor sets his own time for talking with students, reviewing their work, or even setting their examinations. The caprice of a professor can and does extend the time a graduate student must spend in an institution from four to occasionally fourteen years. This arbitrariness, of course, is also found in the undergraduate college through the grading function, which is operated at best capriciously and at worst vindictively. An individual professor can alter the entire adult life of a student. Given the unvalidated significance of grades, a professor personally irritated with a student can determine whether or not the student will enter medical school or achieve other aspirations for which he is just possibly quite well qualified.

While students typically have not been as articulate as they might be in criticizing the college curriculum, they have said enough to suggest that for the most part college curricula are arid, professor-centered, and of scant interest or relevance to students. In study after study, the college curriculum and college instruction are judged by students as being of the least importance to their own personal development. Outside of a few charismatic professors, students judge instruction to be somewhat less than adequate and courses to be just so many hurdles to be overcome in the process of gaining a desired certification. Most students will submit to the drudgery of courses because they do intend to fit into the system of American society; but the precocious dropouts tell us something is wrong.

Then, too, colleges and universities have been almost dishonest in their claims as to what they can do for students, even as the establishment has been dishonest in its claims for democracy. This dishonesty extends from catalogues that advertise professional programs without adequate staff and equipment to make good these claims, to the claims of prestigious institutions to develop wisdom. There is even some suspicion that there has been considerable dishonesty in the sorts of research tasks that institutions have undertaken for the federal government. One observer estimates that perhaps three-fourths of contract research in the social and behavioral sciences has proven completely useless for the purposes of the sponsoring agency.

Although theorists for American colleges and universities argue that higher education should be the critic and the leader of society, the history of higher education does not really support such a claim. Merle Curti stated that major educational leaders in America had never been in the forefront of society with respect to their social ideas, but rather codified the conventional wisdom of even the class of which they were a part, particularly with respect to the two issues most di-

visive of contemporary society.[2] Higher education has been far from
the vanguard of thinking about resolution of either war or civil rights.
It was not until several years after the 1954 Supreme Court decision
that higher educational organizations began to pass resolutions to support an end to segregation. Even as late as 1960–61, votes within such
organizations could be evenly split. In 1965, colleges across the country
were beginning to talk about the possibility of trying to do something,
at some time in the future, about the college education of American
Negroes. In 1967 the same picture had not changed. It was only the
death of the Reverend Martin Luther King that forced colleges and
universities seriously to reconsider their stand and to seek ways of extending educational opportunities to Negroes. Also, institutions have
occupied ambivalent positions with respect to war, particularly the
Viet Nam war, as an instrument of policy. Universities conducting a
large amount of research have accepted, frequently without question,
defense-based research, and at times have seemed likely to become a
willing instrument of political policy. Whether or not institutions
should take an institutional stand regarding such things as the Viet
Nam war is, of course, moot. If an institution does enter the arena of
political decision, then it may very well open itself up to the action of
other rules of political life. The fact that it has not as an enterprise
been able to decide whether or not it should take stands, and has been
unable to develop policies regarding appropriate and inappropriate
governmental research affiliation, has forced militant students into
making judgments.

There is more than a small suspicion that institutions have been
overly sensitive to the demands of politically or economically powerful
elements in the society, even when those demands jeopardized the
rights and needs of less influential people. With a few notable exceptions, Southern institutions, even after the Supreme Court decision of
1954, moved with maddening slowness toward integration, for fear
that a more precipitous action would bring down the wrath of the
politically powerful. A number of the observers of the 1964 Berkeley
upsets have suggested that several of the crucial decisions made by the
university administration were prompted by powerful Republican
forces in the Berkeley-Oakland area, and several institutions have
moved slowly on such matters as the extension of parietal rights, the

[2] Merle Curti, *The Social Ideas of American Educators* (Paterson, N.J.:
Pageant Books, 1959).

large scale integration of the student body, or the hiring of controversial professors, for fear of what attendant publicity might do to potential donors. Now, this is not to say that institutions have been supine in the face of the power elite, but is to argue that there are enough verifiable cases to allow critically militant students to raise the charge of a double or multiple standard.

The next matter is even more difficult to document but it has to do with the several roles of a college professor. He is expected to be a teacher, a scholar, and occasionally of service to his society. However, much of his system of ethics and most of the procedural rights he has emphasized have to do with protecting his right as a scholar and with augmenting the prerogatives for scholarship. Such issues as permanent tenure, academic freedom, and self-determination of the scholar say little about the role of the professor as a teacher and a member of a helping profession. Thus, there are institutionalized justifications for the scholar to place "his own work" first, after which he may attend to the needs of students. Now, it is true that when professors have sought to make themselves available to students, students have frequently not availed themselves of this service; but students make enough demands for greater contact with their professors to lead one to believe that they are criticizing the entire ethical stance regarding the helping of others.

The organizational and administrative structures of institutions of higher education seem admirably contrived to delay decision on critical educational matters. If an institution attempts to remodel its curriculum, it must anticipate that the task will require anywhere from five to ten years; and to attempt such a radical proposal as improving college teaching would likely exhaust the tenure of one or two sympathetic presidents. This slowness to change is in some ways a by-product of the collegial system of government, but it can particularly frustrate the young who are looking for quick solutions to quite complex educational problems. It could well be argued that the present system of organization of colleges and universities is simply inappropriate to accommodate the rapidity of change currently necessary.

It is possible to catalogue still other failures of higher education that contribute to the confrontation evil. The cost of education has increased more rapidly than has the gross national product or other measures of economic function; thus parents, students, donors, legislators are faced with inexplicable rises in costs. Effectiveness has been

assumed just from the existence of the enterprise, and some have begun
to ask, Is it worth it? But perhaps enough failures have been described
to suggest the dimensions of this part of the confrontation syndrome.

Students themselves have contributed enormously to their own
problems. First, there is a strong tendency for students to expect the
university to be something it is not. Some of the protest students seem
to want the university to become the modern church and to provide
a theology to help them cope with temporary conditions. Others want
the university to be clearly a political action agency, taking stands on
both major and minor political questions. Quite a few students see the
university almost as a clinic capable of providing therapy for the
psychic wounds that a complex and somewhat impersonal society has
imposed on them. And, more recently, there seems to be a demand for
the university to be a sanctuary. Students have rejected as doctrine
the *in loco parentis* position but at the same time seem to expect the
university to provide them freedom with some degree of protection
from the intruding outside society. Simply illustrative are the students
who plan on campus a sit-in demonstration in another city, and then
expect the university to provide bail and legal services. Actually, the
university is simply one institution of many in society, and has a restricted range of functions. Institutions themselves have sometimes mis-
led by claiming more than they can actually accomplish, and some of
the more militant students seem to be misleading themselves by expecting the university to be something other than what it is. The university
is a device for teaching or screening people, for enculturating them,
for providing certain limited kinds of services, and for conducting some
kinds of research and scholarship.

Second, perhaps more so in recent times, there appears to be
a strong romantic vein in contemporary college students. They seem
to believe that absolute justice is possible, and that it can be achieved
immediately if only the wish is somehow expressed. This justice somehow takes on the attributes of a justice they imagine existed in a more
primitive, less complicated society. Thus, there is a worship of the simple life of primitive goods and artifacts, and a belief that expressing a
wish should automatically produce complete accomplishment. One of
the reasons students have been adopting direct protest techniques is
because the more laborious task of reform through bureaucratic structure takes too long for their youthful impatience. And in their impatience students have been somewhat remiss in developing a set of cri-

teria or moral or ethical standards that they can use to judge the relevance or appropriateness of their activities. Hence the inclination to use the same techniques used in civil rights demonstrations in the South to obtain a change in check-in hours for women or to oppose recruitment efforts by corporations holding defense contracts. A very good case can be made that civil disobedience and the more extreme forms of direct action protest, such as sit-ins and even revolutions, can be justified only when there is a matter of high moral importance at stake, and when no other plausible recourses to action are open. Americans thought so in 1776 and 1861. Thus, one can support civil disobedience, massive parades of protest, sit-in tactics, and economic boycotts on the part of Negroes in the South to gain the simple political rights which open up other recourses. Without direct tactics these advances could not have taken place, so tight was the White supremacy society. But on a university campus such conditions generally do not prevail. There are channels by which administrative attention can be drawn to rules regarding student conduct, and there are appropriate ways by which student minorities can express their disbelief about campus recruitment. If the minority is defeated on an issue on which procedurally correct steps could be taken, it would seem there is no justification for more direct approaches. Some would say that the issue of Viet Nam is of such a nature that it is parallel to the civil rights movement in the South. If this be so, then the protests should be directed with full awareness of consequences to the most relevant social agencies rather than against the university, which typically is not in a power-generating position. Thus, in place of a sit-in in the administration building of a university, the protest might be directed against military installations, ports of embarcation, draft headquarters, and the like.

Then, too, students have opened themselves to charges of superficiality when they have not really criticized fundamental weaknesses in the university but rather have tilted at relatively minor matters. There is much that is wrong with the contemporary college curriculum. Much teaching is so useless that it might better not have been done. Much counseling is and has been simply ritual designed to attend to bureaucratic details. But students all too frequently have focused their ire on the quality of food in residence halls, on parietal rights, on regulations regarding relatively minor aspects of human conduct. This is not to say that some of these matters are not deserving of attention; but it is to say that if students want really to be taken seriously as partners in governing the collegiate enterprise, their ordering of priorities ought to be somewhat different. One can be quite sympathetic with students who galvanize themselves to action in support of a highly effective teacher and who at the same time do not care too deeply whether or not co-eds are in at eleven or twelve o'clock on given days of the week.

This next point may be an individual aesthetic reaction, but it does appear that student militants have been too frequently addicted to the flouting of relatively inconsequential conventions, thereby jeopardizing their effectiveness on more important issues. Long hair, somewhat atypical clothing, abstinence from bathing are not of themselves necessarily good or bad, but rather are matters of individual choice. But if the generally accepted conventions indicate that for some occasions certain styles of dress or grooming are appropriate, the politically sensitive individual is likely to attend moderately to those conventions. This is brought home to me by a number of quite talented graduate students who clearly want to become college presidents and undoubtedly have the talents to become effective administrators, but who will not condescend to adopt the personal mannerisms necessary to gain appointment. It is possible for persons to be quite individualistic in the way they think, in the solution to problems they invent, and still conform to the superficial conventions of society.

The last point involves student inconsistency regarding the college as a parent surrogate. Students clearly want greater freedom, and should have it. But many of them also want protection against the consequences of their actions. This expectation is reflected in many ways ranging from students wanting the institution to take action in cases involving marijuana to institutions providing a kind of parent image to whom students can go when they are in trouble. Students must realize that they can't have it both ways. The greater the amount of personal freedom, the less the institution should be expected to interfere between the operation of the larger society and the conduct of students' private lives.

Out of these and similar errors an impasse is clearly in the making. However, there is time for solutions to be found. First, faculty and administration might very well engage in greater introspection to determine their own motives for the role they occupy, and to concentrate on developing a system of ethics that emphasizes the helping roles of the teacher. There has been a high degree of professionalization of college professors and in some prestige institutions they have gained the right almost to set whatever tasks make sense to them and them alone, and to reject all others. This is a happy sort of situation for the individual occupying it, but perhaps a little introspection might suggest that it is not socially defensible. Or deans of students might engage in a bit of introspection as to why they like the role of controlling the behavior of others.

Second, institutions might develop a more parsimonious statement of goals so as not to mislead students, parents, the larger society, or themselves. Such an action might make the institution more effective overall, and could certainly give the institution a more honest stance in the eyes of its constituencies.

Then, it is possible to find better ways of assessment of the outcomes of education so that malfunctioning can be detected more quickly. Such detection is likely to be forced on institutions as the supporting society demands evidence of need for additional resources.

But students also should change. First, they could be expected to demonstrate a greater willingness to accept the consequences of the exercise of freedom. If protesters violate university regulations and are expelled from school, and if this expulsion makes them eligible for the operation of the draft law, the possibility of draft should be accepted as a consequence. If students elect to opt out of the middle-class achieving society, the consequence is living in poverty. One has the feeling that too many students expect the largesse of achieving society to support their nonachieving style of life.

Students can also be expected to work within the system to carve out new roles appropriate to extended childhood which must accommodate their own needs as well as the rights of the adult society. In a very real sense the duration of childhood has been extended from ten or eleven years old in the nineteenth century to seventeen years old before World War II to the middle twenties now, and it is possible that this childhood—defined as not having full economic self-sufficiency—could extend into the late twenties or early thirties. Physiologically and emotionally, individuals are mature at this point—yet traditional roles no longer suffice. In some way or other the youth's need to be helped to develop new roles to accommodate the lack of economic self-sufficiency, the very real needs of the self-sufficient adult must be met.

CHAPTER 6

Students
and Governance

The claim that students should have a major role in actual academic governance is based upon a false premise: that students can plan, with reasonable awareness of the outcomes, the essentially professional service they receive from the college and university. The falseness of this premise can be illustrated by considering realistically whether freshman medical students have the background to plan courses in surgery, or business students to plan their work in accounting, or students in the physical or biological sciences to plan sequences of work in physics or bioengineering. That students may take from a curriculum those courses that seem of value to them does not mean that they possess the necessary background, insight, and awareness of consequences actually to be given a share of responsibility for decisions about the curriculum or about the skills of those professionally charged with making the curriculum operative. Becker, in *Boys in White,* revealed that medical students functioning within a student subculture would decide which of the laboratory work they would actually do, and which lab problems they would fake or copy from their classmates.[1] A student who wanted to enter psychiatry would state that nothing in his future professional practice would require him to have a firsthand knowledge of nerve tissue; hence, he would leave detailed dissection of a cadaver only to those proposing to enter surgery. And one must assume that students in the other sciences and the vocational curriculum will from time to time inject their own thinking into the functioning of the curriculum by similar devices. But, by and large, one does not have the impression that these students, oriented toward developing a specific set of skills, are asking for or expecting a substantial voice in the planning of the institution.

The students who appear most desirous of directly modifying their educational experience are those non-vocationally oriented who are majoring in the traditional liberal arts subjects. Robert H. Somers remarks in connection with the 1964 student protests at Berkeley that "social science and humanities students predominate on this campus, together accounting for nearly half of its students, and these two groups are the most likely to be found in the more militant camp, with physical science majors coming close behind. Indeed, in our sample, these three groups accounted for three-fourths of the militants we identified, and only a little over one-third of the conservatives. Support for the conservatives is most likely to come from business administration, engineering, architecture, and agriculture, which together account for nearly half of them."[2] And Rose K. Goldsen makes the same point when she remarks that:

> College students are asked to go through a great deal of drudgery. Their motivation to endure the drudgery is complex to be sure, but one element in that motivation is the conviction that the drudgery they are asked to go through is relevant to a desired outcome. The outcome may not always be an intellectual one in their eyes, but it often is. And, since one of our tasks as university professors and administrators is to upgrade the value of the intellectual payoff in a student's value systems, I am going to discuss only that intellectual payoff. Thus, let me rephrase my previous comment. They must be convinced that the drudgery they

[1] Howard S. Becker and others, *Boys in White: Student Culture in Medical School* (Chicago: University of Chicago Press, 1961).

[2] In Charles Muscatine and others, *Education at Berkeley: Report of the Select Committee on Education* (Berkeley: University of California Press, 1966).

are asked to go through is relevant to some desired intellectual outcome; that it is not nonsense.

Right now, what we call the hard sciences are not on the defensive in this regard. Students are willing to accept on faith that the drudgery they are asked to go through in these fields is not likely to be nonsense; that it will have a relevant intellectual outcome. Students do not really expect a Hans Bethe to supervise their laboratory work in Physics 101.

It is the social sciences and humanities that are on the defensive. Students look to these disciplines to help them approach answers to the explosive questions that trouble all of us, world peace, distributive justice, the nature of thought, control of atomic weapons. We tell them at least two things that cause them a lot of misgiving. First, we tell them that they must learn some abc's before they can intelligently examine each problem in any serious way. They must go through some paces that they see as drudgery to get themselves background and skills.

They don't always believe us. Undergraduate students are more convinced than their professors are that they can already read a document critically, analyze an argument, think independently, marshal and evaluate evidence, clearly engage in constructive exposition and clarify a dialogue about a problem. We tell them they are mistaken and turn them over to graduate assistants to help them develop skills and background. But these skills are not so concrete as though involved in say solving an equation or analyzing a chemical element. They are sharpened by bringing to bear informed judgment and judicious evaluation which the graduate assistant often doesn't have.

We tell students they are mistaken in another regard. That their explosive questions are really unanswerable. They want to examine the dynamics of international tensions. Let's look at games theory with statistics and calculus as prerequisites. Distributive justice interests them. It's a normative question and should be rephrased. What about the discrepancies between American ideals and the workings of our social system? Likewise, how did fascism come about? They must begin with an earlier historical period and a seminar on how to evaluate the authenticity of documents. The best students get restless. This is not what they meant at all.[3]

One can agree with Goldsen and put her point even more sharply. Professors in the professional fields and in some of the hard sciences seem to have made a reasonable attempt to conceptualize the

[3] In L. E. Dennis and J. F. Kauffman (Eds.), *The College and the Student* (Washington, D.C.: American Council on Education, 1966).

outcomes desired from an educational experience or a curriculum, and with a number of clearly false starts, have attempted to arrange a sequence of courses that will bring students up to some predetermined level of competence. Professors in the "soft" areas have just not done this, even though the catalogue may indicate prerequisites for courses in the humanities and social sciences. These prerequisites are generally quite meaningless, and students with little or no experience can compete quite effectively in advanced courses with students who have followed a full sequence in the field. Students in these "soft" areas are therefore likely to resist the kind of drudgery that they accept in the hard sciences and professional fields, and to believe that they can know as well or perhaps even better than their professors how courses should be organized.

Actually, the college or university is most properly considered an agency for rendering professional services. These services may be to develop literacy, certain vocational competences, certain skills of analysis, or even an internally consistent, personally satisfying set of values. These professional services are provided by a cadre of professional workers who may, if they wish, select from a large number of techniques and devices for rendering the service required. It may be that for certain desired outcomes it is desirable to have students teach someone, and for other outcomes, to engage in independent study; or to prepare a paper, to conduct a laboratory experiment, to live in a residence hall, to participate in faculty debate, to work part-time, to go to an art museum, or to read a chapter. But each one of these activities most properly should be viewed not as of essential worth in and of itself but as a device selected by a professionally competent person to achieve a desired outcome. This thesis—that the college or university is an agency for rendering professional service—is a fundamental one with respect to both the argument concerning student role in governance and the hypotheses explaining some of the student unrest currently plaguing American college campuses. One can theorize, on the basis of a good bit of the protest literature and conversations with students, that there is generally an implicit recognition of the professional role of the college or university. Student unrest is probably not over the fundamental notion but rather over implementation. College professors have never really seen themselves as members of a helping profession—which is essentially what they are. They have tended to view themselves as spokesmen for this or that or the other discipline.

Even the elements from which might ultimately be fashioned a professorial code of ethics are more related to the role of spokesman for a discipline than to that of member of a helping profession. The concepts of academic freedom, tenure, and authority over the curriculum seem rooted in the values of the discipline rather than in the relationship with those who receive professional services. Professors, not clear in their own minds about their professional role, have tended to be quite crude in the selection of techniques for administration of service. Thus, lecturing, discussion, outside reading, and limited laboratory exercises are the most frequently used devices, and students are quick to see that some of these are irrelevant to their needs for professional help.

To this false premise—that students are capable of planning an education for themselves—should be added a number of misconceptions or even myths. The first of these is that students are generally dissatisfied with their education and really want to change it. Although one could argue that students should really be dissatisfied, they just aren't. This point may be documented in a number of ways. At the very time that the student movement at Berkeley in 1964 was gaining national prominence, questionnairing of students on the Berkeley campus revealed some interesting findings:

> If one supposed that the student protest rose from some general feeling of dissatisfaction with the university this supposition is damaged, if not thoroughly destroyed, by the fact that 82 per cent of our samples report themselves as "satisfied" or "very satisfied" with courses, examinations, professors, and so forth. In addition there is almost unanimity, 95 per cent agreed that although people don't think so, the President of this University and Chancellor of this campus are really trying very hard to provide top quality education experience for students here. In retrospect, it is amazing to find this much appreciation of the intentions of the top administrators some five weeks after the police car incident, and only a few weeks before a widespread strike in sympathy for the Free Speech Movement.[4]

Although Paul Potter does have some unkind things to say about the quality of education being offered, when he attempts to probe the sources of student discontent he reveals that they are not directly re-

----

[4] Muscatine, *op. cit.*

lated to the academic or to the professional mission of the university. Says he,

> By 1960 [student interest in social and political issues] had built up to the point that unleashed in the same spring the sit-in movement, the San Francisco demonstrations against the House Un-American Activities Committee, and the West Coast vigils against the execution of Caryl Chessman. The same spring saw the awakening on a number of other campuses of more campus-directed reform activity, *but in overall significance it paled beside the on-campus issues.* Nonetheless, on a number of campuses significant battles were being waged against compulsory ROTC, fraternity and sorority discrimination, and the loyalty and disclaimer affidavits in the National Defense Education Act, three of the more obvious and vulnerable indignities that universities had been content to tolerate. . . . What has emerged out of five years of growing protest is a clear critique of the society, a more articulate enunciation of some of the contradictions in American life. The naive belief in the myths of freedom and abundance that suburban life and patriotic school teachers had inculcated could now be confronted by the stench of Southern justice or the burning flesh of children, napalmed by American bombs in Viet Nam.[5]

It is true that some adult commentators on student affairs have suggested that students want and can handle concerns for the academic mission of the institution. Thus, Paul Woodring can say, "The recent student protests have reopened an ancient question: 'Who runs the university?' "[6] And Paul Goodman, speaking for other student apologists, can argue that "Thus far in the Berkeley revolt two new factors have emerged: (1) the students want to extend the concept of academic freedom from the freedom of professors to teach according to their lights to include the freedom of students to ask for what they need to be taught, and if necessary to invite teachers, including advocates of causes."[7] But when one goes to the student idiom itself, the conclusion is unmistakable that even the most militant protesters are

[5] Paul Potter, "Student Discontent and Campus Reform," in *Order and Freedom on the Campus* (Boulder, Colo.: Western Interstate Commission for Higher Education, 1965).

[6] Paul Woodring, "Who Makes University Policy?" in C. G. Katope and P. G. Zolbrod, *Beyond Berkeley* (Cleveland: World, 1966).

[7] Paul Goodman, "Thoughts on Berkeley," in Katope and Zolbrod, *op. cit.*

concerned about matters other than the academic functioning of the institution.

This misconception about what students want is related to another misconception about the ability of undergraduate students to cope with the realities of conducting a complex organization in an even more complex society. Once again, recourse must be had to the growing volume of student protest literature. Otto Butz, who in the fifties edited a collection of Princeton student essays under the title, *The Unsilent Generation*,[8] has now edited a series of polemics about life and education uttered by students at San Francisco State College under the title, *To Make a Difference*.[9] The students Professor Butz selected first of all are clearly not representative of undergraduate students. Their average age is somewhere around twenty-four or twenty-five; but their remarks do reflect or permit inference about student judgment regarding the nature of society and what must be done to rectify its problems. Let us sample a few analytical comments: One student reveals the romantic strain when he says that he no longer feels a part of America because "My America is me, alive and living, wading upstream, crashing through brush, chasing grunion, watching salmon leap, screeching my brakes on the freeway to watch a flight of Canadian geese, picking up a hitchhiker and asking him where he's going, having coffee with a trucker, finding an arrowhead, and being attacked by a blackbird because I passed too near her nest. America is me getting up tired and driving thirty miles to meet someone on time, or hiking up mountains just to do it." And there is a nostalgia for the simple life: "Those who have moved out of town to a small village have forgotten their TV, radio, and newspaper subscriptions but have brought their kazoos, marbles, tops, kites, jacks, and Monopoly, and are attempting to get clean and simple." Another student reflects another strand in the syndrome when he describes the fears he experienced during a lightning and thunder storm by saying, "I was aware of a vague but strong feeling of anger, an anger which stemmed from a total feeling of helplessness. I could not defend my wife from what was happening nor could I deal with it. Anger and fear were where confidence and faith should have been." The same student, when he inadvertently boarded a wrong bus that could not make a stop where he wanted to get off, again responded in anger and re-

[8] Otto Butz, *The Unsilent Generation* (New York: Harper, 1957).
[9] Otto Butz, *To Make a Difference* (New York: Harper, 1967).

marked, "I felt alienated from the whole damn bus." This feeling of frustration as well as indecisiveness is reflected in another student's comment: "Upon my return to San Francisco State College, I was confronted with the decision as to what I was going to do. I had come to believe that I had to do something, not merely work for someone. I thought of perhaps going into psychology since I was interested in rehabilitation work of some sort. I also considered teaching but was afraid that I wouldn't be able to stomach the restrictions of a public school classroom."

Then there is the tendency for a number of student writers to develop *a priori* conclusions. One reveals this strand when he says, "The primary concerns of an intellectual leadership today, if it is to be a vital force in society, ought therefore to be the formation of knowledge about the destructive nature of social structures, plus the development of theories of social change through which the great brutalizing forces of our era could be molded to fit human hands and minds and thus be brought under control." Now, one feels with the romantic urges of students their frustrations at major and frequently minor irritations, and their impatience with some of the quite apparent malfunctioning of a post-industrial society, especially when that post-industrial society is juxtaposed with primitive and developing cultures. But the hard decisions about allocation of resources, the grubby, endless hours of committee work needed to contrive a curriculum, and the delicate diplomacy needed to mediate among various pressure groups found within such a complicated organism as even a liberal arts college, just cannot be handled by romanticism, frustration, and a sense of outraged social injustice. It is true that students in their late teens or early twenties occasionally reveal blazing insights as to how education could be better, and these should be attended to; but the overall impression that student utterances reveal is that their experiences at this point are just too limited to allow them to make responsible and binding decisions.

A third misconception concerns the proper role of a collegiate institution. The central thesis in this argument is that the college or university is a social institution designed to provide a limited number of functions which the supporting society wants. Overly simplified, the college or university is a device for enculturating the young and for developing in the young certain essential survival values, some of which are vocational and some of which apply to one's nonvocational life.

Second, in certain areas the college or university is an agent of social change charged with and supported for research and scholarship designed ultimately to solve human problems. And third, the college or university, particularly in the American context, is charged with rendering limited kinds of service to the supporting society, such as retraining workers, disseminating certain kinds of useful information, and making its facilities available for certain kinds of community activity. Where the misconception comes, and with the misconception student unrest, is ascribing to the collegiate institution inappropriate roles.

Let us consider several of these misconceptions. The college or university is not a clinic, although it may provide clinical services for relatively minor physical or emotional disturbances that interfere with student achievement of academic goals. But a collegiate institution would be misusing its resources and jeopardizing its own essential character if it provided sustaining therapy for all students who wanted or needed it. One institution, which must be nameless, some ten years ago stressed personal counseling. It began to attract a student body composed of a disproportionate number of emotionally disturbed youth. The emphasis had to be modified. Second, the college or university is not a church even if it is church-related or church-affiliated. One can argue that the essential function of an organized church within a society is to provide theory and assistance in mediating between perceived reality and the unknown or imponderable aspects of human existence. Certainly, one can even argue that the university is not properly a major research installation for large science or large scholarship. There are more efficient ways for providing certain kinds of research services, which a complicated society needs. To the extent that the federal grant university comes to resemble the independent research institute, the university jeopardizes its essential educational function; and to the extent that a research installation comes to resemble the federal grant university, it also jeopardizes its effectiveness. Fourth, the American college or university is not a sanctuary free from imposed sanctions regarding political activity. In other societies the university has from time to time taken on this quality; but within the American society sanctuary is provided by other means. The expressed provisions of the Constitution seem in a very real sense to provide sanctuary which in some Latin-American countries is provided a limited number of people by the university campus. One could indicate many other things that the college or university properly is not. Although big-time football belies it, the college or university is properly not primarily concerned with entertainment; but perhaps enough examples have been given to make the point.

The last misconception is that the current generation of students is qualitatively different from previous generations. It is true that the curriculum they study is considerably more enriched, as is their diet of food, cultural events, and opportunities for recreation. But since collegiate education is a human institution dealing with a human condition that has remained relatively stable, the similarities between generations appear quite marked. In 1966, Vice-President Hubert Humphrey encountered severe student resistance on the Stanford campus when he attempted to argue a point of view regarding Viet Nam. "When Lucy Stone, feminist and abolitionist, came to Princeton with her husband the year after Appomattox to plead the cause of Negro suffrage and women's rights, the meeting was broken up by boys and young men said to be students of the College of New Jersey."[10] Students from medieval times on have quarreled with their parents, complained about the quality of food, let off late adolescent energy through acts approaching sheer vandalism, have pondered the issues of their time with the long, long thoughts of youth, and somehow managed to survive and become the leaders of the next generation. Students at Princeton in 1860–61 were concerned about whether the Civil War was right. The Oxford Peace Movement in the 1920's reflected a student worry as to whether war could ever be morally justified. As the world moved toward the holocaust beginning in 1939, American college students who were enrolled in advanced ROTC tangled with the various militant peace groups seeking to emphasize an isolationist stance. It is true that there are some differences between student activists at various times, but fundamentally those differences seem to fade in significance.

There are a number of matters about which students have or should have registered complaints. These provide a partially valid base for student demands for a greater voice in governance. Colleges have repeatedly impinged on student personal lives and personal prerogatives. In more than a handful of colleges, students have been required to take lie detector tests as college administration sought to

[10] George P. Schmidt, *Princeton and Rutgers* (Princeton, N.J.: Van Nostrand, 1964).

solve cases of stealing, alleged use of narcotics, and the like. Residential colleges frequently still maintain the right to search students' rooms. Students have been punished for acts committed off campus and even during vacation periods, all without any form of due process. Student personnel workers have all too frequently imposed their own esthetic standards as they dictated standards of campus dress and of personal conduct. A dean of students at a state university insisting that a boy and girl not walk arm-in-arm around the campus somehow seems to invade a student's private life.

And college courses are frequently arid, dry, rehashes of material contained in textbooks. All too frequently the two-textbook system of instruction is used, having students purchase the poor text while the professor uses the better one as a basis for his lectures. And this is understandable. Expecting college professors to teach three or four different subjects, as a number of liberal arts colleges and junior colleges still do, is expecting more creativity than most teachers possess. There are still too many campuses across the country on which the first lecture in beginning psychology commences with the warning by the professor that students who are expecting insights into themselves from a course in psychology are doomed to disappointment. There are still too many courses in foreign language featuring vocabulary drill, the singing of simple little songs, and the achievement of neither comprehension of language nor insight into culture.

And much of college teaching leaves much to be desired. All too frequently lectures are filled with the professor's reminiscences of his experiences in World War II, with rambling discourse, or with rapid-fire presentation of facts that could be better assimilated through the printed page. All too frequently discussions are really "lecturettes," that is, lectures interspersed every twenty minutes with a student question. One still finds too many examples of capricious faculty grading, with students understanding neither the ground rules on which grades are based nor the manner in which they are implemented.

And college officials frequently have reached quite unwise decisions about matters which students viewed as of critical importance. The entire Berkeley controversy, in one sense, may be said to have stemmed from a decision in the Dean of Students Office regarding a piece of property that should have been disposed of and transferred to the City of Berkeley some time earlier, but through an oversight in the business office was not. There have been too many examples of college presidents applying double or multiple standards to decisions about who could speak on campus, what the student newspaper might publish, what group could and could not recruit on campus, and the like.

And much of the student demands that their education should be relevant is based on the kinds of idiom found in college texts and lists of readings. The paperback revolution has made it possible for professors to require that students purchase long lists of books frequently classical or semiclassical in character, and students respond as people generally do regarding the classics: they are frequently revered but rarely read. The student interested in a career of counseling who was told by the head of a sociology department that sociology, as studied and researched at that institution, had no relevance for real life concerns, since the department was theoretically oriented, was making a point one wishes more students would apprehend.

Then, too, the present generation of college students, having been able to travel, to see worldwide events as they happen, and to explore more widely than other generations, have become concerned about the moral dilemmas facing the society. In a very real sense, much of student protest on college campuses is not directed at the institution so much as it is directed at these moral dilemmas. It just happens that they are on the university campus and the university frequently gets in their way. The concerns about the war in Viet Nam, the civil rights movement, the concerns about the very real invasions of privacy, the uneasiness about the contradictions between the ideals of democracy and the facts of the poor of Appalachia, the slums in the cities, are all involved.

Then, too, college regulations have tended to exhibit a fairly marked cultural lag. There is a revolution taking place in standards of personal conduct, there is the phenomenon of urbanization, which allows quite young people to enjoy a high degree of personal freedom. There is the revolution of discontinuities in the lives of college students, which allows them at various times to experience quite complete personal freedom. There is the revolution within middle-class families toward a generalized sort of permissiveness and understanding of children's needs, and colleges have been overly slow in recognizing these changes. Too many colleges still insist upon a protective role that was much more appropriate a century earlier, when entering college students were much younger, fourteen or fifteen on the average. Young people from permissive middle-class homes, who have been allowed to set their own hours and standards of behavior, feel quite understandable resentment when forced to check out of a residence hall or be back in a residence hall by 10:30 or 11:00 in the evening. The use of alcohol is a particularly marked example. Institutional regulations regarding alcohol simply have not kept up with changing social standards regarding the role alcohol plays in social intercourse.

And colleges, college and university professors and administrators, have been remiss in listening to students and developing channels of communication by which student opinion can be moved some place so that some action can be taken on suggestions. Students develop intense feelings of frustration as they talk among themselves about perplexities, but have no real way of channeling these ideas into positions where decisions are really made.

The list of collegiate malfunctionings could be extended. The relatively ineffective but universal physical education requirements, the system of prerequisites in programs where courses really do not build one on the other, the tendency for too many professors to be vindictive as they work out their own feelings of inadequacies on students, the preoccupation of professors at some institutions with their own research and consulting work rather than with students, are simply further examples. Perhaps, however, enough have been listed to suggest that there is need for some kinds of changes but that these changes need not necessarily include direct and responsible student involvement in governance.

It is now proper to ask and to attempt to answer what should be the student role in academic governance. There are a few institutions that, because of historical accidents, use students successfully in a governance capacity. In general, where this is true, the involvement of students stems from some quite practical problem in the solution of which they assisted at some earlier time. Where students have been used as members of committees, or even as members of boards of trustees, there can be no objection; but very likely most of the colleges and universities in this country do not have such a tradition, and no valid reasons have thus far been advanced to suggest that such a tradition should be contrived and developed.

With respect to academic governance, one should repeat the argument presented here that the collegiate institution is designed to provide professional services, and that it should be governed by all professional individuals who have a professional relationship with someone. Within the American tradition the faculty and the administration represent these professional people. Ideally, the wisdom of the faculty and the dynamics of the administration should be brought together in a corporate faculty structure which allows for shared responsibility in academic governance, to the end that the best professional services can be provided students.

To this notion of governance as a professional matter should be added a conception of relative student freedom over their personal lives. As an ideal one might suggest that the college student should enjoy no more and no less freedom over his personal life than he would if he were not in college, functioning as an individual either at home or independently of his parents. Such a notion may be difficult for some protective institutions to adopt, but even those institutions could set as a goal that by the time students became seniors they should enjoy every single personal right and freedom which young adults, having reached their majority, enjoy in a relatively open society. Several institutions, it should be noted, have moved in this direction. The University of Kentucky has developed a limited list of specific offenses concerning which the University takes cognizance and imposes sanctions. Except for those, students are free to act as they will and, of course, are free to experience sanctions imposed by government if they violate law. If this single matter of guaranteeing students freedom in their private lives could be solved, one could theorize that much of campus unrest would disappear.

But other elements are also needed. The university must test its performance through the reactions of those who receive its service, just as any other profession must ultimately test its performance by what happens to its clients. Within the entrepreneurial professions, consistent failure to meet expectations means that clients or patients disappear. The academic profession is of a somewhat different order in that it is not entrepreneurial but institutional. Thus ways must be found for students to express judgment of what they have received after they receive it. Here, such things as student rating forms of teachers seem wise. Student consultation with administrative officers over how things seem to be going makes sense; and student opinion regarding the total functioning of the institution should be sought. A good case could be made for each institution to maintain a public polling agency that periodically through the academic year would test student reaction about a number of real or potential concerns. Relatedly, the institution needs to develop channels of communication by which students can know that their opinions and suggestions are at least heard and considered. This seems to be much more important than whether or not specific action is taken on a specific proposal.

E. G. Williamson has developed a concept that seems to epitomize at least part of the argument presented here.[11] He suggests that the *in loco parentis* doctrine is no longer appropriate but that a university does have a peculiar responsibility for its clients (students). He calls this a fiduciary relationship according to which the institution makes decisions and renders services for the ultimate good of the student. This does not imply unlimited rights to control student behavior of the sort that parents at least legally have, but it does imply a limited number of areas within the domain of professional service in which the institution may take action.

Part of the institution's educational responsibility is to prepare the young to assume certain kinds of responsible roles as adults. Derivative of this, a case can be made that some students, or perhaps even large numbers of students, should be given some roles in governance, should be given some opportunity to participate on committees, should be given some responsibilities for leading fellow students, or should be given some responsibilities for teaching others, simply as a device by which they can be trained ultimately to assume such roles as responsible adults. But viewing student participation in governance in this light is substantially different from seeing student involvement as necessary and essential for the professional functioning of the institution.

[11] Personal conversation.

PART THREE

Institutional Reform

CHAPTER **7**

Challenge and Response

To a large number of recent student demands, higher education has not been particularly responsive nor is it likely to be responsive in the future—partly because so many of the demands students are making are really beyond the pale of institutional powers. Militant students are concerned over materialism in American life, the war in Viet Nam, the plight of the American Negro and other minority groups, and the deterioration of the central city. While collegiate institutions can be involved to a limited extent in such issues, genuine alleviation of them far transcends the financial or organizational resources of colleges and universities. Nor are professors really professionally qualified to deal with such matters in any consistent way. Students seem to expect college professors to serve them in ways inappropriate to the background, training, and experience of scholars. Students also almost seem to want the college professor to be a clinician or a priest or a father-surrogate while the professor's training equips him to understand a single domain of human knowledge and hopefully to transmit some of what he knows. But even if professors could respond professionally to the categories of student demands, the whole tradition of American colleges and of their professors makes impossible responding to nihilism, and it is really nihilism for which a number of the more articulate militant students are arguing. Somehow college administrators can't quite bring themselves to believe that the entire American society, including its universities, is so completely rotten that it and they should be destroyed.

But within student protest literature and the articulated demands of thoughtful students there are valid requests, and institutions and their professors have been somewhat insensitive to these and slow in responding once aware of them. There are relatively few effective channels of communication by which students have been able to approach faculties and administrations, and even if the message gets through, the organizational structure of a college or university is just not capable of responding rapidly. The departmental style of organization, with its attendant necessity of satisfying a large number of pressure groups, each having quite a discrete array of vested interests, determines that least common denominator solutions will be the rule, and the least common denominator is not really what idealistic youth is requesting. It can be argued that in some respects the American collegiate institution is one of the most autocratic and authoritarian institutions in the society, lodging almost complete power over individuals in the hands of the professors. Since a number of student demands imply a reduction in this autocratic power, it is quite obvious that professors tend to resist, thus the shrill rejection of student evaluation of teaching, particularly if sanctions are implied. Then, too, the American professoriate has become almost a completely professionalized guild with its own members setting their activities and in turn evaluating them as long as a gullible society will provide the funds for professors to do what they wish without nonprofessional supervision. Such a condition is quite pleasant for the individual professor, even though it might not be of value to society. Hence, any suggestion that an outside group, whether it be government or students, has the right to assess what professors are doing is likely to be resisted and resented. While, of course, the roles professors play vary according to the type of institution that supplies their salaries, the role of the major professor in a federal grant university seems increasingly to be the ideal toward which all lesser mortals aspire. Consider the professor in a well-endowed private university having access to large amounts of federal funds. The professor, through the project technique of allocation of funds, looks directly to one of the federal agencies for the support of his activities and feels little loyalty to the institution in which he currently resides. If the institution makes such an untoward suggestion as to his spending more time teaching students, the climate is such that the professor can pick up his grant and go elsewhere. Thus, the academic revolution has provided professors in some institutions sinecures and made these seem plausible goals for professors in other institutions. No one really wishes to surrender a sinecure.

The bleakness thus far implied, however, is relieved by a number of quite serious attempts on the part of a few institutions to respond rationally to the sensed demands and disturbances of youth. Students have remarked on the impersonality of the large mass-style university, and a number of institutions have begun to experiment with new ways of grouping students so that some primary group values can be achieved. The Santa Cruz campus of the University of California is organized by colleges of between 600 and 1,000 students. The institutions in and around Amherst planned and helped launch the small experimental Hampshire College. Even the 2,000-student Stephens College saw the need to create a house plan that allowed 100 students to live and study together under the tuition of a cadre of five teachers. Michigan State, the University of Michigan, and the University of the Pacific have all created smaller living and learning units, and are trying desperately to maintain these at costs comparable to those involved in handling students on a mass basis.

Gradually the fact that large numbers of students find typical residence hall arrangements unsatisfying, and indeed repulsive, has been documented. Katz and his associates find that students both at Stanford and the University of California at Berkeley exert strong pressure to leave residence halls and to find more congenial living arrangements.[1] Co-educational residence halls represent an early response to living conditions, featuring more amenities, as did the houses at Yale and Harvard. A few institutions such as Michigan State have created apartment-style residence units, not only for graduate students but for undergraduates as well. Beginning in the fall of 1969, Antioch

[1] Joseph Katz and Associates, *No Time for Youth* (San Francisco: Jossey-Bass, 1968).

College, using a variety of residence units, will be completely co-educational, and the students themselves, unsupervised by adults, will decide how to regulate their own group living. Stanford also is moving in the direction of complete co-educational residence arrangements, and institutions are becoming more tolerant of the styles of living that students adopt on campus. The Barnard case of an unmarried student living with a male from Columbia College symbolizes de facto acceptance of cohabitational residence arrangements; and at this point it is possible to speculate that the legitimating provisions for such arrangements lie in the not-too-distant future.

Students have also asked for courses that transcend disciplinary lines and which focus on problems as they perceive them. Both graduate and undergraduate schools have begun to experiment with interdisciplinary courses ranging from the general education sort of courses in the humanities to special ad hoc sorts of courses such as "The Idea of a University." In all candor it should be pointed out that there is greater anticipation than actual experimentation. Most of 156 universities surveyed regarding the future of graduate and professional education indicated that they would move into interdisciplinary course work; but relatively few have solved the perplexing problems of staffing and stimulating discipline-oriented faculty to attempt a broader offering.[2] Two good examples are Drake University and San Jose State College, each of which have created interdisciplinary programs for a limited number of students as a means of satisfying general education requirements. However, the majority of freshmen will still do the bulk of their work in disciplinary and sequential curricula.

The student uneasiness over moving directly from high school into college and pursuing a steady academic program to graduation has at last been recognized, and institutions are beginning to provide or to think about providing ways by which students can interrupt their education and gain perspectives from which to view their academic work. The cooperative work-study programs of Cincinnati, Antioch, and Northeastern Universities allow students to intersperse formal academic studies with work experience, and student testimony praises this as one of the more important educational experiences they have had. A semester abroad, or the junior year abroad, is another device judged

[2] Lewis B. Mayhew and Robert Chapman, *Expansion of Graduate and Professional Education 1966–1980*, unpublished confidential report (Stanford: School of Education, 1967).

by students in the more successful programs as one of the highlights of their undergraduate career. A number of institutions such as Beloit or Florida Presbyterian have rearranged the academic calendar so that each year students will have an off-campus experience of several months between the fall and spring periods of on-campus work. While not generally practiced, there is growing awareness that perhaps a break between high school and college is desirable, and a few institutions have begun to investigate ways by which this break can be accomplished for larger numbers of students. The mandatory leave of absence from Dartmouth and the growing acceptance of Peace Corps, Vista, or military service as not necessarily harmful are all reflective of colleges struggling to make legitimate what students are doing anyway. At several state institutions, for example, some 30 per cent of entering freshman classes graduated with a bachelor's degree at the end of four years; but an additional 35 per cent of that same entering freshman class had received a bachelor's degree from some place ten years later.

Almost reluctantly, institutions have begun to relinquish the *in loco parentis* doctrine and to allow students greater responsibilities for their own lives. Cornell University and the University of Kentucky have each worked out a code of behavior whereby the institutions take cognizance of only a few limited matters. All other matters of student behavior are left to individuals with, of course, attendant responsibility to the state and civil authorities. Institutions have gradually moved to extend to women students the same sorts of personal freedoms that male students have long had. Parietal rights are gradually being extended as is assignment to student groups of judicial responsibility over nonacademic variations in student behavior. Just somewhat in the lead of other institutions is Antioch College, which states in its *College Handbook:* "One of Antioch's goals is to encourage achievement of high standards of interpersonal relations both on and off campus. Within this framework of standards, decisions about private sexual conduct are essentially personal and the persons involved must assume responsibility for them."

Students increasingly expect to attend college with persons of the opposite sex, and if institutions will not provide this opportunity, students increasingly take their custom to those places that will. This phenomenon has resulted in such bastions of single-sexed education as Princeton, Yale, and Vassar searching for means by which to become co-educational and finding some. Even Roman Catholic women's institutions have begun to accept male students, and several male and female institutions located close to each other have merged or have begun to merge to insure a much more normal intermingling of the two sexes. Although there will probably always be a few single-sexed institutions, particularly those with a specialized clientele (such as novices for religious orders)', it now seems clear that single-sexed education as a major strand in higher education is almost a thing of the past.

As high school programs have been enriched, and as heterogeneous quality of college enrollments expanded, students have demanded greater flexibility in satisfying requirements for a bachelor's degree, and a few institutions have begun to investigate modifying prescribed sequences of courses by creating several different tracks, each one appropriate for some kinds of students. For example, Stanford has modified its freshman English program so that three tracks are now open, and very likely will modify its History and Civilization requirement in the near future. While it seems to be generally accepted that a baccalaureate degree should imply some common materials, a few institutions are seeking multiple ways to provide the desired common experiences.

Also reluctantly, a few institutions have actually responded to the demand that their programs should be more relevant to the needs of the disadvantaged or culturally different segments of society by creating special programs of study and even special admissions and guidance procedures. Thus, the University of California at Berkeley has mounted an intensive program to enroll more Negro students and to meet their unique needs. San Francisco State College has created curricula dealing with Negro history and Mexican-American culture. The death of Martin Luther King has resulted in a flurry of effort on the part of institutions to create new programs.

Also on the credit side is the fact that the institutions, at least a few of them, have begun to make intensive study of the functioning and malfunctioning of undergraduate instruction in the hopes of bringing about needed reform. Perhaps the first of these, accomplished as a result of student pressure, was the so-called Muscatine Report of the University of California at Berkeley, which ended in making a series of radical recommendations such as easier approval of *ad hoc* interdisciplinary courses and the creation of a Center for the Improvement of Undergraduate Education. It has been followed for the most part, one must assume unwillingly, by other major universities seeking to head off student outbreaks and to make undergraduate education more relevant to contemporary needs.

In spite of these rather impressive attempts to respond, higher education generally has not reacted to a number of student demands and complaints. Study after study has suggested that college teaching is not very effective nor regarded as very significant by students, and student testimony suggests that most of their formal classwork is arid, routine, and not at all inspiring or helpful. In spite of this, college teaching continues in rather much the style that has characterized it since the late nineteenth century. The lecture or lecturette still prevails as the chief mode of instruction, in spite of student contention that most teachers really can't lecture, and in spite of evidence that lecturing is a quite inefficient way of transmitting information. Professors have been reluctant even to experiment with some of the newer media that might enrich teaching. A résumé of experiments suggests that after outside support for an experiment using, say, television has ended, the equipment goes into disuse.

Students also testify that at the point of entry into college they are quite confused and need a great deal of help and guidance in understanding themselves and deciding on their subsequent careers. Perhaps half of the students are, as freshmen, undecided as to the field in which they wish to concentrate; yet, with the exception of a few experimental colleges such as Bennington, Sarah Lawrence, St. John's, or Stephens, institutions have simply not discovered ways of providing the intimate, sustained guidance students wish. This seems true of many types of institutions. The City College of San Francisco is a junior college stressing counseling and guidance as one of its six major objectives; yet it provides a cadre of only twenty counselors to attend to the needs of an 8,000-member student body. Obviously the guidance is going to consist of almost rote handling of registration details. Few institutions have felt disposed either to provide the needed, specially trained counseling staff or to insist that all or a large majority of faculty counsel students and become somewhat professionally competent in the activity. Adequate counseling or advising of students is an expensive undertaking, but it is one which students say they want and need. Relatively few institutions have been willing to rearrange the deployment of their resources to provide this effective service.

With the exception of a limited number of institutions that have

really attempted radical curricular reforms, for the most part departmental offerings are designed more with the interests of faculty members in mind than the educational desires of students. Students want
some personal help from their psychology for some insights in understanding their families, from sociology, some enjoyment from their
courses in literature, but are told such outcomes are really not appropriate for college-level courses. Thus, psychology emphasizes animal
experimentation; sociology, theoretical constructs; and courses in literature, historical interpretations about works of literature rather than
the works themselves. The sciences seem to have persuaded students
that there must be a payoff from suffering through the drudgery of
introductory courses, but in the social sciences and humanities the payoff is yet to be successfully accomplished. Very likely this shortcoming
may be related to the fact that a preponderance of students majoring
in the humanities and social sciences have been in the forefront of the
more militant student protests, but even the nonmilitant vast majority
of students are eloquent in their testimony, or lack of testimony, concerning their curriculum. Only between 2 and 5 per cent of Stanford
students mention course work or student-professor relationships as
among the most meaningful experiences they had while at college.[3]
And that generalization can be replicated in virtually every survey of
college senior opinion.

Students have long criticized grades and grading, although they
have quite obviously been motivated by grades. They contend that
grading is unreliable, frequently capricious, occasionally vindictive and
demanding of the wrong kinds of studies and intellectual activity.
Their complaints have been validated by studies that indicate that professors are inclined to use intuition, hunch, or feeling as a means of assessing student performance; and on the basis of studies that indicate
that for any given paper a number of different professors will each
assign different grades ranging from A to F, it has generally been established that a three-point grading scale is about the largest number
of points a professor can comprehend reliably. Yet there is still the
widespread insistence on at least a five-point scale, with the possibility
of adding pluses and minuses to each letter grade. Now, a few institutions have been forced to experiment with a Pass or Fail grading system, but have done so hesitatingly and with so many restrictions that

[3] Katz and Associates, *op. cit.*

there has been no real gain. One major university received considerable publicity when it announced a Pass-Fail system, but then in faculty meeting established the actual meanings of *High Honors, Honors, Pass, Low Pass,* and *Fail*—in effect, perpetuation of the grading system.

And students have indicated that they expected there to be some relationship between what they studied in a professional school and what they subsequently did as a professional person. Yet, professors in professional schools, particularly as they attempt to emulate the most prestigious institutions of their type, try to move the curriculum farther and farther away from the realities of work. Schools of Engineering begin to stress engineering science and ultimately become more science than engineering. Schools of Medicine stress basic biological science, and Schools of Education, as they become more respectable, discount the requirements of the practitioner. The evidence, which suggests little or no relationship between successful passing of courses in graduate and professional schools, and subsequent professional achievement, has been largely overlooked. Or, if not overlooked, simply disregarded, since it implied that the professors themselves should look to practice for curricular guidance.

The paradox in this analysis is that higher education seems to have been more responsive to student demands with respect to peripheral matters and less responsive regarding what might be considered the central professional facts of education. Thus, new living arrangements, new groupings of students, the provision of off-campus experiences and allowing students greater responsibility for their private lives, have received considerable attention, while teaching, counseling and guidance, and the curriculum, as they affect the majority of students, and, of course, grading, seem not to have changed appreciably. Probably several reasons can be advanced. The first is that college teachers are really not prepared for their role as members of a helping profession. Regardless of whether they receive the doctorate or stop at the master's or master's plus, future college teachers are trained to understand a body of information and to conduct research in it. They are certified in it, through the conferral of degrees, to be teachers. When they enter into their professional roles, they are very likely to imitate the most significant individuals in their academic pasts, who are likely to be their graduate professors; and regardless of whether they teach in a predominantly undergraduate institution or one offering post-baccalaureate work, the styles of teaching, grading, counseling, and course building seem emulative of the graduate school.

Second, however, is the fact that institutional budgets have typically not allowed for on-the-job improvement. Recent experiments involving teaching by television have revealed the critical need for considerable prior preparation before a teacher feels comfortable and is able to teach naturally before the television camera. This preparation, however, takes time, and unless it is budgeted for, the time simply won't be spent. Other similar examples could be presented. It does require time to search for appropriate visual aids. It does require time to build a theory and competency in handling discussions or other interactive kinds of instruction; and it does take time for a faculty to develop an adequate theory of the curriculum, and then prepare courses to achieve curricular ends. Since budgets don't allow for the extra time, the curriculum is likely to consist of imitations offered in whatever prestige institution is being imitated.

Third, there is the impact of the graduate school on undergraduate teaching and on professorial styles of life. Earl McGrath remarks that the graduate school was a major contributor to the decline of liberal arts education. The argument goes that the graduate school expects its students to have had prior disciplinary work to prepare students for graduate study even at the expense of more broadening sorts of course experiences. Graduate courses are inclined to be highly specific, frequently with a strong tinge of scientism about them, and the undergraduate colleges seek to duplicate these highly specialized courses.[4] Then, too, the graduate professor is conceived of as one who spends his time in research and scholarship, with teaching being only a hack-work kind of activity necessary to provide the basic salary for the professor. And, since the graduate school is viewed as the highest pinnacle in academia, professors in all other collegiate institutions seek to model their professional styles after those of professors in prestige graduate institutions. This point may be illustrated by noting the 300 or 400 liberal arts colleges that have recently entered graduate training even though many of them lack the requisite fiscal and library resources to support the graduate program. The reason simply is that the existence of graduate programs is a necessary prerequisite if the

---

[4] Earl J. McGrath, *The Graduate School and the Decline of Liberal Education* (New York: Teachers College, 1959).

institution is going to be able to recruit the faculty it needs to conduct its undergraduate program. Somehow working with graduate students seems more prestigious than working with undergraduate students.

Related is the impact of the concept that improvement of institutions of higher education is synonymous with higher selectivity, whether this selectivity be exercised at the point of entry or through an enforced attrition rate during the first several years. Thus, in the name of standards, institutions seek to exclude large numbers of students who conceivably could help; as institutions in fact become highly selective, they of course acquire a student body that can educate itself and whose members when graduated can develop successful personal careers. The phenomenon operates something like this: An institution becomes highly selective and finally accepts students who will be able to succeed almost in spite of anything the institution can do to them. The students acquire their own education and indeed testify that this is in fact so. Their subsequent successful careers are then used by the institution to justify continuation of its existing mode of education. Institutions which have not yet become so highly selective using limited criteria as to life's success, see the products of selective institutions succeeding and then seek to follow the prestige model.

Professors have been quite understandably reluctant to modify their practices with respect to teaching, the curriculum, grading, and counseling, because there really is not good evidence to suggest that what they are now doing is wrong, or at least no evidence that professors themselves will accept. There just is not any good evidence that a well-developed program of general education is better than an undergraduate program consisting of quite specialized courses. It is true that recently such writers as Sanford,[5] Katz,[6] Heist,[7] and the older book by Jacob[8] presented evidence that students didn't very highly regard their curricula or instruction; but there have been relatively few experimental studies suggesting the effectiveness of change.

The central thesis of this analysis is that although institutions of higher education have responded to some of the emerging needs and demands of students, they have not done so consistently and have actu-

[5] Nevitt Sanford, *Where Colleges Fail* (San Francisco: Jossey-Bass, 1967).

[6] Katz and Associates, *op. cit.*

[7] Paul Heist (Ed.), *The Creative College Student: An Unmet Challenge* (San Francisco: Jossey-Bass, 1968).

[8] Philip Jacob, *Changing Values in College* (New York: Harper, 1957).

ally failed to respond to needs involving the central educational mission of higher education. Quite clearly, rectification of this situation, if it is to take place, must ultimately be the responsibility of the institutions themselves. However, one can have grave doubts that institutions, without outside pressure, will be able to generate the energy or the motivation to bring about change. One of the characteristics of recent student unrest is that it has generated an external power that is forcing some institutions to reconsider the traditional ways of doing things. Other agencies and institutions in the society can be expected to exercise power in forcing institutions to change, particularly if remedy of long-standing abuses is not forthcoming. Quite clearly, for the public sector, state legislators represent an important constituency and properly should be concerned with how well the institutions they support are functioning. This is not to say that legislators should involve themselves individually or collectively in the internal workings of the university. The history of political interference is much too vivid to allow advocacy of that. However, legislatures can exercise considerable healthy influence to make institutions be more responsive to students.

Third, legislatures could take the initiative and provide funds for legislative-sponsored conferences within a state to which legislators, college administrators, professors, and students could come and confront one another with their needs and expectations. So frequently there has been a wall of antagonism between legislative bodies and college faculties. Perhaps a series of conferences held annually could suggest both to legislators and faculty members that the others are really human.

Legislators might seriously consider appropriating reasonable substantial funds for institutions to use as incentives for improvement of instruction or curriculum. In 1965, the Oregon legislature appropriated a half-million dollars to reward outstanding undergraduate teaching. The appropriation caused a little consternation within the universities but several accepted funds and the funds did apparently have the impact of making faculty members a little more sensitive to the problems of instruction.

Fourth, when legislators are asked to appropriate funds for state studies of higher education, they might well appropriate enough so that many of the underlying assumptions of state studies could be tested. In the last six years, a majority of the states in the union have authorized or conducted surveys or studies of higher education. These have come to be quite similar one to another, and not particularly helpful because they all seem to be based on the same sorts of assumptions regarding such things as how students will flow into various types of institutions if once they are created. Legislatures could do considerable good by insisting on and supporting more searching inquiries into the nature of higher education.

Lastly, legislators can recognize that struggles for improvement must be accompanied by mistakes, sometimes quite costly ones. Legislators thus might be a little more tolerant of error so as to open the way for experimentation.

CHAPTER 8

Changing Structures

It is a truism, although one frequently overlooked, ignored, or even repressed, that the curriculum of higher education is determined by its structure, which, in turn, rests on the needs of society. Higher education, like all other forms of education, is a social institution designed to provide services to the society that created it. At times, social needs change, and society asks its institutions to assume new responsibilities. Unless the institution involved does shift to accommodate such new orientations, it loses its viability and effectiveness. Thus, it can be argued that student literary societies, organized athletics, and the fraternity system came into existence to provide demanded educational needs that colleges in the nineteenth century failed to provide.

American colonists created colleges in the remembered image of Oxford and especially Cambridge because of two principal needs stemming from two prevailing social forces. The Reformation created the need for an educated and scholastic ministry, and the Renaissance, the conception of a gentleman as a humane scholar. Curricula reflected both strands, offering Latin as the fundamental discipline (as well as the medium of medicine), law, and a basic knowledge of Greek philosophy. But Greek also had its place, and knowledge of these two languages early became the sole entrance requirements. Hebrew, too, was stressed, although it never really competed with the other two classical languages. A resulting typical curriculum consisted of Latin, Greek, logic, Hebrew, and rhetoric during the first year, and Greek, Hebrew, logic, and natural philosophy the second. During the third year would come mental and moral philosophy, and in the fourth, a review of languages and a start in mathematics.[1]

The Enlightenment and the Revolution upset the ordered tranquillity of such a curriculum, and the practical demands facing an unsettled country made natural philosophy a naturally ascendant portion of the curriculum. Possibly one can see this pattern repeated throughout the nation's history. Thus, Jefferson's notions that a college should teach anatomy, medicine, chemistry, modern languages, and the laws and history of nature were entirely consistent with such developments as those at Columbia (formerly Kings College), which introduced economics, natural history, and French. The University of North Carolina planned chemistry, agriculture, mechanic arts, belles-lettres and, amazingly, English.[2]

During the Revolutionary and Constitutional periods many discussed the idea of a national university, the curricula of which would follow these lines. However, the American response rather was to create hundreds of small institutions as the frontiers moved to the West. The reasons for this response are clear. The twin forces for pluralism, a federal system of states and militant religious denominationalism, were dominant. Thus, it became a matter of state pride that students were not obliged to seek education outside state boundaries. And the missionary movement urged men to create new models of images they well knew and of which they were proud. Thus, eleven colleges were established in Kentucky, twenty-one in Illinois, and thirteen in Iowa before 1869.[3]

Here, however, dysfunction appeared. The structure of higher

[1] Frederick Rudolph, *The American College and University* (New York: Knopf, 1962).
[2] *Ibid.*, pp. 40–42.
[3] *Ibid.*, pp. 53–55.

education responded to the conditions of society—but its curriculum
did not. Although a few recognized the need for reform, the curriculum in most of the better-known colleges atrophied in the form in
which it had been crystallized during the Revolutionary War. The
college had come to be viewed as the proper training ground for the
rich and the well-born, who could take pride in refraining from any
practical study. The Yale Report of 1828 became the dogma for an
unchanging curriculum which, among other things, eventually required colleges to pay students to attend in order to stay open at all.
Using the phrases of "discipline and furniture of the mind," "parental
superintendence of students," "values of studies not having immediate
connection with future professions," "exclusion of professional studies
and adherence to principle over practice," the Report pointed the road
to collegiate impotence. It assured the profession: "As long as we can
maintain an elevated character, we need be under no apprehension
with respect to numbers. Without character, it will be in vain to think
of retaining them. It is a hazardous experiment to act upon the plan
of gaining numbers first and character afterward . . ."[4]

    If the private college would not change, society's needs con-
tinued to do so, and society created new ways of providing the educational services it required. The Morrill Act of 1862 provided the
resources for land-grant colleges to offer curricula that ". . . without
excluding other scientific and classical studies, and including military
tactics to teach such branches of learning as are related to agriculture
and the mechanic arts, in such manner as the legislatures of the States
may respectively prescribe, in order to promote the liberal and practical education of the industrial classes in the several pursuits and professions in life."[5] The colleges so created emphasized the laboratory
method and concentrated on the sciences, especially the applied ones,
required by agricultural experts, civil and mechanical engineers, and
managers. Earlier, the federal government anticipated its interest in
practical and scientific curricula by creating the military academy at
West Point, which for several decades provided the only engineering
talent to map rivers and build the bridges and railroads needed for the
West to be truly settled. And slightly later the religiously suspect Harvard, under the leadership of Charles William Eliot, adopted the elec-

----

    [4] "The Yale Report of 1828," in T. R. Crane, *The Colleges and the
Public 1787–1862* (New York: Teachers College, 1963).
    [5] *Ibid.*, p. 192.

tive principle, which in essence was a device to allow the sciences to compete with the more philosophical studies and ancient languages that had been stressed in the collegiate prescribed curriculum.

The new curricula, allowed to compete through free election of courses by students, and force-fed through the research emphasis and concepts of professorial freedom imported from Germany, succeeded all too well. Curricula became overspecialized and student courses of study lacked balance, especially in the once mandatory humane and philosophical studies. This, coupled with the changing nature of society and modes of life after World War I, provided the challenge to which the general education movement was the response. Once again the principle of prescription was invoked in order to insure that the competitive advantage of the sciences and applied subjects would not destroy completely those parts of the curriculum deemed essential for man's nonvocational life. This change is still being effected in many places, but meanwhile the society is changing in other directions—all of which are having or will have curricular implications for the liberal arts. As is so often true, the structure of higher education is responding first to the new conditions. How the liberal arts curriculum will be modified is still to be established.

Although the public has always given some support to higher education (on over one hundred occasions before 1789 the General Court of Massachusetts appropriated public funds for Harvard and state lotteries were created to support private colleges in New Jersey, Pennsylvania, Connecticut and South Carolina),[6] privately supported institutions have been the most characteristic expression of American higher education. Until approximately 1956–57, the majority of all students received their education in privately supported colleges and universities, and the images of these institutions were (and still are) the stereotypic ideal of what a collegiate institution really is. The power of alumni to provide resources and to control or affect policy has been used in directions dictated by collegiate experiences in private institutions. Now, however, that power is changing. At a rate of approximately 2 per cent a year, the proportion of students attending public institutions is increasing over the proportion of those attending private institutions. The present 38 to 40 per cent thus will drop to 20 per cent or lower before the end of the next decade. Whether any save the

[6] Rudolph, *op. cit.*, pp. 185–186.

most prestigious and wealthy of the private schools can survive and remain viable is at this time moot.

And higher education, in keeping with the agrarian myth, has been actually and perhaps is now idealized as being rural in character. Early colleges were deliberately located in out-of-the-way places in the belief that country life was better for the character of students than city life, with its many temptations. But higher education in America has in practice renounced its British ancestry and has come to follow the pattern of continental European institutions, which have always existed as part of the fabric of city life. The large majority of college students are enrolled in institutions located in urban centers of 100,000 population or more.[7] Further, the trend continues and even such bucolic locations as Stanford have become engulfed in an expanding megalopolis.

To anticipate still another element of change, Alvin C. Eurich makes this point about urbanization when he predicts that by the year 2000, "the largest universities, with their clusters of professional and graduate schools and research institutions, have . . . become virtually self-contained cities. Some, like New York University, [will] enroll more than 200,000 students. We continue to wonder whether these institutions are getting too big."[8]

Size is a little understood phenomenon, partly, one suspects, because of the myth of higher education. Although America is creating many new institutions of higher learning (over 100 in the past five years), it is doing so at a rate much less than the rate of expansion of the student body. At present over 75 per cent of all college students are being educated in less than 25 per cent of the total number of institutions, and the trend continues. The University of Minnesota expects 50,000 students on its Minneapolis campus this decade and Michigan State plans for 40,000 students in East Lansing by early in the 1970's. John Folger predicts, on the basis of present trends, that the modal institution will be one of 20,000 students.[9]

Size and urbanization of higher education are reinforced by the

[7] Allan Nevins, *The State Universities and Democracy* (Urbana: University of Illinois Press, 1962).

[8] Alvin C. Eurich, "A Twenty-first Century Look at Higher Education," *Current Issues in Higher Education*, Washington, D.C.: National Education Association, 1963, p. 40.

[9] John Folger, "The Urban Sprawl in Higher Education," *Journal of Higher Education*, September 1963.

post-World-War-II involvement of the Federal government in higher education. Twenty per cent of the total collegiate budget now comes from federal sources and is distributed to at least 80 per cent of the institutions in the country. Typically, however, these funds have been concentrated in a relatively few institutions with strong graduate and professional programs, especially in the natural sciences. For example, of 287 institutions, five received 57 per cent of the total funds, twenty received 79 per cent, and sixty-six received 12 per cent. The federal grants, contracts, and the like have changed those institutions receiving them to a point from which there can be no return to older modes.[10] The sciences have been overemphasized, research has been rewarded more than teaching, and graduate education has become the chief preoccupation of those schools receiving major federal assistance. The true curricular implication of this development is that the institutions receiving the greatest aid are the ones that have served and continue to serve as the models toward emulation of which other institutions are striving. They are the ones producing the largest number of future college teachers who will carry with them to their professorial appointments visions of a collegiate institution similar to the one in which they received their training.

So serious is this pressure that Jacques Barzun has argued that the liberal arts tradition is dead or dying. The general education movement of the post-World-War-I period has transformed pre-collegiate schooling. The better secondary schools now offer history, social science, great books, and mathematics through the calculus. With the growth of graduate and professional education, "what we see," says Barzun, "is the thinning and flattening out of [the college's] once distinctive curriculum under pressure from above and below, the high school taking away the lower years, the graduate and professional schools the upper."[11] This does not mean that liberal studies have to die. At the time when liberal arts colleges are squeezing out the old liberal education, some of the professional schools are asking that it be in their students' backgrounds, and if it is not, they attempt to provide it. Barzun remarks that ". . . the only true believers in the liberal arts tradition are the men of business."

And this is consistent with another major structural change.

[10] Based on "Harvard and the Federal Government," *The Graduate Journal,* V, 1962, supplement, 113–147.
[11] Jacques Barzun, "College to University—And After," *The American Scholar,* Spring 1964.

At one time the college was in essence a single-purpose institution existing alongside of other single-purpose institutions such as teachers colleges, technical schools, business schools, and the like. Currently, however, a regression toward the mean is observable. Thus, liberal arts colleges have created, first, teacher education programs, then business offerings, and in some cases, programs in engineering science and agriculture. At the same time that teachers colleges became liberal arts colleges, as they have in New York, technical institutes began to grant degrees in the humanities and social sciences, and within the universities, separate schools and colleges created complex programs of both a technical and liberal nature. The offering of degrees provides another example of the movement toward a single model; liberal arts colleges are beginning to offer master's degrees, and a few hopeful members of their faculties dream of a day when their first doctoral degrees may be granted.

It is as though all of higher education were seeking to resemble Clark Kerr's multiversity. "Today the large American university is, rather, a whole series of communities and activities held together by a common name, a common governing board and related purposes."[12] This thing, says Kerr, is the product of both Greek Sophists and Pythagoreans, of the reborn German universities, of the land-grant movement, of the establishment of Johns Hopkins, and of efforts like "The Wisconsin Idea" to extend the reach of the university to the entire community. Out of these trends and developments has come a highly inconsistent institution consisting of many different communities whose edges are fuzzy. There is no touchstone by which one can decide what should or should not be included in the list of services it should perform or of activities in which it should engage.

Another factor that must ultimately have major influence on curriculum content is the extension of the democratic ideal to its logical conclusion in higher education. With few exceptions, the American college has always sought to extend its services to larger and larger segments of the population. However, there were always some limits placed on this trend. A college does focus on conceptualization, analyses of abstract problems, and many secondary school graduates were presumed to lack requisite abilities or inclinations to deal with these matters. A major shift in emphasis came with the report of Truman's

12 Clark Kerr, *The Uses of the University* (Cambridge: Harvard University Press, 1963).

Commission on Higher Education, which claimed that at least 50 per cent of all high school graduates possessed the ability to handle post-high-school work. The structural response to this claim was a rapid expansion of junior colleges so that in some states, such as Florida or California, junior colleges were to be so located as to be available to all students in the state. Further, there were to be open-door establishments requiring only high school graduation for entrance. And these establishments were to be a part of higher education, not secondary education, which eventually, in the minds of the most extreme exponents, would provide the lower level collegiate education for the majority of students.

This development flowers at the same time secondary schools are changing. Once the high school was primarily college preparatory in its function, and its curriculum reflected this purpose. Then it became comprehensive, the chief agent of enculturation for a mixed population. Only a small proportion of the graduates of most high schools intended to attend college. It was during this period that a variety of new curricular offerings appeared, only a few of which seemed to have relevance for the intellectual life. Now, another change is upon us. A majority of high school graduates will attend college, and colleges quite understandably are concerned with their preparation. The curricular revisions in physics, biology, chemistry, mathematics, and more recently English, are reflections of this concern. So extreme has it become that a number of high schools are now offering work of what was collegiate level a generation past. Strong liberal arts colleges have had to seriously question some of their best courses, as did Amherst its American Civilization course, because feeder high schools were already offering courses covering the same materials at about the same level.

Two more factors in this changing complex must be mentioned, although many others, such as the impact of internationalism, could also be cited. The first of these is the rise of adult education as the biggest sector of post-high-school education. In 1964, the 4,600,000 students in colleges and universities must be compared with the seventeen million taking some form of adult education. The increased amount of leisure and the rapidly changing vocational patterns mean that more and more adults will attend school for avocational purposes, for retraining, or for bringing vocational skills up-to-date. The significance of these changes for the curriculum is that they remove the last possible criterion for deciding what should and should not be the proper subject of collegiate study. Some junior college theorists, for example, believe that their institutions should offer work on whatever subject its supporting community wants and is willing to support.

The second is the secularization of society and of religiously related colleges. While perhaps many would not go as far as David Riesman, who suggests that the more an institution is higher education, the less it can be religious,[13] it is nonetheless true that the greater the religious emphasis, the less the higher educational one. Yet, even in the most cloistered schools, such as those sponsored by Seventh Day Adventists, old religious notions are falling. In the past, a religious orientation provided synthesis for a college curriculum and served as one criterion for curricular change. As the force of religion to do this weakens, nothing so far has been discovered as a substitute, although many things such as citizenship, or critical thinking, or Western thought have been suggested.

In response to these structural changes, higher education has experimented with a number of curricular modifications and is faced with serious curricular perplexities. General education, once regarded as a panacea for fragmentation of the curriculum, overspecialization, and overemphasis on science and practicality, is presently in an uneasy state. The action of Columbia College in suspending Contemporary Civilization B, of Chicago in restoring undergraduate responsibility to the divisions, of the seminar effort at Harvard as a fit substitute for general education courses for some students, and of the University of Minnesota in abolishing the essential power of its division of general education, all suggest that that movement has expended its dynamic. However, the curricula of the newer institutions such as the University of South Florida, the Santa Cruz branch of the University of California, the Monteith College of Wayne State University, and the New College of Hofstra University have all been based on the general educational model of interdisciplinary courses, comprehensiveness, search for integration, and relating educational effort to behavioral objectives. At the moment those in liberal arts colleges have no way of knowing whether a program consisting wholly or mainly of such courses is viable for their institutions.

Nor is the more traditional curriculum consisting of sequentially

[13] Christopher Jencks and David Riesman, *The Academic Revolution* (New York: Doubleday, 1968).

arranged disciplinary courses a more assured pattern. So great have been the pressures (real sometimes, but sometimes imagined) from graduate and professional schools that subsequent student success at that level has come to be the criterion for undergraduate curriculum building. And this criterion would go unquestioned except for several disquieting facts. First, the relationship between undergraduate preparation and graduate specialization is not as clear in reality as it is in the university catalogue. For example, it comes as a surprise to most college faculty to learn that well over a third of the students who attend graduate school specialize in fields other than their undergraduate major.[14] Second, the newer advances in such fields as physics and mathematics and newer approaches in language and literary study, in philosophy and in other fields, have rendered obsolete or irrelevant much of what was formerly taught in undergraduate courses, although textbooks continue to stress such matters. Third, the sheer increase in the subdivisions of older disciplines and the consequent expansion of the number of college courses have virtually denied a faculty the opportunity to define a liberal education as involving exposure to an organized set of significant experiences.

Gradually colleges have reasserted a concern for student values and for character development. In the face of convincing data that colleges were not having much impact on essential parts of students' lives,[15] college officials have sought in a variety of ways to modify their programs. Courses in personal adjustment, counseling and advising programs, involvement of faculty with student groups, emphasizing values in some classes, religious emphasis days or weeks, and renovated orientation procedures have all been attempted. A few theoreticians, such as Joseph Katz, have even suggested radical revisions of curricular structure to facilitate personal development of students, especially with respect to values and abilities to cope with emotions.[16] Thus far, however, a concern for values without the sanction that prescribed religion allows has encountered the serious ethical implication of the democratic respect for the value of each individual. Thus, the college faculty is caught in the impasse of wishing to affect a student's character, his

[14] Bernard Berelson, *Graduate Education in the United States* (New York: McGraw-Hill, 1961).

[15] Kenneth A. Feldman and Theodore M. Newcomb, *The Impact of College on Students* (San Francisco: Jossey-Bass, 1969).

[16] Joseph Katz and Associates, *No Time for Youth* (San Francisco: Jossey-Bass, 1968).

attitudes and values, who does not yet wish to impose a particular philosophy or point of view. In view of such ambivalence, it is no wonder that attempts at curricular reform thus far have yielded, as the researchers say, no significant differences.

For generations, American education was dominated by the Western intellectual tradition. Its logic was Aristotelian, its philosophy and art were that of the West, as were its political theory, history, and emphasis on science. Language study was limited, with the early exception of Hebrew, to Greek, Latin, and the three or four commonly taught languages of Western Europe. World War II and the realization of the potential power and significance of Africa, the Middle East, and the Orient suddenly presented curriculum theorists with a dilemma. No one could argue for long, although a few have tried, that the non-Western world was unimportant. However, the translation of that concern into curricular terms has presented a major problem in curriculum planning—one that remains as yet unsolved. To add a few courses as electives affects only a few students. To infiltrate non-Western materials through the extra curriculum and through existing courses is a goal that is hardly ever implemented, for most faculty do not have appropriate training. To set up required courses forces out other substance of considerable importance; moreover, not enough well-prepared teachers are currently available to teach the courses in non-Western history, languages, or culture in the large institutions if they were to be required of all undergraduates. Among other reasons why Contemporary Civilization B was dropped at Columbia College was precisely that—there were too few teachers prepared to offer the work.

As research in the various disciplines has progressed, combinations, recombinations, and completely new subjects have appeared, and older subjects have come to resemble each other in ways unforeseen a generation ago. Thus, a medical faculty concerns itself with learning theory as an outgrowth of surgery; biology has become basically chemistry; and mathematics and philosophy or botany and zoology are seen as parts of a larger whole; and language study now has interrelationships with mathematics and psychology, which came into existence only in recent years. Yet, these new alliances have not been given curricular expression in undergraduate colleges, for many of the same reasons that have blocked the inclusion of non-Western materials. Time, teachers, and traditions are difficult obstacles to overcome. Yet, they must be overcome, for the interrelationships among the fields of knowledge at the highest levels become daily clearer and more exciting. Even graduate schools have not resolved this issue and their faculties have had to set up institutes and centers as the organizational means of overcoming departmental fragmentation.

A last development is only in a sense curricular. This is the development of technical aids to instruction and radically divergent views of instruction. Thus, television, films, tapes, teaching machines, language laboratories, large-scale transparencies, information retrieval systems, and computer-based teaching devices are all available and all have curricular implications. But the precise use to which these will be put depends, in the long run, on a unified theory of personality and human development. Psychologists have not yet found it. But Skinner's behavioristic psychology, Bruner's search for intrinsic substantive structure, and the "developmental" psychologists' emphasis on self-generation and actualization all have curricular significance. If Skinner is right as he sketches his ideas in *Walden Two*—if teaching machines can be used to teach most of what students need to know—then the present curriculum must be severely altered in the direction of simplicity. If Sanford and Katz are correct that age and stage development need to be related to appropriate curricular modes, a different modification is essential. If Bruner is correct that subjects do have essential structures and that these can be exposed by even nonverbal means, then still a different curriculum will result.

Thus the future form and substance of the liberal arts and the liberal arts college are obscure. Present evidence reveals that crystallization is not imminent and contemporary theorists show little agreement. There are those who say that the mission of the liberal arts is as it always has been, to free the human mind through the disciplined study of the basic learning in language, mathematics, history, science, and philosophy. If the liberal arts college will simply remain true to its tradition and insist on offering rigorous study in those subjects, it will succeed. Arthur Bestor argued in essence this position when he criticized the American high school,[17] and Russell Kirk places himself in the same camp.[18] Words of representatives of this persuasion sound

[17] Arthur Bestor, *Educational Wastelands* (Urbana: University of Illinois Press, 1957).

[18] Russell Kirk, *The Intemperate Professor* (Baton Rouge: Louisiana State University Press, 1965).

quite similar to those in the Yale Report, which nearly destroyed the liberal arts college.

A second option is reflected in the notions of Robert Wert, who believes that the fact that high schools and graduate schools have each claimed a distinct share of the educational effort allows the undergraduate school to experiment and develop new modes. If the high schools teach the basic courses in history, mathematics, and languages, and if the graduate schools teach the specialized knowledge needed in the professions, then the undergraduate college can become properly philosophical. If students came to college having had four years of French, collegiate humanities in French is a possibility. As more and more high school students experience the new mathematics, the way is open for offering mathematically sophisticated interdisciplinary courses in science. The general educational level of entering college students may become such that field experience, foreign travel, and independent work are viable as means of synthesizing high school experiences before moving into graduate or professional education. While Wert's ideas attract some thinkers and college planners, it is likely they will run into problems, since he has minimized the effects of the present status system in higher education, which offers the highest rewards to scholars who work at the graduate level alone.

And, of course, there are the Cassandras such as Barzun, already cited, and T. R. McConnell. McConnell, seeing the distribution of the functions of the College of Science, Literature, and the Arts at the University of Minnesota to the professional schools, has judged the future to be indeed bleak. He feels that the specialized tendencies within the traditional disciplines are so consistent with the professional work in the professional schools that the drift is complete and inexorable. The tendency of faculties of independent liberal arts colleges to allow demands of graduate schools to determine curricular policy seems to add support to McConnell's position.[19] McConnell and Barzun, however, may have overlooked a latent vitality and potentiality for renaissance within the liberal arts colleges.

Such a renaissance seems possible in view of continued needs of human beings for experience beyond that of preparation for vocation. As we have seen in Chapter One, higher education currently serves several needs. It is the way by which people are selected and

[19] T. R. McConnell, *A General Pattern for American Public Higher Education* (New York: McGraw-Hill, 1962).

screened for the higher vocations. It is a place in which people may occupy themselves usefully until the labor market can absorb them. And it is a place in which young people can search with some tranquillity for a sense of personal identity. The graduate and professional schools meet well the first purpose. It is with respect to the second two that the liberal arts college can best orient itself.

Residential colleges obviously are well equipped to provide the custodial function, although many fail to exploit their potentialities. However, even commuter colleges in urban areas can also respond to this need. Through libraries, student centers, lounge rooms, classrooms as well as independent study rooms for each student, and a rich cultural events program, they can provide personally satisfying experiences for students throughout the day and evening.

In its program, the liberal arts college can perhaps best achieve its mission if it states, as parsimoniously as possible, its objectives. One sometimes has the feeling that the liberal arts colleges are in difficulty because they claim to do too much. Claiming all, they succeed in little. The liberal arts college might assume these few responsibilities:

1. To provide the languages necessary for contemporary man to describe his conceptions of reality in a nonprofessional way. Courses that feature highly specialized languages appropriate to a single discipline only should be reserved for graduate or professional schools.

2. To provide contemporary man a body of cognitive and symbolic knowledge, appropriate to reality, that can provide a common universe of discourse. As what is significant for man changes, the content of the curriculum should also change. Lunar orbit and cybernetics are appropriate topics for the 1960's; vertical and horizontal trade unions are no longer so relevant.

3. To provide means by which one can learn to cope, in a mature way, with the full range of human feeling and experience, from great joy to deep grief, from enmity to religious ecstasy, from deep hostility to love.

4. To provide a view of the various ways of knowing reality, from the rawest empiricism to revelation.

In the years ahead the liberal undergraduate college can prevail if: (1) it seeks its own objectives, provided they are consistent with the prevailing social climate; (2) it recognizes the realities of staffing, perhaps even to the extent of rejecting the Ph.D. as the normal preparation for college teaching; (3) it seeks to do what it can do as economically as possible; and (4) it produces individuals who are demonstrably better—as human beings living lives in the complex world of tomorrow—than individuals who have not had the liberal arts experience.

CHAPTER 9

Learning Environments

An analysis of institutional factors affecting the collegiate learning environment might begin with a straightforward résumé of factors comprising that environment. One would expect that size of student body and faculty would affect conditions of learning. The University of California at Berkeley is a different kind of place from Goddard College in Plainfield, Vermont. While the evidence about the effects of class size is inconclusive and even at times seems to favor large classes, one feels that the impact of a place in which a student knows all other students should contrast with the impact of a place in which a student will never even see the vast majority of the student body. And, of course, size of the campus itself (with such exceptions as Brooklyn College with its 18,000 students on fourteen acres, or Stanford, with its 10,000 students on 9,000 acres) is related to numbers. A large campus like Michigan State University, on which some students may rarely come to the central campus during the freshman and sophomore years, can be expected to influ-

123

ence learning differently from a campus like Earlham on which all
student trails cross daily.

Then, the educational philosophy and, when relevant, the religious stance of an institution are presumed to influence learning both
directly and indirectly. Harold Taylor once classified educational philosophies as rational—exemplified by some Roman Catholic institutions
and possibly by St. Johns College; neohumanist—a position favored by
the majority of liberal arts colleges; and instrumentalist—suggested by
the General College of the University of Minnesota, Sarah Lawrence
College, and certainly Goddard College.[1] One must believe that an
institution seeking to place Dewey's pragmatism into educational effect
must have a different effect on students from one that seeks to make
manifest the postulational truths of medieval scholastics. Just as one
feels that a liturgical campus, stressing daily mass and surrounding
students with visual representation of religious faith, leaves an educational imprint different from a place in which even prayer at cere-
monials is eliminated. And a college stressing a vigorously specified set
of standards of personal conduct, like Wheaton College with its pledge,
is a sort of place surely different from an institution like Bennington
College, which has from its inception allowed students adult latitude
in setting personal dimensions to their conduct.

Although the evidence about the effectiveness of college faculty
can at times shake professorial egos—in one study teachers were not
even mentioned by students in response to an open-ended query about
educational influences—nonetheless, intuition and reason suggest that
the kind and quality of a faculty are somehow involved. If a majority of
faculty members are in the senior ranks and spend much time off campus on research, in pursuit of funds, or on consultations, one presumes
a different set of relationships than would obtain if faculty members
were daily in their offices and were constantly available in their close-
to-campus homes. Faculty members who place institutional loyalty
above disciplinary loyalty could be expected to feel differently about
students than do professors whose professional satisfactions come chiefly
from national professional recognition.

Similarly, administrative structure and the personal roles adopted
by administrative officers may be involved in the educational outcomes
an institution typically achieves. If the president, vice-president, and

---

[1] Harold Taylor, "Philosophies of General Education," in the National
Society for the Study of Education, *Fifty-first Year Book,* 1952.

deans are preoccupied with off-campus relations, fund-raising, and the details of managing a complex establishment, a different sort of place exists than if the president's door were always open to faculty and students. The fact that a president lives on campus and opens the door of his home to students or faculty several times each week night says one important thing. A president who lives in a different part of a large city away from his campus and who each night joins the commuting rush says something else. The campus that is pervaded by a sense of community on which central administration, clerical and grounds workers, and faculty and students are on first-name basis, should contrast with an institution on which friendships and social life are organized hierarchically. At one institution, for example, assistant professors and above were always "professor," instructors with the doctorate were "doctor," and instructors without the doctorate were simply "Smith" or "Jones" or "Brown."

Since college students experience a range of problems from routine academic ones to those of a deeply disturbing personal nature, one must also presume that colleges that differ from each other in how they help students solve problems should differ in their impact. Stephens College insists that each student see her adviser at least six times during the academic year. At Sarah Lawrence, each student will see her don at least once a week. Surely, logic says, these places affect students differently than would an institution in which advising is limited to registration time and in which the dean of students handles counseling cases in his spare time. Or, as colleges differ from each other in staffing residence halls—house mothers, faculty in residence, trained resident counselors, graduate students in residence, or peer supervision—so should they differ in influencing student attainment of educational outcomes. The college that views most student problems as being rooted in theological concerns and issues obviously approaches the resolution of them differently from the college whose large counseling staff is oriented in the psychoanalytical tradition. Presumably such differences will be reflected in how and what learning takes place.

Institutions can presently be classified on the basis of admissions policies as open-door, selective, very selective, or highly selective. Further, they can be classified as community, regional, state, or national in their appeal to students. Or obviously they could be described as nominally integrated, deliberately integrated, or essentially segregated with respect to race, religious involvement, or even social status.

Whatever the bias in admissions policy is, one must assume it will affect the learning environment. A college that deliberately seeks a specified percentage of foreign students, that overtly solicits culturally disadvantaged students even to the extent of using a double standard admissions policy, and that tries to insure a range of academic and other talents in its student body should affect students differently than does one that selects chiefly on an academic dimension.

To these, other considerations might be added. The City College of New York or New York University, just by virtue of their locations and access to a metropolitan culture, should differ from a Hiram College or from a Stanford. The relative affluence of institutions has long been considered important by such agencies as the regional accrediting associations. The amount of available funds limits, if it does not determine, the richness of program, which, in turn, is supposed to condition learning. The physical plant of the college may also be operative in learning. The location of the engineering and agricultural colleges on least desirable campus land many affect feeling and, indirectly, learning. Collegiate Gothic may say one thing to students exposed to it while "California Tranquillity" may speak in a completely different idiom. And the overall image a college projects conceivably affects learning. If a public junior college is viewed as a high school with ash trays, to be attended by students only as a last resort, this image could affect learning. A college that is generally regarded as offering good counseling services may attract a disproportionate number of students with deep personal problems. College for them is therapy and a clinic surely achieves different educational outcomes than does an academy. If fraternities, football weekends, partying, and social life loom large in the public's picture of an institution, the type of student attracted may be affected just as much as if the college is seen as the right road to a limited number of highly specific vocations. And a college that features a year-round academic calendar and stresses acceleration of graduation may provide a different climate than does one that alternates periods of intense on-campus effort with periods of leisure for research, travel, or reading.

Presumably the curricular and extracurricular emphases of colleges ought to make some differences. One has the feeling that the particular course structure of the College of the University of Chicago during the 1930's and 1940's made that student body different from students in colleges still stressing the free elective system. A college deliberately emphasizing non-Western elements should be different from those based on the premise that only the Western intellectual tradition has real validity for American students. While the effectiveness of overseas experiences has been variously evaluated, their very existence testifies to a belief that somehow experiencing a different culture is important for some students. A campus sponsoring an elaborate program of cultural events—lectures, concerts, plays, art displays, and artists and writers in residence—may condition learning differently than does a Spartan campus on which the weekly grind of course work is relieved only by the weekend flight from campus. The college that accepts and provides for the discordant thoughts and ideas of gifted students may appear different to students from those institutions that enforce an intellectual conformity. Or a college that assigns no grades to freshmen ought, one theorizes, to affect performance differently than does the institution that uses first semester grades to accomplish a difficult screening task.

These are all surmises, however. To evaluate such theories or practices, more verifiable information is needed. While there is no comprehensive body of research that can explain how institutional factors affect the learning climate, there are a number of discrete studies or speculations based on research the results of which may help illuminate the problem.

The visibility and even specific nomenclature of curricular programs seem to have some impact on student academic performance. Dressel and Mayhew, after studying test performance of students from nineteen different colleges, suggested that greatest gains in general education took place on campuses that (1) were residential, (2) clearly designated the general education program as a unique and separate part of the college, (3) assigned full-time faculty to teach general education courses as full-time duty, and (4) emphasized a reasonably elaborate, formal evaluation program.[2]

But while discreteness of various parts of an academic program appears to be related to the learning climate, the sheer size of the curriculum does not. Earl McGrath and his associates studied strong, well-established, and recognized liberal arts colleges and found an enormous variation in the number of courses offered by departments in different colleges. Yet, the size of course offerings appears unrelated to such

[2] Paul L. Dressel and Lewis B. Mayhew, *General Education: Explorations in Evaluation* (Washington, D.C.: American Council on Education, 1954).

factors as student enrollment, number of courses required for a major, satisfaction of department chairmen or deans with curricular effectiveness, or student achievement in graduate school.[3] McGrath believes that curricula in liberal arts colleges could be kept relatively small and still be effective. Indeed he believes that the undergraduate college might even become less effective if it insists upon offering quite specialized courses, more the province of the graduate school.

The outcomes of education implied by McGrath are roughly those that Stern lists in his studies of various college campuses under the heading of intellectual climate. In a high intellectual climate, there is strong motivation for academic achievement, considerable opportunity and desire for self-expression, and high achievement of academic awards such as subsequent graduate degrees and scholarships. Colleges that demonstrate this climate typically are small, residential, independent liberal arts colleges located in the Northeast or Midwest. But more importantly, high intellectual climate seems associated with factors that could be replicated in other types of institutions. Faculty members are personally committed to scholarly activity and communicate to students an enthusiasm for a subject. They define high standards of performance and provide students with ego support to achieve them. They serve as critics or judges of student mental effort but are more concerned with person than with regulation. These effective colleges also reflect a permissive atmosphere regarding student conduct, an absence of a detailed and rigorously administered code of student behavior, and an absence of suspicion of students on the part of the faculty. The physical plant offers students places to withdraw in privacy yet provides uncomplicated access to faculty so that interaction may take place informally. And the student body is unique. Even as freshmen, students at these effective institutions demonstrate superior intelligence, breadth of interest, high motivation, and a spirited independence.[4]

The environment that leads to a high intellectual climate possesses many dimensions. The organization of the curriculum of the freshman year seems especially critical. "The first year, indeed the first months, can be a revelation, a grim disillusionment, or just another routine stage to be endured. Some students [speak] of how imagination was kindled at the very beginning—and how that made all the

___

[3] Earl J. McGrath, *Memo to a College Faculty Member* (New York: Teachers College, Columbia University, 1961).

[4] George S. Stern, "Student Ecology and the College Environment," *The Journal of Medical Education,* March 1965.

difference. A good many look back on that year with distaste and resentment."[5] Those colleges in which the freshman year is rewarding to students have made a deliberate effort to make the freshman year important. Devices may vary from the Harvard Freshman Seminars to the Hofstra course, An Introduction to Science and the Humanities, to the social science sequence at Monteith, to programs designed for the gifted. The important element is that the unique needs of freshmen are recognized.

Another dimension is the size of institution, or rather, the size of the unit within which students function. It appears that only in the context of smallness do students have a true opportunity to establish the relationships with teachers that they believe to be important.[6] Students who are becoming educated do not like nor accept the experience of being ignored by teachers. This does not mean they want to associate on terms of complete equality. There is always a distance between the adult teacher and the almost adult student. But they do want and value working with a professor on an intellectual problem to which each can devote himself. Teachers who have a passionate commitment to a subject and to life and who can communicate this to students are the ones students value most. Students quickly distinguish between an impersonal teacher who cares that his students become engaged in their work and those whose impersonality cuts off communication. What students want and value most are teachers ". . . who not only [give] them knowledge but who [share] the experience of knowledge, who [communicate] their own intellectual vitality, their conviction of the worth of ideas, and the importance of feeling the sense of life."[7]

But students themselves serve as an additional institutional factor contributing to educational outcomes. John Bushnell, drawing on the Vassar studies, makes explicit the significance of the student culture and some of the mechanisms through which it operates.[8] A student body possesses characteristic qualities of personality, modes of interacaction, and systems of belief, which are passed on from student generation to student generation. This culture is a prime educational force

[5] Esther Raushenbush, *The Student and His Studies* (Middletown, Conn.: Wesleyan University Press, 1964).
[6] *Ibid.*, p. 129.
[7] *Ibid.*, p. 136.
[8] John Bushnell, "Student Values: A Summary of Research and Future Problems," in Marjorie Carpenter, *The Larger Learning* (Dubuque, Iowa: W. C. Brown, 1960).

for assimilation into the student society and is a prime concern of new students. This does not mean students are uninterested in the curriculum—for the most part they are dutiful, hard working, and ready to accept the value the college places on courses. "However, except for a minority, the fundamental philosophy of the College and its academic and intellectual aims do not enter primarily into the formation of the central values and habits of life of the student body."[9]

> . . . student bodies in our colleges and universities function in a fashion which bears an intriguing similarity to the group behavior of an American colony located in a foreign capital. I call this parallel the "market place analogy" and, while it may have mildly humorous overtones, I think it does underscore one of the basic problems besetting our institutions of higher learning. The tourist who arrives in a foreign country has, putting it broadly, two directions in which he can go. He can accept the canons of the local enclave of Americans—eat American food, wear American fashions, drink American cocktails—or he can go native to an extent, that is, interact with the urban and rural population, set about to learn the language and to familiarize himself with indigenous customs, dress, food, and the like; try to cull what, for him, is best in the "new" way of life which he now sees on all sides. However, "going native," or even an approximation thereof, is generally frowned upon by the colony membership as something which is antithetical to their identity as Americans. One cannot, at one and the same time, immerse oneself deeply in the foreign experience and maintain active ties with the American colony.[10]

This phenomenon operates not only in liberal arts colleges but also in professional and graduate schools as well. Medical students, for example, quickly form a society that has a culture discrete from that being offered by the faculty. Medical students decide what is important to study. They decide what shortcuts are possible and which ideas of the faculty are worth accepting.[11]

Although there is a tendency currently to minimize the educational significance of the college president and to consider him merely a mediator and a fund-raiser, some observers of higher education still consider him to be influential. Dana Farnsworth is one who believes the president is the single most important influence in building a help-

---

[9] *Ibid.*, p. 56.
[10] *Ibid.*, p. 58.
[11] E. C. Hughes, H. S. Becker, and B. Geer, "Student Culture and Academic Effort," in N. Sanford, *The American College* (New York: Wiley, 1962).

ful environment to stimulate student responsibility. A good president is one who thinks first of student welfare, who treats students fairly, and who considers them as individuals. When faced with student behavior having possible public relations implications, such a president would likely take the point of view not to worry about the institution's reputation but rather be concerned as to what is best for an individual student. This kind of president would entrust considerable authority to students and would maintain informal contacts so as to know how such authority was being used. A president who is inconsistent in decisions, who responds unwisely to pressures from parents, alumni, or publishers, who interferes with the decisions of subordinates, who is afraid of students, and who keeps to himself will inhibit the development of students.[12] And one can assume that the same general point of view can be applied to other administrators. Deans, department heads, and the like can, by the conduct of their offices, determine the institution's learning environment.

Until recently an overlooked strand of institutional influence was the campus itself and the buildings and space it comprises. Gradually, however, has come an awareness of the idea of Neutra that "The Shapes on a Campus Are Not Extracurricular."[13] He and the faculty of St. Johns College thought deeply about the modes and purposes of education at that institution. They finally decided that there were two ways of advancing wisdom. One was through dialectic and the other through observation. To accommodate both he designed a lecture hall and discussion room to reflect the central purpose of that college and to each laboratory he attached a seminar room to symbolize dialectic and observation. In doing so he was trying to show that the shapes of campus architecture ". . . mean a soul impact on the young people who go here to learn and on the older people who here go through their lives to teach." Harold Gores makes the same point with his remark that ". . . a college is people, ideas and a place—and in that order. A college aspiring to completeness in all things will somehow find a way to cast up a physical environment that supports and sustains its mission."[14]

[12] Dana L. Farnsworth, "Who Really Helps Our Students?" in *Personality Factors on the College Campus* (Austin: The University of Texas, 1962).

[13] *Current Issues in Higher Education 1957* (Washington, D.C.: National Education Association, 1957).

[14] Harold B. Gores, "Bricks and Mortarboards," in *Current Issues in*

Actually, the buildings of a campus tell much of the essential spirit of the institution. Architects shown unnamed photographs of brick buildings at the University of Missouri, Christian College, and Stephens College were able to separate them just on the basis of knowing the educational philosophy of each.

The single factors of curriculum, professors, students, administration, and facilities do not operate in isolation. Increasingly it is clear that satisfaction or success of a college experience is a result of the interaction process between students and the total college environment. Students act on the environment and the environment acts on students and each is affected by the reaction of the other. One can observe this process by focusing on students who seek to satisfy certain needs through manipulation of the environment, satisfaction being achievement of those needs. Or, one can observe the same phenomenon by focusing on the environment that poses requirements to which students must adjust. Satisfaction here would be the measure of fit—of how successful students are in meeting the requirements.[15] From such a conception it is possible to study the degree of student satisfaction as one measure of institutional influence on learning. While a study from one institution cannot be generalized to apply to all, it may suggest leads or hunches of relevance. Four classes at Yale were each asked to fill out a questionnaire during the spring of their senior year. The responses from all four classes proved to be highly consistent. For the majority of students, the senior year was most enjoyable and the freshman year least so. Junior and senior years were most rewarding, and freshman and sophomore years least so. The elements of the Yale experience that contributed most to enjoyment of each class, arranged in rank order, were roommates and friends, social activities, junior and senior departmental courses, extracurricular activities, other junior and senior courses, athletics and sports, and courses taken during the freshman and sophomore years. The listing of the same factors ranked according to student development revealed a similar ordering but with a few differences. Junior and senior departmental courses led, followed by roommates and friends, other junior and senior courses, social activities, extracurricular activities, courses taken during the freshman

---

Higher Education 1963 (Washington, D.C.: National Education Association, 1963).

[15] Bryant M. Wedge (Ed.), *Psychosocial Problems of College Men* (New Haven: Yale University Press, 1958).

and sophomore years, and athletics and sports. When asked about improvements they would like to see at Yale, each class seemed to want more personal contact with faculty, more personal direction in courses and studies, and fewer lectures and more discussions.[16]

How the student and the collegiate environment interact is still unknown in any precise detail, but current research and theory are beginning to suggest some of the ways. It now seems possible to identify at least four student subcultures, each of which is affected differently by the various other elements of a particular institution. The collegiate culture, which emphasizes fraternities, sororities, social life, football and campus fun, is not hostile to the college. Indeed, it may generate strong loyalties to it. Rather it is resistant to serious academic demands from the faculty. Then there is the vocational subculture, which flourishes on many urban campuses. This is a world in which students, many of whom are married, work part-time and take courses leading to a degree that will mean a better job. Students have little attachment to the college and also are resistant to the intellectual demands the college might make unless these demands appear to contribute directly to attainment of the vocational goal. The third subculture is the academic one and is composed of serious students who have accepted the intellectual values of the faculty. Members of this group work hard, earn good grades, talk about their course work, and manifest strong emotional ties with the institution through identification with the faculty. Products typically aim at graduate and professional school. The fourth is the nonconformist subculture. Members are often deeply involved with ideas but use off-campus groups and currents of thought as points of reference. They demonstrate a rather aggressive nonconformism and maintain a critical detachment from the college. This subculture offers a temporary but genuine alternative for rebellious youth who must reject the other three subcultures.[17]

The collegiate environment interacts with each of these subcultures and affects members along several dimensions, perhaps the most significant of which is the institutional ethos, which is derived from present and historical purpose, distinctiveness of character, the interests and orientation of faculty, and administrative concerns and interests. Single-purpose liberal arts colleges have generally been the

[16] *Ibid.*, pp. 19–30.
[17] Martin A. Trow, "Student Cultures and Administrative Action," in R. L. Sutherland and others, *Personality Factors on the College Campus* (Austin, Tex.: The Hogg Foundation, 1962).

locales for the collegiate and academic subcultures, while tax-supported colleges and universities serving cities or states have encouraged the vocational subculture and tolerated the other three through curricular offerings that would allow members to survive. For example, the curriculum in a large urban institution will consist of a large number of vocational courses but enough soft courses so that a collegiately-oriented student can stay in school. A college that has developed a distinctive character, as has Reed College, will tend to be supportive of the subculture most consistent with that character. One cannot visualize a strong collegiate, nonconformist, or academic subculture on the campus of Pace College, to which students go to receive the specialized training needed for work in the New York financial offices. And, of course, faculty interests are important. One can visualize a range of faculty from those who are locally oriented and who see their chief role as helping students to cosmopolitan faculty whose chief interests are off-campus. With a predominantly local faculty, student subcultures blend and come to be one with the total institutional culture, while cosmopolitan faculty would tend to allow student subcultures to develop and exist independently. Generally, until recently college administrations have tended to favor and to encourage collegiate subcultures over others as being more predictable, routine, and acceptable to important constituencies. A collegiate student government, for example, is not nearly so dangerous as would be the urge of an academic or nonconformist group to assume some measure of student responsibility. Big-time athletics, an important part of the collegiate way of life, has typically received administrative support as being a safety valve for student emotions and a way of marshalling powerful alumni support.

But factors other than ethos are also operative. The authority structure through the support of values and interests does much to determine which student subcultures will flourish. Four-year state colleges are likely to be characterized by strong presidential authority exerted in favor of vocationalism. Private liberal arts colleges having strong academic subcultures are likely to manifest strong faculty control. But in the large universities with a marked bifurcation of faculty and student interest, little or no relationship between control and institutional style exists. In some universities, faculty power predominates, and in others, presidential or board influence is greater. A second dimension of the authority structure is student involvement. Colleges having a strong academic subculture are likely to have strong student government, while colleges of strong student vocationalism appear generally at the other extreme.

Then, size and complexity, requirements for admission, and the relative autonomy of the institution also contribute to various student subcultures. Large institutions that have not deliberately broken students into smaller groups—as has Harvard through its houses—seem most supportive of vocational subcultures. Highly selective admissions policies will be inclined, although not absolutely so, to support the dominance of academic subcultures. While there are some notable exceptions, colleges that seem to merge with the larger society and whose students commute are likely to support the vocational subculture and to tolerate nonconformist groups, but to discourage collegiate or academic groups. It is in the autonomous, residential college, located somewhat away from other social influences, that one finds the climate most sympathetic to an academic ethos.[18]

The presence or absence of any of these subcultures on a given campus suggests a chicken-and-egg sort of dilemma. Do the student-composed elements in the learning environment become that way because of other factors in the institution, or are they that way before college? Is Darley's remark that, "Without cynicism, one might state that the merit of certain institutions lies less in what they do to students than it does in the students to whom it does it."[19] The evidence on such questions is mixed, but the tendency seems to support the belief that differential productivity of different institutions is determined by concentration of different types of students. Dressel and Mayhew[20] found that experiments involving highly authoritarian and highly nonauthoritarian students could not be conducted on some campuses because authoritarian students tended either not to attend or to leave early in the freshman year. Holland compared National Merit Scholarship winners and near-winners who attended high and low productivity colleges and found differences in academic motivation and differences in parental values placed on study.[21] More recently, the Center

[18] *Ibid.*

[19] J. D. Darley, "Diversification in American Higher Education," (Lawrence, Kansas: National Association of Student Personnel Associations, 1956), pp. 45–66.

[20] *Op. cit.*

[21] J. L. Holland, "Determinants of College Choice," *College and University,* Fall, 1959.

for the Study of Higher Education at the University of California has studied the colleges selected by scholarship winners and near-winners with substantially the same results. "In general . . . it was concluded that high-ability students attending highly productive institutions have a pattern of traits, values, and attitudes which is more closely related to serious intellectual pursuits than do high-ability students attending less productive institutions."[22]

If such elements of the college do affect the learning environment, then it becomes necessary to discover how they interact and what the dynamics actually are. Currently one can only speculate, but the experiences of some institutions do provide limited basis for speculation.

One has the impression that certain of the colleges roughly describable as experimental have had a peculiar and lasting impact on the lives of students. Colleges such as Bennington, Bard, Goddard, Sarah Lawrence, Reed, Stephens, and Antioch are among those identified by Jacob,[23] Eddy,[24] Stern,[25] or Newcomb[26] as being influential. It is possible to reason that the one thing all of these institutions possess in common is that each operates from a consistent and pervasive educational philosophy. The existence of considerable personal freedom for students, a sense of community, emphasis and respectability accorded the performing arts, a fusion of academic and off-campus or work experience, a preoccupation with individual and small-group problem solving, and a concern with the personality or character outcomes of education all seem to represent a definite educational point of view. Someone has remarked that these colleges seem to represent the intellectual confluence of Dewey's educational point of view and Freudian psychology. But whether this particular judgment is warranted or not, a progressivism does seem to operate and to do so effectively. David Boroff sensed this in his remark that "Colleges, then, have been catching up with Sarah Lawrence, but the latter—along

---

[22] Paul Heist, T. R. McConnell, Frank Matsler, Phoebe Williams, *Personality and Scholarship*. (Unpublished manuscript, Center for Study of Higher Education.)

[23] Philip Jacob, *Changing Values in College* (New York: Harper, 1957).

[24] Edward D. Eddy, *The College Influence on Student Character* (Washington, D.C.: American Council on Education, 1959).

[25] George Stern, "Characteristics of the Intellectual Climate in College Environments," *Harvard Educational Review*, Winter, 1963.

[26] Theodore Newcomb, *Personality and Social Change* (New York: Dryden Press, 1943).

with Antioch, Bennington, Reed, and a few others—is still way ahead of the academic procession."[27]

One also has the feeling that the existence of appropriate role models with whom students can identify is involved in the influence or lack of influence the collegiate environment seems to have. The point is made negatively by the lament of the University of California students that the sheer size of the institution denied them the chance to relate to and identify with mature, professional adults. Only when the faculty and students made common cause in December 1964 did students feel they belonged. Or, the point can be made positively through David Riesman's analysis of the effectiveness of certain Midwestern liberal arts colleges in producing scholars, Ph.D.'s, and college teachers. Young people from relatively unsophisticated homes in small Midwestern towns, farms, and villages viewed their college professors as urbane, indeed glamorous figures who represented a life-style worthy of emulation. The same phenomenon did not operate in institutions attracting more wealthy students from homes in the urban East. To those students men in business, finance, law, and medicine seemed more worthy models. Undoubtedly this condition is changing, but the dynamics underlying it continue viable. An institution that faces young women with a faculty of older and somewhat disillusioned female teachers attuned to standards prevailing at the turn of the century denies itself the potent educational tool of possible student identification with faculty. Similarly, an institution that encourages its senior faculty to be off campus more than on, and that presents students with young instructors or graduate students, may also be jeopardizing one strand in its learning environment.

This phenomenon of identification may also be involved in another sort of influence, which comes from grouping students, for academic purposes, into units small enough to allow intimacy to develop. Stephens College has developed its House Plan in which 100 students and five faculty pursue a common curriculum while living or having their offices in a single residence hall. The Raymond College of the University of the Pacific lodges 250 students in a single complex and provides them with a full-time faculty. The College of Basic Studies of Boston University organizes its student body into groups of 100 students and assigns eight faculty members to guide the students through a two-year prescribed curriculum. And New College of Hofstra Uni-

[27] David Boroff, *Campus U.S.A.* (New York: Harper, 1958).

versity is based on a similar scheme. Each of the efforts has resulted in greater learning, greater longevity in college, more expressed satisfaction with the collegiate experience, and more marked changes in measured values than have other parts of the same institution. Paul Dressel made the same point when, after studying a number of liberal arts colleges, he remarked that the best liberal education was being provided by a small school of journalism of a large private university. The school was located on the edge of the campus where the small faculty and student body worked at studies in which each had an intense personal and professional interest.

Perhaps a reason why these small groupings of students and faculty have been effective is that the total environment is small enough to be operative on each student. Regardless of how many Nobel prizewinners a campus boasts, of how many lectures or concerts come to the campus, of how rich are the library holdings, of how many courses are in the college catalogue, they are not educationally effective unless students interact with them. Perhaps there exists a point of diminishing returns beyond which size, variety, and frequency of activities, events, and academic opportunities simply become confusing stimuli to which students cease to respond. Or, perhaps the timing of activities is such that the attraction of other, less intellectual matters is compelling. For example, a commuting college that schedules most of its cultural events in the evening hours very likely denies those elements of the environment of any lasting educational significance. Or, a large university that spreads its residence halls on the far edges of the campus but concentrates its art displays, its library, and the offices of its counselors and major professors on the central campus may cut most students off from an operative environment.

Then, the prevailing reward system on a college or university campus must be considered as a major influence. Whether faculty members like it or not, students are highly motivated to obtain passing grades. Students seemingly will learn whatever is necessary to get the grades they want. "If teachers base their grades on memorization of details, students will memorize the text. If students believe grades are based upon their ability to integrate and apply principles, they will try to acquire such ability."[28] The power of such motivation can, of

[28] W. J. McKeachie, "Research on Teaching at the College and Uni-

course, have favorable or unfavorable effects. Recent evidence suggests that at least half of all college students have engaged in some form of academic dishonesty. While typically students believe cheating to be morally wrong, they do so in response to the pressures or motivation of the academic system. Those who have difficulty adjusting to the role of student, as evidenced by poor study habits and low grades, are more likely to cheat than are good students.[29]

The reward system may, of course, possess other dimensions. At one graduate school of education, students believe that the only acceptable form of doctoral research is statistical and experimental in nature. Despite disclaimers of the faculty, students believe that the central power figures are those preoccupied with research methodology; hence they respond to the direction from which rewards flow. An institution that prides itself on the number of its graduates who enter the strongest graduate schools encourages student selection of courses most likely to insure high grades and adequate preparation. A junior college that emphasizes the success of its transfer students encourages student preoccupation with the transferability of courses elected.

The elements of the collegiate environment that seem to have especial relevance for learning, then, are the visibility, balance, and organization of the curriculum, the total college climate or press, the size of the unit within which learning takes place, the degree of personal interaction with some faculty, the student subculture and the various subgroupings within it, the administrative point of view, the campus itself, the interaction on the campus, the self-selection which creates a given student body, the prevailing educational philosophy or lack of it, the presence or absence of role models, the blending of learning and living, the operative environment, and the reward system. It becomes relevant to discover whether these elements can be so juxtaposed as to have validity for the many different sorts of institutions that comprise American higher education.

In one sense, such an effort might be judged to be fruitless. One of the glories of American higher education is its diversity. Thus, there are liberal arts colleges, teachers colleges, state colleges, state universities, private universities, junior colleges, and a variety of tech-

---

versity Level," in N. L. Gage (Ed.), *Handbook of Research on Teaching* (Chicago: Rand McNally, 1963).

[29] William J. Bowers, "Student Dishonesty and Its Control in College," *Education Digest,* No. 70, April 5, 1965.

nical and professional institutions. There are secular and religious colleges, large ones and small ones, single- and multipurpose institutions, and institutions whose faculties represent the full spectrum of philosophic positions. Yet, in another sense, all of these institutions are seeking to do approximately the same thing. The techniques and approaches just seem to be different. One might assume, or at least hope, that all institutions of higher education might seek several attributes, each of which implies transcendent educational objectives. First among the attributes is a climate in which ideas are believed to be important in and of themselves. Obviously, ideas that will lead to action of some sort are not to be discouraged. A university is an instrument of society that trains people in the skills of a vocation, of citizenship, and of the arts of successful living as determined by that society. The university will, of course, assume that many ideas are of worth simply because of their relevance for their practical purposes. However, a university should also foster another attitude toward ideas. It should be a place where the abstract refinement of a concept is accepted of as great worth as building a house or auditing a set of books. Further, the university should possess a tone in which students and faculty feel a desire to invent, explore, and discuss ideas. Nor should the source of ideas be primarily verbal. Ideas first expressed in sound, color, or line are to be valued as well as those explored through verbal or quantitative symbols. In addition, ideas need not all be of "high seriousness." The campus should not make people ashamed of the pursuit of the light and fanciful any more that it should discourage pondering of questions on the nature of man and of the significance of justice. The making of epigrams or discussion of a Steinberg cartoon may have as appropriate a place in the collegiate environment as a massive construction in the plastic arts or a commentary on the conception of God by Buber.

Second, the campus should provide conditions and should sponsor a spirit in which leisure is enjoyed and respected. It is not the goal of a university to keep its students and faculty at assigned work all of the available time. For that matter, to attempt to do so would be foolishly impossible. Rather, the university should accept leisure as an essential in the lives of men and should provide ways to use it creatively. One can contrast a desirable use of leisure with simple time-killing or with filling leisure hours with activities that anaesthetize people to the reality of experience. The university would not reject television, nor consumption of food and drink, nor complete idleness. Indeed, these can each be used appropriately as leisure-time activities. It would, however, seek to have its students and faculty select wisely from the many leisure-time activities and enjoy them as complete and worthwhile experiences. This is a difficult concept to express and even more difficult to achieve. One can contrast the individual who spends hours before the television screen indiscriminately, only in order to pass the time, with someone who watches Godfrey Cambridge, Dick Gregory, Redd Foxx, and Flip Wilson because he is interested in the role of the black man in contemporary American humor. Similarly, the use of alcohol as a means of dulling one's response to reality can be contrasted with the consumption of beer because good beer tastes good and doubly so when it is shared with someone else who also likes the flavor of the drink. Passive participation in sports, watching a game because one's friends are also doing it, can be contrasted with participation in games for the sheer joy of feeling one's body respond to the challenges of the game.

Third, the university should create a climate in which academic work is viewed as of essential value rather than as a tedious means of some pragmatic end. Again the university does not reject its purpose to prepare its students to do the many things that they and society need. The university should help students keep in mind the need to become effective teachers, skilled draftsmen, or accurate accountants. However, if such ends are the chief motivating forces in the academic program, the university may be successful but will not be a great or vibrant institution. In some way the sheer aesthetic pleasure of working a statistical problem or the complete personal involvement in preparing a research paper should be cultivated. Again, this abstract idea perhaps can be clarified by examples. The course in Functional English, which is generally regarded chiefly as a hurdle to overcome on the road to a degree or as preparation in skills needed in other courses, would be less consistent with the ideal than the same course viewed as a tough, demanding, but nevertheless pleasurable experience in itself. Perhaps *pleasure* is the wrong word. Courses may prove vexing to students, but if accomplishment of long, hard assignments is viewed as a worthy purpose, the ideal will have been in part realized.

Fourth, the university should be pervaded by a spirit that encourages people to accept the uncertainties of not knowing how things will come out. The spirit of the frontier, where there are many difficulties, where the possibility of failure is always present, and where the human emotions are always taxed, is the spirit that is sought. Human beings are always faced with uncertainties and these are never comfortable. They can respond by seeking to find some more clearly understood way or they can develop a toughness of character that allows them to live with not knowing how the story will end. It is the latter, almost stoical, ideal that should characterize the university. To make this concept more specific, the university should be a place in which students and faculty can see their most vital beliefs scrutinized and still not flinch. It should be a place in which change of vocational plans is regarded as simply one other uncertainty with which people must live. It should be a place in which theory can be pushed to the furthest limits of human comprehension without driving students to infantile compensations for the tension of not knowing. The university should be a place in which teacher or student can ask why until it forces the other to the basic presupposition upon which all belief rests.

Fifth, the university should be a place in which intellectual and creative effort is valued for itself. It should foster the belief that the artist should be more than tolerated. He should be encouraged to pursue his efforts even though the resultant abstractions seem to distort traditional concepts of beauty and even though his effort seems to profit no one, not even himself. It should encourage students to investigate the most esoteric subjects if those subjects seem to have genuine appeal for the student. In short, the university should encourage students to value the experience of creative effort and to value a similar quest by others. This obviously is no easy prescription. To accept the endless theorizing about personality structure when this has little relevance to how people seem actually to behave is difficult. To encourage a college sophomore to delve into religious questions that have perplexed centuries of theologians may seem a waste of time. To allow students to proceed down alleys the professor has already learned were blind calls for a high faith in creative effort. Yet all of these must obtain if the goal of a vigorously alive collegiate enterprise is to be even approximated.

Sixth, the university should be a place in which both cognition and affection are viewed as effective and valuable forces. It should not be preoccupied with conscious reason alone. It should accept and teach its students to respect feeling as well as rationality as a worthy means of human response. It should be possible for students and teachers to become angry with each other. It should accept as good the expressions of sheer joy that can come from a pleasant afternoon at a football game. It should accept the feelings of uncertainty with which students see basic religious beliefs challenged by the findings of science, even when that challenge involves tears. The university should be acceptant of emotional responses to modern poetry whether they are of pleasure or bitter displeasure. However, it should also encourage its students to use reason and feeling as tests for their respective validities.

Last, the university should be a place that makes a significant difference in the lives of its members. Whether one likes or dislikes the particular outcomes of the institution is relatively unimportant in this regard. What is significant is that students and the community should be distinctively different simply because the university exists. By this we do not mean solely the increased purchasing power that a university education brings, nor the increase in numbers of persons from the region listed in *Who's Who in America*. We do not mean even that students should more uniformly accept the beliefs of their professors nor that the larger community should be a macrocosmic version of the university. We do mean that both students and the community should be more willing to consider ideation, to enjoy leisure, to accept academic effort, to encourage creativity, to communicate with each other more freely, and to accept the uncertainties of not knowing.

To achieve such an environment with the tested techniques and practices currently at the disposal of higher education would seem to require adherence to several principles:

1. The curriculum, the extracurriculum, the direct contacts with students, and the interaction with faculty should all be on sufficiently limited scale that the educational impact can be realized. Whether the device be a house plan, a cluster, a college, a team arrangement of teachers and students, or emphasis on the social cohesiveness of major professors and their students, it appears necessary to keep groups relatively small and to allow them to work on projects that are of real significance to them.

2. Although pluralism is an essential in American society and in its supporting institutions, there does seem to be a need for some prevailing ethos, philosophy, or theory that can assign meaning and establish priorities to the educational activities a college or university conducts. It is out of such a backdrop that the total institutional press, which seems so potent in attracting students and in modifying them,

can derive. This is to argue that an institution that manifests a prevailing philosophy, whether it be Roman Catholic, military, instrumentalist, or service to agriculture, is likely to be a more effective agent than an institution that reflects, as an institution, all points of view. Since this seems so central, one other matter should be clarified. An institution may reflect a common philosophy in its educational practices yet welcome a variety of personal viewpoints on the part of its students and faculty.

3. The institution should make clear and explicit the expectations it holds for its students. Just the act of designating a general education program as a unique requirement seems to make it more effective than a collection of similar but undesignated courses. The fact that institutions have recently made public the profiles of their student bodies and are increasingly suggesting the criteria by which students are selected helps fashion the learning environment. Similarly, the attitudes and behavior of administration seem to be effective and probably should be made even clearer. Students, one must suppose, like to know the rules of the game. Once known, they probably adhere to them if they are not too far-fetched in the light of their own understanding of society.

4. Last, an institution should recognize the existence of several student subcultures even on a campus on which one seems to predominate. From what little is known it seems evident that each of these groups search for, and to a certain extent find educational values consistent with their own orientation. Unless an institution wishes to place itself in the difficult-to-defend position of drifting toward a homogeneous student body, it should provide for all such groups activities and outlets that can be harmonized with the main educational thrust. The existence of an articulate nonconformist or bohemian subculture can be a threat to institutional stability or it can enrich the entire institutional fabric.

CHAPTER 10

Innovations

Although innovation in American higher education is not a new phenomenon—witness the land-grant idea, the free elective system, and the variegated ideas that found expression in the experimental colleges of the 1920's and 1930's—it currently proceeds at a more rapid rate through the effects of several factors or forces. Innovation in higher education in the last half of the twentieth century is more possible than at any time in the past, partly because of the general affluence of the society and partly because the technology has produced needed materials. But these conditions have become operative in response to several urgent social demands.

One of those urgent social demands is the sheer number of people demanding higher education. As long as the collegiate enterprise evolved at a slow and steady rate, the techniques of small-group discussions, leisurely use of for the most part unused laboratories, and reliance upon stable library collections sufficed. Graduate schools produced all needed faculty—even at times flooding the market with unneeded Ph.D's. But with the college-attending population doubling every decade or less, these modes and practices have proven insufficient. The current college population of over seven million students and the anticipated twelve million within ten years require new ways of grouping students, new ways of extending the talents of a limited number of faculty, and new ways of communicating knowledge. Consider just the task of teaching mathematics to over a million freshmen when the nation's output of Ph.D.'s in mathematics is just slightly over 400 a year, half of whom will be absorbed in noneducational activities.

Then there is the exponential increase in knowledge the dimensions of which must form the outer structure of higher education. New curricular devices are needed to accommodate valid elements of Western and American culture, Newtonian physics, and descriptive biology, as well as to receive and assimilate non-Western materials, nuclear physics, and microbiology. Techniques of instruction that can develop in large groups of students skills of open heart surgery, facility in obscure languages, and directly applicable principles of management represent a new demand unfilled by older ways of teaching. And the crescendoing volume of research evidence requires different ways of storing information.

To compound this problem is the phenomenon of constantly changing work patterns. From the present, in which adults must typically expect to change vocations three times in a lifetime, it is but a step to a future in which learning five, six, or seven different vocational skills will reflect the normal life-style of Americans. This means that methods must be contrived to keep curricula closer to the needs of the society and to develop quickly in people skills that, in other times, could mature through four or more years of leisurely learning. Men and women in their middle years whose jobs have been rendered obsolete through the almost perpetual workings of the technology cannot afford long periods of inactivity to learn a new set of skills, nor can a suddenly modified industrial style wait overly long for people to assume new tasks.

But these demands, if met, present yet another urge for innovation. As new materials are added to the curriculum, as many more people with varying needs are accepted by higher education, and as new equipment is brought to the service of teaching, the cost of education must go up until even the most affluent of institutions will falter. This condition is intensified by the market forces that have made professional instructional talent so expensive and by the expansion of collegiate interests to research and service, all of which are reflected in basic educational costs. Somehow, if the society is to meet its many obligations of helping underdeveloped societies, rebuilding obsolete and decaying cities, and creating adequate transportation systems, ways must be found to provide better education at lower per unit cost. And ways should be discovered to charge these costs equitably to parents, students and the larger society.

But perhaps the most profound force of all is the fact that the lifespan of human beings is increasing so that even now many females must expect to live to well past eighty years, and some have speculated that a norm of 100 years is not an impossibility within the present century. These human years are not needed by the productive institutions, yet they must be filled with humanly satisfying activities. A higher education that might reasonably extend from age seventeen or eighteen to age seventy or eighty cannot rely on traditional concepts of a four-year span, a residential situation, or a rigid system of prerequisites. Nor can it apply to the educational needs of men and women in their fifties the instructional techniques devised for late adolescent students.

Of course, other forces could be enumerated. A culturally impoverished segment of the society is now insistently demanding higher education. These demands simply cannot be accommodated if older concepts of intelligence and prediction prevail. An urbanized people will require different campus organization and different calendars than did a people whose agrarian style of life was set by the planting seasons. And new ways to develop new values in a culture in which traditional value systems have atrophied seem imperative. One problem will be how to teach, for example, the values that derive from the similarity in gene patterns and functions among all living organisms including man when previous value systems placed man in a unique role on earth. But perhaps enough has been indicated to make clear the challenges to innovation.

Some educational innovation began at the end of World War II as colleges and universities sought to satisfy the educational needs of veterans through general education courses, books of readings rather than textbooks and accelerated programs leading to degrees in less than four years. However, the full flood of innovative effort dates from approximately 1957–59, when the technological supremacy of the United States was challenged by Russian achievement and the predictions of numbers and complexities in education began to come true. In 1959, Stephens College conducted a consultation with people presumed to know the state of the technology of psychological theory, and of educational readiness for innovation. Their opinions serve as a description of the levels of innovation reached by that time and a suggestion of things to come.[1]

First it is quite apparent that American technology has produced a wide variety of devices that could be used in education. Motion pictures, television and its more recent developments of video tape and effective kinescope, tape recorders, electronic information-storing machines, test-scoring devices, and recording devices of high fidelity are all in existence. The amazing thing is that they have been so little used that an institution actually contemplating the adaptation of any one of them to a college situation is regarded as a pioneer. It is true that some research workers and some theorists have argued for the significance of educational television or of foreign language laboratories. Relatively few colleges have taken the leap actually to experiment on any large-scale basis.

A second issue perhaps helps to explain the first. Adaptation of new devices to the process of education requires adequate theory to undergird experimentation and a definite reconsideration of the role of the teacher. Traditionally, the school has operated on fairly simple theories of how people learn. A teacher is one who knows—one who by various methods informs students of the substance of that knowledge. Knowledge and the mental processes by which it is manipulated were seen as the prime concerns of teaching. As the use of such things as television, motion pictures, and the like are studied further, analyses should be made of the processes of communication, the processes by which people reach decisions, and the processes by which personal identification of student with teacher take place. As devices are created that transmit knowledge more efficiently than can individual teachers, some consideration must be given to other tasks that do require a teacher. It may well be that the typical teacher of the future will spend only a small part of his time providing information. Such time as he does spend may be in a carefully rehearsed demonstration or lecture. The rest of his time may be occupied in conferences with individual students or with small groups of students. If teachers can discover personally satisfying new roles in which they can facilitate learning, they

[1] Lewis B. Mayhew, *New Frontiers in Learning* (Columbia, Mo.: Stephens College, 1959).

will be better prepared to accept new theory and new media of instruction.

A third theme is the clear need for students to assume greater
responsibility for their own education. Language laboratories, filmed
courses, learning machines, and even televised courses demand that students be able to function without the close supervision of a teacher.
This, of course, is not a new concern in collegiate education. However,
it seems clear that if some of the newer devices are to be used on any
large scale in colleges throughout the country, teachers must accept
the fact that students should do independent work. Students therefore
must be led to the same conclusion and must be motivated to assume
this responsibility. This, of course, is no easy task. Indeed, some leaders
in higher education have stated that greater independent study is but
an idle dream. Students, because of the kinds of homes from which
they come and the kinds of schools they attend, have become conditioned to a teacher-dominated learning situation. The participants in
this conference thought otherwise.

A fourth problem to be faced is the great cost of using some
of the newer electronic devices. The enormous expense to a college in
setting up a closed-circuit television arrangement is relatively small as
compared with the now-available refinements like video-tape equipment. When equipment is installed that can allow several colleges to
cooperate, costs increase still more. The only way colleges can afford
to use modern equipment is to increase the number of students educated in part by such means. Thus within a college large numbers of
students must be enrolled in single courses simply to justify the expense
of providing programs that fully tax television potential. Large courses,
which meet at a single hour, play havoc with scheduling problems for
the rest of the curriculum. This problem, however, can be solved if
the faculty accepts the values of television. Colleges can also justify
the expense of newer devices if the larger population of several different institutions can share in a particular learning program. For example, an hour-long video tape costs $300. A single college budget cannot
afford making many such tapes to preserve particularly effective teaching. However, if several colleges have agreed on a plan to pool their
tapes, the cost does not loom as such a large consideration. One college cannot afford elaborate library equipment. If, however, a central
repository that serves the research library needs of a number of schools

is created, rather complicated storing and retrieving equipment may be justified. If a college can save faculty cost or construction cost through new media, it can afford much modern equipment.

A fifth theme reaffirms the point that colleges must understand themselves and their own unique educational problems before they can reasonably expect help from technological experts. There are many devices that have relevance for education. Which devices are precisely suitable for a particular college can be decided only after a college understands what it is hoping to accomplish. A college must know not only the number of students and faculty it has with which to operate, but also its subtle educational objectives. A college dealing with students most of whom work, which is trying to accomplish much of its impact in a classroom, has a different problem from a residential school in which a wide variety of out-of-class influences are brought to bear on students. A college offering language instruction chiefly to develop reading proficiency for graduate work might value a language laboratory less than a college seeking to give students simply a broad awareness of language as an aspect of foreign culture. The college must answer many questions for itself before it can hope to ask intelligent ones of those who design equipment.

A sixth theme is almost a warning. A sharp distinction must be made between the device itself and the content communicated through devices. It is useless to argue that motion pictures are or are not good educational devices. They are simply the means by which certain kinds of student behavior can be modified. The first question to be answered involves substance. If it can be agreed that certain kinds of information should be communicated, then the relevance of different kinds of equipment to communicate that information can be examined. Several times during the conference the analogy of a railroad system was used. The device is comparable to railroad tracks. The information is analogous to whatever travels down those tracks.

A seventh theme, much less clear, involves the relationship between function and space. The participants in the Stephens College conference were somewhat reluctant to endorse the notion that the way space is organized is completely a product of the function it is to serve. On the other hand, space and function, some maintained, were not to be divorced. Very likely this correlation can best be guaranteed by emphasizing flexibility in planning.

An eighth theme is, in a sense, a tension between the reality principle in education and what might be called the aesthetic or non-utilitarian principle. To serve the reality principle, course materials should be arranged and taught so that immediate application to the lives of students could be perceived. Thus, courses in engineering would present processes that students would likely encounter shortly after leaving school. Courses in social problems would take up those issues about which young adults should realistically be concerned. The other principle posited that there were some activities that were so valuable in themselves that although they might be inefficient they nonetheless should be encouraged. It might, for example, be most efficient to move to microfilm collections for libraries. However, to do so would deny students the aesthetic satisfaction of handling books and browsing. It might be most efficient to show an expert technician conducting a laboratory experiment. To do so might sacrifice the value of students fumbling with apparatus in conducting their own experiments. While the conference did not resolve the tension between these two principles, it did underscore its existence and the necessity for its resolution.

Ninth—and last—there is no magic device that can simplify the teaching-learning process; it is unusually complex and will remain so. There are many aids to learning and much that can be done to smooth the process. Learning, however, still consists of modifying human behavior, which is always a long and laborious process. A tranquilizer can reduce student anxiety so that he can concentrate on his schoolwork. It can't learn for him. A film can help students visualize how things were. It can't synthesize materials for him. Education has always been and will always be a difficult process.

The intersection of the population born during the low birthrate years of the 1930's as the pool of teachers and the needs of the World-War-II-born population as the pool of students has created a strident necessity to extend the reach of a limited number of professors to larger and larger audiences. Closed-circuit television at such institutions as Pennsylvania State University, Miami University, and the University of Houston has been used to offer full courses assigned full academic credit with no appreciable difference between student achievement in a televised course and those in more orthodox situations. The Chicago City Junior Colleges have offered credit courses to several thousand students over open-circuit television—students whose sole contact with the campus proper was at registration and examination time yet who out-achieved students who faced their teachers in person each day. In other institutions such as the College of Wooster, heavy emphasis has been placed on independent study, partly in the hope that a professor directing independent study could really reach more students on an intimate basis than he could in a formal classroom setting. At the University of South Florida, major lectures are tape-recorded and the tapes then played continuously in a vacant room so that all students may hear them at their leisure. To allow mathematics professors to spend more of their time with advanced courses, Michigan State University has assigned programmed textbooks for elementary courses and made students responsible for developing basic competencies with only the occasional aid of a graduate student. And Stephens College has brought distinguished lecturers for courses in both the sciences and humanities to as many as ten different college campuses at the same time, through an amplified telephone device arranged on a conference circuit.

While much learning has taken place through the traditional devices of books and abstract discussion, there has grown up the feeling that classroom experiences should be greatly enriched if even the optimum potentialities of a collegiate education were to be realized. Lecture halls have been wired so that the instructor can gain an immediate reaction of students recorded on a console located beside the instructor, and any student in a large lecture hall can gain the attention of the speaker. The arrangement at the Chicago Teachers College North is said to make lectures much more personal and relevant to student needs. Also intended to bring more life into lectures is the overhead projector such as is in use at Rensselaer Polytechnic Institute. Not only may the instructor show previously prepared transparencies, but he may also write, on the table lodged in the lectern, materials that are then reflected on the overhead screen. Closed-circuit television with industrial-quality cameras has been used to allow a number of classes in educational psychology to view an elementary school classroom in operation. And television has made possible instruction in operating-room procedures to relatively large groups, sometimes with better results than were attained from direct observation of the surgeon in action. And the wide availability of low-cost paperback books has come close to revolutionizing collegiate reading habits. The late David Boroff remarked that there was no single book attracting the attention of college students because paperback books made it possible for them to read so many.

In the past, collegiate life was inclined to be somewhat provincial; college graduates were sometimes regarded as being divorced from the real world. In order to extend student horizons and make students more aware of the relationship of their academic world to the worlds of work and of other cultures, colleges have experimented with a number of programs. In the 1930's, Bennington College allowed for students to spend as much as a year away from campus on research, study, or work, and Antioch College created its Cooperative Work Program, which demanded that every student alternate periods of study with periods of work. Slightly later, several Eastern colleges sent students for a junior year abroad. Similar attempts at other campuses evolved slowly until the advent of the jet airplane, which made rapid, relatively inexpensive transportation possible. During the past ten years there has been an almost rank growth of programs designed to get students off the home campus for a period. These range in size from the Earlham College delegation working at the Hoover Library half a continent away to Stanford's attempt to send at least half of its undergraduate population on some kind of foreign experience.

It was the University of Pittsburgh that first made higher education conscious that using a physical plant twelve months a year might be less costly than purchasing expensive urban land for the buildings needed if a more leisurely procedure were pursued. And it was the Western Conference and the University of California Study of Space Utilization that made higher education aware of how profligate it had been in maintaining unused space. Since the middle of the 1950's, colleges and universities have experimented with a variety of techniques to make higher education more efficient. Individual institutions have moved to the quarter or trimester system and have encouraged students to finish their bachelor's work in as few as two and two-thirds years. State systems, such as that in Florida, have placed all state universities on a year-round calendar. Colleges have conducted studies of space utilization with forms prepared for national use and have compared their results with normative standards accumulated through foundation-supported studies. The College Entrance Examination Board, in response to a study made by several Eastern preparatory schools and universities, has developed its Advanced Placement

Program, which allows a growing number of college freshmen to enter as sophomores.

The American society, speaking through the aspirations of parents and the pronouncements of its educators, has demanded that a larger proportion of its youth receive some form of post-high-school education. The same society, speaking through its college students, has suggested that education, to be truly effective, must recognize the validity of small-group experiences. And the society, sensing the growing amount of leisure in the lives of most adults, has indicated a willingness to support education for people at whatever age they choose to pursue it. Psychological research has validated these interests by showing that college-level work is appropriate for even modest ability levels, that face-to-face interaction is necessary for personal feelings of security, and that intelligence does not begin to decline at age twenty as once was assumed. The result has been several innovations, begun at an earlier time but currently being exploited, which may prove to be the most revolutionary of all. State after state is following the lead of California in creating junior colleges within commuting distance of every child in the state and making these open to all high school graduates. These same institutions, using the older example of land-grant college extension and short course effort, also provide adult education in such measure that a typical pattern is for the number of people taking adult evening courses to double the number of students enrolled in the regular day program. And even the largest institutions are experimenting with small units within the university that allow students and teachers to come to know each other. The University of the Pacific has created three 250-student colleges on the edge of its main campus. An anticipated 20,000 students at the University of California at Santa Cruz will be divided into separate colleges, each having 600 to 1,000 students. Michigan State University, the University of Minnesota, and Wayne State University are each creating smaller clusters of residence halls, classrooms, and libraries in an effort to recapture the tone of the small residential college while still retaining the intellectual and economic advantages of the large university. It should be emphasized these are not new ideas. The junior college dates from the 1920's; Woodrow Wilson wanted to create houses at Princeton before World War I; and high schools have long offered adult education. The innovation lies in a more universal application of the concepts.

As long as higher education was relatively small and relatively inexpensive, the American traditions of lay control and local institutional autonomy could prevail. But as higher education became one of the most important instruments for state or national policy, as higher education became a potential concern for everyone, those traditions became ineffective. The society could not support excessive duplication of effort nor could it leave to chance the flow of students from one level to another. Currently both tax- and privately supported institutions are experimenting with new ways of inter-institutional coordination and control. In California, higher education is divided into four sectors—the state university, the state colleges, the junior colleges, and the private institutions. Broad statewide policies are set by a Coordinating Council. In the Midwest, the Great Lakes College Association attempts to coordinate some of the more expensive efforts of a group of private liberal arts colleges. And in New York City, the freedom of the individual city colleges has been restricted by the creation of a supra-institutional chancellor. Even in Michigan, the two constitutional universities have seen fit to join with other state institutions and limit their freedom for the sake of a better coordinated state educational effort. At present, no pattern has emerged that could gain nationwide acceptance as did the idea of lay control.

Traditionally, higher education has been the gift of the older generation to the newer. Through parental payment of tuition and taxes, and through individual philanthropy, students have been granted an education at little cost to themselves. And, traditionally, higher education has been assumed to be an uneconomical enterprise to which the rules of business could never apply. As the cost of higher education has mounted, and as more and more people have demanded higher education, these traditions have come under serious scrutiny. Some believe that since higher education typically results in greater individual income, the individual should pay for it through long-term loans or work while in school. Others believe that for some such a scheme is appropriate, but since society reaps important rewards from its talent, bright students should be supported through fellowships and scholarships. Those who believe that students should be given free or low-cost higher education by the state also see the limit to what an individual state can supply. Hence the search for ways that federal support can come to the aid of higher education. Experimentation is under way regarding all points of view with some form of packaging of financial aid perhaps the most innovative. Thus, the college calculates the best mix of tuition, loans, work, and scholarship in assessing each student. To complement the concern for income, colleges are also experimenting with controls over expenditures. Parsons College in Iowa actually tried to establish itself as a profit-making enterprise. Theorists such as Earl McGrath have shown how control of the curriculum can result in major institutional economies,[2] and national educational organizations such as the American Council on Education seek to help colleges and universities to regularize accounting procedures. The State of Florida is seeking to find methods to cost account even the use of professional time in its state universities.

American higher education is diverse with a range of types of institutions available for the enormous range of talents and interests that a pluralistic society yields. In the past, the flow of students to the various colleges and universities has been left to chance, individual initiative, and economic and geographic factors. One result has been a steady 50 per cent attrition rate over the decade. Now that so many more students need higher education and groups previously denied it expect soon to receive it, better methods for mediating between student desire and ability and institutional capability are necessary. The College Entrance Examination Board and the Educational Testing Service not only seek refinement of admissions tests but also are reaching for tests appropriate to facilitate movement from the lower into the upper level of the undergraduate college. Further search goes on for reliable devices to measure noncognitive factors such as personality or motivation, which might be relevant in predicting academic success. The widespread use of the College Characteristics Index is indicative of interest in this domain. But perhaps the most urgent quest is for techniques of assessing an individual's talent potentiality even when it has been concealed by the grossest sort of cultural deprivation. Moderately and highly selective institutions, using existing screening devices, virtually deny access to large proportions of the Negro population and thus help to perpetuate the cultural deprivation of Negroes in America. Somehow this deprivation must be overcome and devices must be found to help disadvantaged youth overcome quickly the results of too few books, too impoverished schools, and too early leaving the educational process.

Innovation is also finally striking possibly the most conservative

[2] Earl J. McGrath, *Memo to the College Faculty Member* (New York: Teachers College, 1961).

facet of college life—its architecture. For generations, the ideal of collegiate Gothic or collegiate Georgian and the ideal of the self-contained, even walled, campus conditioned stereotypes of college attending. These relics of the past seem not only presently inefficient but inconsistent with the needs of colleges increasingly located in urban areas. Hence attempts are made to find new and more appropriate architectural forms. One college creates a library in which there are no reading rooms or closed book stacks. Another creates a science building with four lecture halls, each backing to a common preparation room. An engineering college creates a round building of four stories with the mechanical parts fully displayed as things of interest to engineering students. Colleges are jointly occupying many-storied buildings with businesses and finding that the mix of town and gown can be healthy and invigorating. Even more radical are the learning resources centers such as those at Stephens College or at Florida Atlantic University. These structures, centrally located, house the library, collections of films, pictures, and tapes, language laboratories, closed-circuit television studios, and automated lecture halls with remote controls for movie projectors, slide machines, television equipment, and overhead projectors. The one at Stephens also maintains automated study tables at which students can gain quick access to book, sound, or visual resources by using electronic request systems. Yet to be fully tried is the idea of breaking completely from the walled camp concept of college organization and spreading college buildings amoeba-like throughout an urban area. The idea, which is not new in western Europe where the University of Paris is a good example, is a departure from the American experience.

One last innovation must be mentioned, one that could have radical effects on the entire structure of higher education. This is the assumption of responsibility on the part of business, labor, government, and the military services for offering work previously the almost exclusive province of colleges and universities. One California corporation, for example, now maintains a catalogue of courses that is larger than that maintained by the local public junior college. Corporations frequently assume that a recent college graduate's first year of employment will be spent attending corporation-maintained schools. Spokesmen for even small industries foresee a time when they will provide the needed technical education of college graduates, leaving to the undergraduate college either no functions or a markedly different set.

The curriculum is, of course, central to the mission of higher education, and currently there are innovations in that sphere. New relationships of liberal arts subjects to professional schools, area studies, integrating courses, and interdisciplinary seminars all receive attention. As yet, however, there is no innovative effort equal to that of the 1940's which assumed the name of general education.

With such riches from which to choose, evaluation and assessment of actual and potential impact of innovation on higher education becomes imperative. In one sense, evaluation should be made of each type and example of effort. But if broad national policy is to evolve, a consideration of the aggregate of innovative effort is necessary.

While there is much experimentation, one has the distinct feeling that thus far none of the innovations has entered the mainstream of higher education. Experiments with television and some of the new media seem to prosper as long as grants support them, but with a few notable exceptions the new media are not much in evidence in the classrooms of most American colleges and universities. A few institutions have tried cluster colleges, but the central tendency is for large institutions to become larger. And so it goes with the other innovations.

During the 1920's and 1930's there was a series of new educational ideas and concepts, which became essential to a group of experimental colleges. Performing arts became accepted parts of the curriculum; students were allowed to develop programs of studies consistent with their interests; students were assigned tutors, dons, or advisers; community government was stressed, and so was continuous, non-grade sorts of evaluation. All seemed consistent with Dewey's educational philosophy, which gave to the various innovations a cohesiveness that made them collectively significant. Currently no philosophy is available to draw present innovative efforts together.

Then, too, large numbers of American faculty members seem unaware of just how much innovation is in progress. Higher education does not have adequate abstracting facilities nor bibliographic aids. Since many of the reports about innovation are published only in mimeograph form, they quickly become part of a fugitive literature and are brought to the attention of only a small group of interested research workers, Nor are the journals that describe innovation in education widely read by faculty members in academic subjects. Perhaps the single most significant collection of new ideas about the practice of higher education is contained in Nevitt Sanford's edited volume, *The American College.*[3]

Some innovations with demonstrated effectiveness have encountered serious resistance from traditional faculty mores and procedures. The Advanced Placement Program is one example that has been adopted widely but used sparingly as a real device for acceleration. And the junior college administrators stand sentinel duty to prevent end-of-sophomore-year tests being used to facilitate the transfer of students from two-year to four-year institutions. This is not to reject such obstacles as lacking validity. It is to contend that the barriers exist and do impede free flow of innovative ideas.

The earliest use of the phrase *general education* is found in the 1830's. The movement gained some support after World War I and programs were adopted at a limited number of institutions during the 1930's and 1940's. General education as a major innovative force did not achieve full power until the publication of the Harvard report on *General Education in a Free Society*[4] assigned the idea respectability. Thus far no similar status has been granted the present cluster of innovations. Until this happens, given the prestige character of American higher education, one can doubt that innovations will gain widespread acceptance.

Then, too, the present innovative efforts are still too new to have allowed for accumulation of cost and other similar data. One of the great unknowns, for example, is whether the Santa Cruz campus of the University of California can maintain small colleges and keep the cost equivalent with the cost at the more orthodox branches of the university.

Similarly, evidence is lacking as to long-term effectiveness of such things as closed-circuit television. Generally, experiments have produced the conclusions that no significant differences exist between the outcomes of the experimental and control classes. But is it possible that one or the other may contribute to the attainment of ultimate outcomes of education?

But on the positive side is the sheer fact of so many innovations and the fact that faculties are interested, once they hear of them. The climate then seems right for innovation to become more impor-

[3] Nevitt Sanford (Ed.), *The American College* (New York: Wiley, 1962).

[4] *General Education in a Free Society* (Cambridge: Harvard University Press, 1947).

tant in all of higher education; but before this can happen, several factors are or need to become operative.

First, it can be assumed that the forces or conditions demanding innovation will not diminish in pressure. Numbers, cost, and changing society have become an essential characteristic of the United States in the last half of the twentieth century. Thus the challenge remains.

Since so much has been accomplished in relatively small experiments, what seems to be needed now is large-scale field trials. A full university might seek to divide itself into small colleges; strong colleges might seek to apply newer funding arrangements; and junior colleges might mount massive adult education programs via open-circuit television.

In addition to field trials, the research insights of a number of disciplines should be brought to bear to study the impact of innovation. Have, for example, a sociologist, anthropologist, economist, psychologist, and architect look at the new campus architecture and campus planning to determine its full significance for learning.

Then, there should be search for and ultimate agreement on the most vexing educational issues for which innovation might provide resolution. To suggest a few possibilities: access of disadvantaged to higher education, higher education for urban conditions, and education for new and unknown institutions and traditions.

Out of such activities should come, as must always come from innovation, specialization and refinement. Just as the transportation industry finally settled for a time on the jet airliner, so higher education must settle for a time on some one or few innovations which will be centrally significant. Whether this be television, junior colleges, cluster colleges, or cooperative work activities, higher education as an industry needs and will find some focus for the synthesis of its innovation.

At present, the most likely candidates for becoming central expressions of the revolutionary spirit in higher education might include one innovation not previously mentioned—the book. Time was when libraries guarded their contents from possible users. Presently, librarians have rejected their preoccupation with the archival ideal and seek to insure widespread use of books. This tendency, coupled with the easy availability of paperback books, has provided students with immediate access to the richest possible intellectual resources.

Then, there is the concerted effort for even the complex institutions to reestablish the small college ideal. Through cluster colleges, team teaching, and living-learning residence halls, higher education seeks to recapture the virtue of education by primary groups.

Last, a shift from a psychology of poverty to a psychology of abundance seems likely. This implies that intelligence or aptitude, instead of being a static thing, is merely an indication of potentiality *at that time*. Change the cultural conditions and the individual's potentiality changes toward unknown limits.

CHAPTER 11

Preparing Teachers

College teaching in America
is a paradox. When college professors are seen through the haze of
mythology, they represent a complex of many virtues. Professors are
kindly scholars who join with their students in patient but exciting
search for truth. Their own research and scholarship on the frontiers
of knowledge they use to keep their teaching fresh and significant.
Their personal characteristics of tranquillity, love of learning, and
faith in man make them models with which the best impulses of youth
can identify. Their dedication to truth and to education, sometimes
acting in mysterious ways, ignites similar dedication in their students
and transforms the questing young into self-actualizing, mature adults.
Through personal commitment to freedom—individual, academic, and
scholarly—they show students that ideas have consequences and that
the life of the mind is necessary for true human development. By personal example, they teach the young that the examined life is the only

life worth living. Professors speak of their models of Socrates, Jesus, Abelard, St. Thomas, and even Mark Hopkins, and imply that they also possess in some degree the same qualities.

But when viewed as reality, a different vision appears. Some observers of the college professor, however, paint a different picture. They point out that college teachers usually don't make much of an impact on the academic or subsequent personal lives of students. Classroom lectures are rambling excursions into personal histories that have little relevance for their students or their subjects. The mythology of the college teacher's dedication to research and scholarship is belied by the fact that few do any original work after their graduate thesis. The textbook is the principal source of information, which they reconvey in lectures or lecturettes and only the more sophisticated use the two-textbook system—the poorer book for the students and the better as a teacher resource. Their short office hours and quick retreats after class imply the attitude that the campus would be a wonderful place for work and study if it were not for the students. Their ferocity in campus politics is such that Woodrow Wilson could remark that compared with faculty politics, the smoke-filled rooms of national politics were citadels of light, and the behavior of government politicians almost saintly. Their own sense of personal inadequacy and of marginality frequently is reflected in vindictive, carping, sarcastic castigation of students for displaying their own vices of sloth, vanity, and lack of scholarly interest.

Truth obviously must lie somewhere between these two extreme pictures—but where? Some recent statements suggest it is much too close to the latter.

The 1964–65 report of the Danforth Foundation claims that,

> nearly every discussion of student unrest points out the relation of that problem to the poor teaching that is often found on college and university campuses. Once the recognition is gladly given that able teachers exist everywhere and probably in considerable number, the fact of the current situation must also be admitted: poor and uninspired teachers are plentiful, and no one type or size of institution has a corner on the market. In the weaker colleges teachers often do not know their discipline; on supposedly stronger campuses they often do not know their students. Whatever the fault, they fail to communicate either their subject matter or, more importantly, the joy of learning—which they themselves may not possess. Thus the students get short-changed, and

sometimes grow cynical about the educational process. Bad teaching is another major problem of the day, and it is important to emphasize that no college, not even the most prestigious, has escaped it. But what is good teaching? How can it be defined, identified and properly rewarded? The Danforth Foundation shares with many other agencies and institutions a deep concern with such questions and a desire to contribute to their solution. Only a bare start has been made, but even a modest beginning represents a rejection of the absurd though sometimes popular notion that good teaching cannot really be defined and identified.[1]

Earl J. McGrath agrees and suggests at least some reason (the responsibility of graduate schools) for the situation:

The most common dissatisfaction these administrators expressed related to the lack of knowledge the products of the graduate school exhibit concerning the professional activities of their chosen occupation. Of the 302 college presidents, 235 or 77.9 per cent endorsed Statement C: that holders of the doctor's degree were "uninformed about the nature of undergraduate instruction." When nearly four-fifths of the employers of holders of the Ph.D. degree consider them unprepared for the professional duties which they, by accepting appointment to the staff, have at least tacitly agreed to perform, it would seem reasonable to suggest that graduate faculties reassess their present practices.

The voluntary remarks on the subject by many respondents suggest that new college teachers, however well versed they may be in their limited specialized field, know little about such things as (1) the types of students they will encounter in their classes, (2) the motivations of these young people and their social, economic, and even educational backgrounds, (3) the character of the present college curriculum and recent trends in its development, (4) the extra-class responsibilities the teacher in one of the smaller institutions must assume in the academic as well as the more inclusive social community, and a host of other matters included under the term "undergraduate teaching" used in its most comprehensive sense.

Many beginning college teachers, fresh from their graduate experiences, would, of course, deny that they had any responsibility other than teaching their subject as they conceive it, without relation to the other subjects in the curriculum or to the life of the college as a whole. This concept of the functions of the

[1] *The Danforth Foundation Annual Report 1964–65* (St. Louis, Mo.: The Danforth Foundation, 1965).

teacher, imported from the universities of Europe, which operate on an educational and social philosophy quite different from our own, whatever merit it may have in the abstract, does not fit the conditions of life in the American undergraduate college. The large majority of the presidents of the latter institutions rightly believe that graduate programs ought to reflect more fully the activities in which the American college teacher inevitably engages.[2]

Then John Gustad suggests that employing institutions also have some responsibilities that they are not meeting. After surveying policies and practices for faculty evaluation in 584 institutions, he could say, "What was somewhat surprising was the extent and depth of the chaos. The majority of institutions studied said that they placed principal weight on teaching ability, but no even approximately effective method of evaluating this seems to be in use. Scholarship is evaluated by bulk rather than by quality. Other factors are evaluated on a hit-or-miss basis. To say that higher education needs to get its own house in order is something of an understatement."[3]

All of these opinions make the assumption at least that college teaching can be improved and that some improvement could come about through attending to the behavior, activities, methods, and procedures of a teacher as a teacher. Such a point of view has generally seemed unacceptable to professors, especially to those in the liberal arts and sciences and even more especially to those who work in institutions with pretensions of academic excellence. It is an assumption also likely to be rejected by those professors who could be classified as either the teacher-scholar or the consultant. However, the large majority of college teachers could not be so classified nor would they be teaching in institutions which as a matter of policy emphasize research and publication over teaching. To this majority, whose chief means of professing is the classroom, there is the possibility at least of persuading or demonstrating to them that teaching does require sophisticated skills and insights that can be developed through study, practice, and evaluation.

It might be well to indicate some matters about which teachers

[2] Earl J. McGrath, *The Quantity and Quality of College Teachers* (New York: Institute of Higher Education, Teachers College, Columbia University, 1961).

[3] John W. Gustad, *Policies and Practices in Faculty Evaluation* (Washington, D.C.: American Council on Education, 1961).

or prospective teachers might be trained. Obviously, these are matters of organizing, content, selection of reading material, and a knowledge of reading problems of students. It is at this point that prior instruction could be most beneficial in improving the most commonly used techniques. The lecture, potentially powerful, can be spoiled through poor organization, poor delivery, poor timing, or by preoccupation with inappropriate allusions. One student epitomized part of the difficulty by remarking that he was sure Professor X's war experiences were vital to him but that they really didn't contribute much to the course. Even though a few hours with a tape recorder or video tape might make all the difference in the world to a prospective lecturer, such assistance is not likely to be available to a teacher unless there is an organized program of activity. A few more hours of study of what actually happens to students' thinking during a lecture can also change one's approach to lecturing techniques.

A number of disciplines have important insights into discussion techniques. Both substance to be considered and personality needs of individuals are of significance to the discussion method. Group dynamics and group counseling have also produced relevant knowledge. This knowledge should be included in the training of teachers.

Laboratories, long in vogue in the natural sciences, are gradually being adopted in the social sciences and, through studio work, in the humanities. The folkways perhaps have assigned a realistic evaluation of the effectiveness of the laboratory by allowing half as much teaching credit for a laboratory period as for other classroom work. Especially in beginning courses, students testify that required exercises are unrelated to any significant educational outcomes except possibly the development of rudimentary manual dexterity. Yet well-done laboratory work may be among the most important experiences students can have. Therefore, mastering the kinds of problems posed for laboratory experiment, the ways in which the teacher works from one student to the next, and the ways in which laboratory work is related to other classroom work requires special skills. These skills can be taught. They are not learned in doing laboratory work for the essentially different purposes of upper level undergraduate or graduate research.

Similarly, demonstrations also require more than knowledge of content. A demonstration seeks to abstract the central elements of some phenomenon and present them visibly on the ground that students can learn more effectively through demonstration than they can through other means. Frequently a contrived demonstration is more important than a demonstration of the full details of an actual event. Thus, in demonstrating surgical techniques, a television presentation of diagrams of stitching results in greater student achievement than watching the actual process. An insightful person can, if he teaches long enough, learn through experience ways to abstract and to demonstrate content. However, having those experiences vicariously through formal training in advance would seem far better than learning them through trial and error.

In addition to learning about organizing content, selecting reading materials, recognizing the dynamics of reading, and improving lecture and laboratory teaching techniques, there are other elements equally important to the potential college teacher. Some of the more commonly mentioned devices are field trips, tutorials, forums, panels, debates, student reports, dramatization, construction, exhibitions, concerts, recitals, and uses of other people in classrooms as outside resources.

Of recent years such techniques as role-playing, the psychodrama, nondirective class work, independent study, and team teaching have been employed by a few experimenters. New college teachers might well know about them and have some familiarity with the psychological theories on which they are based. Since several techniques either are complicated or involve personality factors, some actual practice under supervision would be in order. The technique of role-playing is an example; it has been used so that students may truly apprehend the feelings of another person or group. On the surface this may seem relatively easy, but unskilled uses have resulted in increasing the anxiety of students above a critical level. For example, having a person whose entire personality is structured by a deep-seated, unconscious assumption of the basic inferiority of certain minority groups play the role of a Negro could cause him to disintegrate on learning that Negroes really want the same kind of life Anglo-Saxon Protestants lead.

For two important reasons, appraisal of the outcomes of education are central acts in college teaching. The college is a certifying agency for technical and professional graduates so that society can rely on the basic competency of these individuals. Appraisal is also necessary because testing exerts such a powerful motivating force on student effort. It has been well said that, regardless of the objectives claimed for a course, students attend closely only to the kinds of things stressed in examinations. Thus, if examinations seem loaded with questions of small, isolated matters of fact, these are what students will learn even though the course objectives stress powers of analysis or appreciation. Yet testing, ineffectively done—whether through poorly written questions that create ambiguity in the minds of students, or through tests distorting the true balance of a course—can jeopardize major educational effort. There is an immense body of fact and principle available about testing. Possibly there is more reliable information on this matter than on any other matter of professional education. Skilled examination writers can prepare tests that are more reliable than many standard physical examination techniques. Questions can be prepared to assess knowledge, understanding, or application, and with some degree of surety. The most effective pattern for the administration of periodic tests can be constructed to gain maximum motivation. Subjective methods of assessment, such as written or oral examinations, can be improved substantially by applying well-established principles. Prior instruction and experience are essential if these methods are to be applied effectively. It is unlikely that many teachers can acquire facility in evaluation simply by teaching over a period of years. But, if there are skills that can be learned more quickly through other means, many teachers would gain through knowledge of them.

The teacher as both teacher and adviser needs to use considerable background information about students. The general academic aptitude, reading ability, and overall cultural level of students is important. In recent years, increasing attention has been paid to the kinds of personality structures students possess and their relevance to classroom techniques. It has been found, for example, that students who might be called authoritarian experience serious difficulties in discussion classes dealing with abstract subjects. The socioeconomic levels from which students derive, the motivations bringing them to college, the problems of adjustment they experience are all of significance. Most colleges and universities, through their testing offices, routinely accumulate this sort of information. It is rarely used by faculty, partly because teachers feel themselves inadequate to use and interpret this sort of information; or, it is used but without full awareness of the strengths and limitations of such data. Yet in a relatively short time teachers can be provided the necessary knowledge and supervised experience that would make them competent to use such information.

They need not become specialists in tests and measurements to do so any more than a medical person needs to be able to make the tests he interprets in diagnosis. But both professions need to use the most precise methods of appraisal and assessment their supporting research and technical services can provide them.

Within recent years, the technology has created many electronic, mechanical, and audio-visual devices to assist teachers. Films and slides can present materials far more graphically than millions of words can. Tapes can record for re-use when needed the speeches of men, the sounds of battle, the remarks of visitors to the campus, or the progress of a college class. Television can reach larger numbers of students and demonstrate phenomena never before visible to classrooms. Special tape-recording equipment can allow language students to practice in the constant presence of models of the best examples of the foreign tongue. Small models can replicate experiments that formerly required large and expensive laboratories. Machines with appropriate questions and answers lodged in them can be used to facilitate the drill that at one time demanded so much teacher energy. Projectors can allow teachers to grade papers with an entire class watching and profiting from seeing errors pointed out. Records can be made and distributed to students so that at home or in their rooms they can play back language laboratory exercises or significant lectures they want to hear again. Photographic methods of printing can enable teachers to reproduce and distribute inexpensively material that in other days would not appear in textbooks until years later.

But this richness will remain untapped if teachers are not taught to utilize the newer media. A variety of skills is needed to do so. Technical dexterity to manipulate the equipment can be taught relatively easily but this teaching does take time. Then the knowledge of what is or can be available is learned. But even more significant is awareness of how to use devices for the achievement of educational objectives. Films when correctly used with a pre-run–post-run discussion can enliven students' understanding of complicated and remote happenings. Amplified telephone interviews can present to students the thinking of those on the frontiers of research or of human activity. Correctly evolved programs of questions and answers can lay clear sophisticated subjects that would otherwise remain hidden from average students. It is to achieve the correctness of use that deliberate education of college teachers should be fostered.

College teachers should have a depth of understanding of what undergraduate students are like. Experience in graduate schools conditions young teachers to expect the same sort of motivation and dedication in those he will teach that he found in his fellow graduate students. Yet the large number of undergraduates will never become graduate students, nor should they. The late adolescent individual in American society who attends college is a distinct entity, differing from persons in other developmental stages in the life process. While research has only scratched the surface, a great many things are known or surmised about undergraduates that could render teachers infinitely more effective if the knowledge were used. Consider such questions as: What motivates students to attend college and to study in the courses they take? Which is more important for a freshman or sophomore, learning to deal with his impulses or learning the rational discipline of knowledge? How do students' previous relations with their parents affect their feelings for college teachers and for the student culture for educational purposes? How does the teacher create situations in which students can learn maximally, and what are the subsequent effects on behavior of such a peak learning experience? What are the essential educational differences between men and women, and how should the teacher comport himself to accommodate these differences? What are the needs of late adolescents for contact with the outside world through news media, and what are their requirements for solitude? What really goes on in the minds of students as they experience the variety of teaching techniques that might be used?

Insight into some of these issues can come through experience in classrooms and counseling sessions. However, there are at least two cultures in college. The student subculture remains somewhat aloof from the faculty world and its true dynamics are inscrutable to all save the most sensitive of teachers. Faculty with family preoccupations, concerns for the larger world, and the other problems of adult life are inclined to drift farther and farther from intuited knowledge of student psychology. The only answer seems to be to provide prospective college teachers with considerable knowledge about undergraduate students. Once they have begun to teach, continuous reinforcement of this knowledge and enrichment as new information becomes available is necessary.

The problem of motivation of teachers is an acute issue. Since few graduate students visualize themselves as teaching "lowly" under-

graduates, they may be reluctant to spend time preparing for this in-
evitability. Later, as teachers, they will feel that their own day-to-day
experience is sufficient to provide the growing insight teaching demands. The fact that it is not sufficient must be demonstrated in many,
but nonthreatening, ways. Of a similar order but requiring different
means for achievement is a teacher's awareness of the forces that motivate him. Psychoanalysts testify that the most important element in
their training was their own psychoanalysis. As they discovered their
reasons for entering a healing profession and for reacting to stress as
they did, they were better able to assist their patients. Now, this example does not suggest that all prospective teachers should have their
heads examined; it does suggest that greater self-knowledge is an appropriate goal in the education of teachers. The act of teaching is a
dramatic role and teachers have a strong urge to perform. Teaching
is also an act of control and prescription as its practitioners seek to
modify and to change their students. It is also a critical act, with the
detection of weakness in performance an essential for improvement.
It is further removed from the mainstream of human activity in order
to insure the leisure for the slow growth that education actually is. It
is also a profession that people embrace late in their own educational
careers for a variety of motives—ulterior and altruistic.

Each of these qualities and forces has impact on how teaching is performed. A college teacher, unaware that he entered the profession to secure a higher place on the socioeconomic ladder, may well
become intolerant of students who do not share his drive. This intoler-
ance breeds impossibly high demands, which in turn are met with the
various techniques of resistance available to students. Or, again, a
compulsive teacher, fearful of repressed sloth in himself, may become
vindictive toward the slightest signs of laziness in students. Torn by the
guilt and anxiety of being unable to make the preparation he feels essential for classes, a teacher may give students impossible assignments,
which, since they are not completed, represent a net educational loss.
At some point within the preparatory experiences of college teachers
some education in the personal dynamics of college teaching ought to
be provided. This might take the form of readings, lectures, group
therapy, or personal counseling. This kind of preparation is possibly
of such significance that it should command the attention of both the
teacher-training institution and the employing institution.

American higher education is a panorama of variegated types

of institutions, and these different institutions attract different types of
students and pose different kinds of problems for teachers. At one extreme is the community junior college, which attracts students from
all ability levels, with vocational aspirations ranging from simple unskilled jobs to the highest professions. The privately supported liberal
arts college, frequently with strong religious overtones, represents a
different task. Complicated state universities with strong service orientation and the complex private institutions represent still other challenges to faculty members. A point of view about teaching that was
formed in a private graduate school might well be so inconsistent with
the demands of a public junior college as to leave both teacher and
student disillusioned and ineffective. Since much is known about the
various kinds of institutions of higher education, it is comparatively
easy to introduce prospective students into the environment they will
likely enter. But, again, to do so requires the planning and conscious
effort of those who are responsible for the improvement of college
teaching.

In one way or another, nearly all college teachers counsel and
advise students. Counseling may be offered through a formal organization in which each faculty member is the adviser to a small group of
students, or it may be offered so informally that the only advising is
done in connection with classwork. But advising does take place.
Further, the skills and attitudes it demands are different from those
that teaching demands. The act of teaching is an act of forming and
creating. Even though the teacher may adopt relatively passive means,
he is likely to have certain objectives that he wishes students to achieve.
Advising, on the other hand, is much more concerned with facilitating
the evolution of goals and solutions to problems of students themselves.
Where the teacher injects his personality, the adviser needs to subdue
his own impact as a person. In classrooms, a subject external to the
student is important to the teaching equation; but the student himself
is the subject in an advising relationship. In teaching, teacher responses
tend to be less subtle than is demanded in the intimate, face-to-face
advising function.

Since prospective faculty members anticipate advising students,
they need instruction to prepare themselves for it. Normally, faculty
members are not conversant with the broad vocational possibilities
open to their students. Further, they need some knowledge as to what
traits of ability and personality are needed by each major vocational

family. They should be able to interpret aptitude and interest test data in ways that will help students to know themselves better. They should know how to conduct interviews and how to deal with the sometimes strongly emotional reactions of students. There is both artistry and science in knowing when to listen and when to respond. To provide these skills, a college teacher should receive requisite instruction somewhere in his education.

If professional education does have relevance for college teaching, it is perhaps appropriate to inquire how. One obvious way is in the pre-service education of college teachers. In some states, California for example, state credential laws require that junior college teachers pass a limited number of courses in professional education—at least a course in educational psychology and one in curriculum and methods of instruction—and do supervised practice teaching. In some institutions, for example the University of Michigan or Oregon State, courses for college teachers are offered as electives or even as prescribed courses for some schools or departments. In others, such as Harvard, a series of seminars or conferences are organized so that each graduate student, before he begins his teaching assistant experience, has at least heard about lecturing, examinations, and the like. "A most promising development seems to consist in the establishment of a variety of forms of internship or apprenticeship in teaching, whereby a graduate school as a whole, or selected departments within it, or one or more departments of an undergraduate college, give careful supervision to initial teaching efforts of students still engaged in their graduate study. Moreover, this teaching-under-guidance is often incorporated into the regular academic program of the doctoral candidate, who is expected to perform creditably under examination here as elsewhere in his work."[4]

But perhaps more importantly, partly at least because the idea of formal work in professional education is a foreign one and is being assimilated slowly into American university life, in-service education of teachers as teachers can be attempted. A few universities have created centers for assistance to faculty members in their teaching responsibilities, if they wish it. The Center for Research on Learning and Teaching of the University of Michigan is one such center; it prepares circulars on teaching problems for the faculty and advises faculty members whenever they request it.

Summer workshops, such as that sponsored by the Danforth

[4] *The Danforth Foundation Annual Report 1964–65,* p. 13.

Foundation for the past nine years, represent another approach. Faculty members, either through institutional nomination or of their own election, spend several weeks working on educational problems of personal significance and attending seminars on such topics as college teaching, curriculum reform, or evaluation. The North Central Association has recently begun a summer workshop for new college teachers. Some colleges, Stephens for example, each year conduct eight or ten faculty seminars that help focus attention on new departures of college teaching and support faculty members for summer work essentially on problems of pedagogy. At Stanford a research project concerning the teaching of the course on Western Civilization has really become a kind of in-service training experience for younger teachers, as was participation in such things as the Cooperative Study of Evaluation, or the North Central Study of Liberal Arts Education. This last, now twenty years old, was initiated originally to improve secondary teacher preparation but shifted to improving college teaching when it became clear that the fault of much lower level teaching lay with ineffective college teaching.

Then, professional education has made some slight contribution through research on various facets of teaching. Institutions such as the University of Washington or Purdue University have long collected data on student evaluation of teaching as one means of bringing about improvement. Michigan State University and the University of Chicago have maintained testing offices, which have, through testing programs, indicated instructional areas needing improvement. The recently emerging offices of institutional research frequently provide evidence on broader aspects of the instructional program upon which discussions of teaching can be based. One example would be research on student characteristics. Then, for the profession at large, agencies such as the Center for Research and Development in Higher Education at the University of California or at Teachers College, Educational Testing Service, the College Entrance Examination Board, the American College Testing Program, or the regional compacts are all conducting research on college education, much of it directly relevant to the teaching components.

In all three realms, the knowledge, insight, and personnel can be employed to improve college teaching. Drawing on existing experience and in anticipation of continuing need for more and more and better and better teaching resources in American colleges and universities, a few elements of a possible program of action can be suggested.

Every institution preparing a reasonable number of future college teachers, either at the master's level for junior colleges or at the doctoral level, might appoint a professor of higher education. Such a person could offer some courses on higher education and on college teaching, open to graduate students, and could, if politically sensitive, actually conduct seminars, conferences, and consultation for faculty members of his own campus. The position should be lodged in the school (college) division of education. Although there have been suggestions that such a role properly belongs outside the professional field, they seem illogical and impossible to put into effect. Even institutions that have created full centers or institutes for the study of higher education deliberately outside the school of education have found that the agency gravitated toward professional education.

As to the kind of person who might occupy the role, the most reasonable one at present is a mature teacher in one of the disciplines who has distinguished himself as a teacher and who has acquired, either through study or trial and error, a command of most of the available techniques. Such a person is not likely to have profound awareness of the history or organization of higher education nor the psychological and sociological bases for it. These he could acquire, possibly through post-doctoral work during several summers or during a sabbatical year at one of the universities featuring research in higher education. Eventually graduate schools of education may turn out young people who aspire to becoming professors of higher education, but for the present that source is inadequate and may, for most, be inappropriate.

If the university maintains a diversified program in higher education, then a second suggestion should be made—that is the possibility that work in professional higher education is appropriate doctoral work for one who would teach a subject in the undergraduate college. Several patterns suggest themselves. One is a doctorate in a subject with a strong cognate in higher education. Such a minor would include courses on higher education, the characteristics of college students, ways of teaching and, obviously, work on the undergraduate curriculum. Or, the converse is possible: that is, a doctorate in higher education with a cognate, but a strong one, in a subject field. Some may object on the ground that such a pattern would weaken the Ph.D. and turn inadequately prepared teachers loose in the classroom. In the absence of any evidence to support such a contention, one could at least experiment with the notion. A third pattern is designed to meet the needs of those who would teach curriculum and instruction courses to future elementary school teachers. It is well that they know a great deal about younger students; they should also know a little about college students, college teaching, and college education. Teachers of teachers, above all others, should reflect skill and artistry in their work. Thus either a full cognate or substantial elective work in higher education seems reasonable.

The third suggestion hinges on two developing situations. One is the tendency for large universities to withdraw from the production of master's degrees in subject fields. Whether properly or not, the argument is advanced that a university should concentrate its efforts on what it can do best—that is, produce doctorates and conduct research. The second situation is the pricing of private liberal colleges out of the market for elementary and secondary school teachers. There once was a time when half of the business of liberal arts colleges was in teacher preparation, but that proportion is slipping. Both of these developments come at a time when the need for junior college teachers having a master's degree is expanding enormously. Now the suggestion follows clearly. Strong liberal arts colleges should, as indeed a number have, enter master's degree work in the most commonly taught fields of the liberal arts and sciences. Such programs should be organized to prepare people to enter junior college teaching or, for that matter, lower division undergraduate teaching. Colleges that elect to organize such a program must, of course, realize that their students with research potentialities will not elect to take a master's degree in a liberal arts college. Once this is understood, faculties in such colleges could provide well-designed graduate programs, have the enjoyment of offering graduate courses, and contribute to solving a most serious problem.

The need for improvement of college teaching is being well established. The insights that can come from the professional study of higher education are increasing in range and intensity. The climate within and without the academy seems favorable. A well-thought-out cooperative effort between those in the academic fields and in higher education might take at least a small step toward better teachers in better colleges for the benefit of better students, who will become better adults.

PART FOUR

Issues in Instruction

CHAPTER 12

Experimentation in Teaching

Even the severest critics of college teaching base their criticisms on the hope and faith that college teaching can be improved. And it is a hope and faith that all concerned with education must share, for such sentiments are fundamental to education itself. Regardless of how one views human nature—as basically depraved, needing controlling and molding, as basically good, needing only freedom to develop, or as basically neutral, taking on the tones and shapes of an encompassing culture—if one believes in education, one must believe that people can change and improve. And if students can be expected to be modified or to modify themselves, the same expectations hold for their teachers.

Such a hope for change in the practice of the profession of teaching is given credence by the fact that other professions have changed their modes of practice to accommodate newer social demands. The American legal profession has turned from solo practice to the organization of law firms in which a number of specialized talents can cooperate and eventually bring competent legal service to larger numbers of people. In order to provide high quality medical care with increased efficiency, doctors are turning increasingly to group practice in which various members play individual roles, the sum of which will add up to a better medical care program than the doctors could provide individually. There is now a national society working to promote group health plans that eventually might be expected to cover the country, affording in reality a national health program on a private basis. In such group practice, much time is saved by staggering the load and keeping doctors busy during their working hours by avoiding duplication and by eliminating lost motion. Even the military profession has modified its time-honored notion that every officer can do everything and has created two relatively discrete categories—generalists and specialists—and has tried to arrange suitable career plans and education for each.[1]

Hope for change is also provided by the fact that presently defects that were once regarded as unchangeable defects in human beings are being modified. For example, a hereditary defect that limited the growth of the central nervous system and always proved fatal has turned out to be controllable by the regulation of diet during the essential period in the early life of the child. Through what might be called physiological aids—including mechanical devices such as glasses or hearing aids and the newer biochemical agents—previously uncorrectable biological inadequacies have been accommodated with attendant enrichment of human life. And an entire range of environmental aids now appears possible. It now appears that such things as intelligence, once believed to be biologically fixed, can be changed radically through modification of poverty of the environment. It is quite possible that the intelligence level of an entire nation can be increased as a result of growth in symbolic complexity of modern urban life.[2]

But the possibilities for change and improvement of college teaching are even more plausible if one ponders the full implications of recent theories or experimentation with college learning. In one experiment at Syracuse University, three classes in social science were

[1] "The Professions," *Daedalus,* Fall 1963.
[2] Gardner Murphy, "The Abilities of Man: A Summing Up," in *Higher Education and the Abilities of Man* (Burlingame: California Teachers Association, 1964).

selected by means of a rough measure of what could be called authoritarianism. The same instructor, who knew that he was dealing with selected groups but did not know the basis on which they were selected, taught all three classes. During the semester he encountered the most difficulty in working with the section composed entirely of highly authoritarian students. They were apathetic, conforming, unresponsive, and completely disinterested in the course. Finally, in desperation the instructor adopted the radical technique of acting more authoritarian than any member of the class. He out-hated them regarding Jews, Catholics, foreigners, socialists, and Negroes. By consistently playing this role, he literally forced an entire class out of an unhealthy stance. The result of the experiment showed that while authoritarian students in all other sections of this multi-sectioned course earned D's and F's, the authoritarian students in this one section out-achieved even normal students and earned C's, B's, and A's. Now here is an example of a type of student frequently not reached by orthodox methods of instruction, who was enabled to develop through the deliberate application of a specific technique. Further, the technique was not the product of the teacher's own intrinsic personality.[3]

In another instance, a bright seventeen-year-old boy was judged by a panel of psychiatrists to be incorrigible; they judged that he should be institutionalized. His aberrant behavior disappeared within three months after he was subjected to a simple and relatively inexpensive sort of therapy. A well-adjusted college student who liked to swim was employed at student hourly rates to go swimming with the disturbed boy every day. Gradually the tutor's enthusiasm for swimming contagiously took with the boy and he began to relate on a deeper and at a more personal level with his tutor. With the personal strength gained from this development, the boy began to relate in more healthy terms with family, school, and the larger society. As the relationship grew, he could yield the antagonistic patterns that had ruled his life. In an effort to apply this technique to a college situation, a number of potential dropouts in a freshman class were matched with well-adjusted sophomores, each of whom agreed to establish one personal contact each week and to do something that interested him in the company of the disturbed freshman. The greater academic longev-

---

[3] George G. Stern, "New Research in Higher Education: Curricular, Instructional, and Organizational Implications," in *New Frontiers in Higher Education,* mimeo. (Berkeley: University of California, 1963).

ity and the slightly better grade-point average of these potential academic losses suggest that here again is a tool for teaching that can be learned and used with considerable effect by a college teacher.

Other studies of college students suggest that sometimes they have experiences not unlike the periods of creativity that Nobel prize-winners have demonstrated. These men were found to work in intensive spurts, after which there were periods of reaction to the great use of energy. In some classes, students seem to attend with only a small portion of their intelligence. In others, they concentrate so that they can recall almost 90 per cent of the substance of the learning experience. In these moments of intense learning, space, time, and surroundings appear lost in the very act of perceiving what is to be learned. Such peak learning situations appear to be of three general sorts. Some individuals will almost by accident become stimulated by an episode in a class and move to this intense level of concentration. Then, there are some experiences that seem to affect a large number of students. The episode may be a random sort of thing. Lastly, there are classes in which these peaks happen year after year. In each type of learning situation, students possess almost total recall even years after the episode. After each type, students seem to spend several hours simply recovering from the experience because of the drain on their energies. These episodes may be in a lecture, a laboratory, a discussion, or even while reading a book. Now if this be generally so, perhaps teachers, by decreasing the frequency of formal contacts with students but enriching those they do have, could radically increase their impact.[4]

In addition, other findings and insights from the behavioral and especially the clinical sciences suggest other ways in which teachers can modify student behavior if they are willing to apply a technique to a specific educational problem. The concept of identification can assist the teacher as he counsels with students, for students seem to be in search of a parent surrogate. The theory of ascribed and achieved roles can suggest ways by which the teacher can modify his own comportment so as to enhance a specific kind of learning in students. One teacher, experimenting with the sort of nondirective class that Nathaniel Cantor has so well described, jeopardized the entire relationship with the class by accidentally stepping out of his assumed role of a

---

[4] Lewis B. Mayhew, *New Frontiers in Learning* (Columbia, Mo.: Stephens College, 1959).

nonthreatening person into the role of a father figure. The simple remark that the class reacted as his children did was powerful enough to cause an end to conversation. And the virtues of reward as compared to punishment suggest many avenues for teacher modification. But in addition to such matters, the evidence that is piling up concerning the use of newer media suggests other ways by which teaching can be improved.

> Teaching—once simply telling, drilling, or questioning—is now seen as a complicated use of motivation, reinforcement, role playing, and other little understood psychological processes. This new awareness of the variety which is teaching and learning has been partly provoked by a desire to understand the uses of the new media. Motivations of teachers as teachers have received close scrutiny simply to understand their reluctance to accept such possible teacher substitutes as teaching machines, closed-circuit television, or video tape.[5]

If the argument can be accepted that the practice can be improved, that the judgment of critics (and, not infrequently, of students) need not be binding for all eternity, then one can investigate ways of contriving this improvement. It could well be that in education, as in war, all things are simple, but that the simplest things are the most difficult to accomplish. What, then, are some simple things that might aid in the improvement of instruction?

First is the matter of time. The way college programs are organized and the way college teaching schedules are fixed seem almost to insure that superficial learning and superficial teaching should be the rule. Students of normal ability required to enroll in five three-hour courses a semester will typically study one course well, another reasonably well, and seek to get by in the remaining three through a glib pen or tongue and native intelligence. Teachers offering three or four courses in a twelve- to fifteen-hour teaching load similarly can be expected to use the easiest techniques simply because they lack the time to contrive possibly better techniques. It is this sheer load that may well account for the predominance of the lecture and the textbook in American higher education. Then, too, expecting a polished performance forty-five times in a semester for each course a teacher handles is

[5] James W. Brown and James W. Thornton, Jr., *New Media in Higher Education* (Washington, D.C.: American Association for Higher Education, 1963).

expecting greater creativity than even the most fertile mind can provide.

Perhaps the greatest way to improve the quality of teaching would be to restrict all teachers to no more than three different courses in any two-year period. This might allow the teacher some chance to keep his knowledge at least reasonably current. Consistently, no student should be allowed to study more than three courses in any one semester. And last, especially for the verbally-oriented classes, no more than an hour and a half of formal classroom contact should be allowed in any given week. Such a scheme would allow for time to study, reflect, and possibly experience some of the essential peak learning experiences.

The resulting amount of time that would be available would permit teachers to organize their instruction to achieve explicitly understood purposes and goals. The Tyler approach to curriculum construction seems eminently rational in calling for postulation of broad goals, specifying them in behavioral terms, and then searching for relevant learning experiences.[6] But that search can be enormously time-consuming. Since time is currently not available, lectures, rather than formless discussions and rigidly structured laboratory exercises, seem to prevail. To make the point, one can ask rhetorically how a teacher might ideally organize instruction to achieve each of several objectives: (1) to develop an understanding of the capabilities and limitations of science; (2) to develop the skills essential for citizenship in a democracy; (3) to develop a consistent and satisfying value system upon which to build a mature and adult life; (4) to develop an appreciation for the good, the true, and the beautiful, or even (5) to develop facility in making research designs for studies in education. One can speculate that rationally one would not expect a lecture or a discussion to be particularly effective. But hopefully proper techniques could be found.

Such a search for relevant learning materials should demand a great deal of reflection and considerable introspection on the part of teachers. It is possible to imagine such an internal dialogue as the following: "Now I would like these students to be able to look at a painting and decide whether it has meaning for them, and if so, what.

[6] Ralph W. Tyler, *Basic Principles of Curriculum and Instruction* (Chicago: University of Chicago Press, 1950).

Now, how can I do this? Clearly if I tell them about the work, they may learn something about my own ideas and tastes, but is that what I want? Or, I could just tell them to go look and report back on what they see. But that will likely leave them frustrated, for they have few guidelines for looking which they can now apply. Perhaps what I should do is first ask them to try to 'say' something in one of the painter's media, one of their own selection. Then, we can talk about the problems they encountered in making the painter's medium talk for them. If we get that far, then we can take a look at several of their own works and several works which generally are regarded as distinguished, and talk about the differences between them. This seems such a long, drawn-out process. Couldn't I just as well show them some slides of great paintings and tell them why they are great? No, that's too easy. I can well recall when I was an undergraduate I would fall asleep in the warm and darkened room every time we had a slide lecture."

And the search ought to include talking with colleagues about the processes of teaching. College teachers, because they are apt to think of themselves first as chemists, historians, or sociologists, have in the past seemed reluctant to talk of their roles and activities as teachers. Yet, when conversation can be stimulated, as it is at summer workshops, such as that conducted by the Danforth Foundation, the subject proves engrossing and productive of many new ideas about teaching. Someone has remarked that a reason why in shortly over a half century psychoanalysis has emerged as a full profession is that analysts spent their days trying out techniques and their evenings talking or writing to their colleagues about their successes and failures.

There have been thousands of experiments dealing with methods of teaching, most of which result in no significant differences between the experimental procedure and a more orthodox one. Students and faculty generally experience a sense of satisfaction from participating in experiments but the results, as measured by standard tests, don't assign particular advantage to one over the other method. Now one conclusion would be that one is justified in restricting practice to the easy, the routine, or the orthodox. Another conclusion might be a feeling of safety that experimentation is not likely to hurt students. This being so, if there is some value in merely participating in an experiment—a Hawthorne effect—experimentation should be attempted.

And some experiments, such as those described earlier, just might yield results or insights that could become part of the standard teaching repertoire.

Styles of teaching, like other institutionalized styles of behavior, derive from the existing cultural climate. John Gardner's strictures about the flight from teaching reflect a climate in which teaching is at best underemphasized and at worst regarded as a positive evil. The same climate produces the young assistant professor who seriously claimed the desire to be regarded as a poor teacher. Such a reputation at least allows the presumption that he was a brilliant researcher. Genuine improvement in college teaching will come about only when the climate of institutions and indeed of all higher education changes. One can frankly doubt that professors will bring this change about by themselves, but one can see public pressures building up, which may force a change. It is likely that the seventies will see colleges receiving the same sort of searching criticism that secondary schools experienced in the forties and fifties.

If there should be a shift that would allow improvement in college teaching, it should be reflected in several facets of collegiate life. The first would be in the ethics of the profession. College professors, like members of other professions, maintain a set of ethical standards, but these are most revelant to the role of scholarship. Academic freedom, professional immunity from administrative pressures, tenure, faculty responsibility for the curriculum are all desirable. But oriented as they are, they do not affect the role of teacher. They don't rule on fairness of grading, being at the service of students, keeping lecture notes up-to-date, responsibility for being understood, or responsibility for effective and accurate counseling. The assumption seems to be that usually the professor is without sin and that student problems result from student failures and never from professorial failures. What is needed is a generally accepted concept of the college teacher as a member of a helping profession whose best energies must be devoted to helping students to develop. Such a concept would suggest that maximum rather than minimum office hours would be kept, that each class and each test would be an evaluation of the teacher, that student failures were really professional failures and that the college existed for students rather than for the more permanent residents.

Such an ethical stance will be possible only if collegiate administration indicates clearly and in material terms that it values teaching.

If each year the faculty became aware that excellent teachers were given substantial raises and promotions even at the expense of the research, the administrative or the entrepreneurial types, professors might see greater virtue in placing students first. If the central administration made clear by such things as classroom visits, consultation with students and discussions with faculty about teaching, even the most obtuse professor would likely get the message.

The third element is even more difficult to describe. It is attitude toward experimentation in teaching. There are several institutions which in every recent study have been described as high impact colleges which seemingly make a difference in the lives of their students. For the most part these institutions can be also described as experimental colleges which have long had the tradition of trying out new ideas. These are not necessarily the prestige institutions. In fact there is a slight suspicion that some of the so-called great institutions make their most important contributions simply by attracting students who would prosper no matter where they went.

Coupled with a favorable attitude toward experimentation should be a favorable attitude toward data about students. In the past, although there are indications of change, collegiate institutions have kept poor financial, personnel, space, or student records. Only if a self-study in preparation for accreditation is to be made are data compiled concerning library use, careers of graduates, scores on national tests and the like. Yet from such information concerned faculty members can tell a great deal about how well they are doing their teaching. Consistently low student scores on the area tests of the Graduate Record Examination, consistently different grading patterns of teachers in different sections of the same course, or consistently low use of the library might well be taken seriously rather than rejecting the results as being based on possibly fallible instruments.

And lastly would be the matter of listening to students. This is not to argue that students should have a voice in making educational policy. On this issue the argument is still moot. It is to suggest that students, as consumers of education, have quite clear ideas as to when and how they are or are not receiving what they want. If each member of a faculty and administration would make a deliberate effort to tap student opinion once every several weeks and then ponder the results, a radical change in education could possibly come about.

CHAPTER **13**

Curricular
Analysis

The establishment, operation, and evaluation of the curriculum ought to be one of the central responsibilities of collegiate faculties and academic administration. It is the vehicle through which the institution seeks to make its most significant impact on the lives of students. It is the organized total of courses, programs, sequences, and their directly related activities that is generally codified in the college catalogue. Yet student testimony does not assign a high value to the curriculum as such. In institutions as varied as Stanford, Antioch, Michigan State, Harvard, and Cornell, other factors are judged of greater worth. Nor are faculties and administrative officers at all sure of how to comprise a curriculum and how to analyze and change it. In many respects curricula, especially those for undergraduates, just grow in response to the organic needs or desires or interests of the individual members of the faculty as it is constituted at any one time. As generations of faculty move on, their

188

memories are perpetuated by the continued catalogue listing of the courses that reflected their individual tastes and styles. It may be that this is as it must be—that there can be no curriculum other than the expressions of faculty interest and talent. But such a premise runs counter to an equally strong conviction that education is, or should be, a rational process. And it is disputed by the serious efforts collegiate administrators make to modify the curriculum.

Perhaps the most widely used technique of curriculum study, other than the administrative review process by which new courses are each year added to the aggregate, is a self-study. Whether it be mounted in response to requirements of an accrediting association, to the offer of philanthropic dollars or to an internal feeling of a need for change, the self-study provides an opportunity to talk about the curriculum. The general pattern is to divide a portion of a faculty into a number of committees, one of which is the curriculum committee and another is a committee on objectives, or purposes and goals. Those committees meet, talk and circulate reports which eventually are bound and become the self-study report. The committee on purposes is supposed to establish the philosophical charter that governs what the curriculum committee decides should be the content in the years ahead. Since committees are talking simultaneously about all parts of the college, it sometimes happens that radical change does suggest itself. But more frequently, since a curriculum does involve vested interests of quite personal significance to power blocs within the institution, the self-study becomes a political action of a conservative sort.

A modification of the full self-study is a specific focus on the curriculum with a few ad hoc committees charged with preparing a set of recommendations for later consideration by the full faculty. Knox College recently undertook such an effort with the aid of an outside consultant. Members of each committee prepare position papers, which are then debated and finally reconciled by a steering committee. Out of this gradually emerge broad policy statements that the college can endorse. In the Knox effort, the first decision was to accept a growth in institutional size as a necessary prologue to curricular reform. But again the mode of analysis is discussion and the method of action is political.

A less frequently used approach, but appealing for its directness and simplicity, is the use of an outside consultant. In one institution the president had been able to develop the physical plant and the financial structure but had been unable to stimulate the faculty to look at the curriculum. He invited a consultant who spent much time with departments and divisions and who then suggested the composition of the curriculum and the ways by which the faculty might prepare itself to offer the curriculum. Another institution secured a small foundation grant to support a panel of consultants with the stipulation that the college would implement whatever curricular recommendations the consultants suggested. Here, of course, the validity of the study rests with the wisdom of the consultant and the effectiveness of the changes with the amount of faculty respect he can command.

In another college, which also experienced faculty reluctance to ponder its curriculum, the board of trustees organized itself into working committees and attempted to recommend curricular structure. Using staff support from a director of institutional research and the critical insights of a panel of consultants, the board committee on the liberal arts attempted to establish policy guidelines on the assumption that the faculty would later implement them. Their scheme possesses the obvious advantage of appropriate power but the clear danger that the faculty will be suspicious of whatever a board would suggest. Further, the board committee, regardless of the dedication of its members, simply cannot spend the enormous amount of time that conversation about a curriculum entails.

One college elected a unique form of curricular analysis that made a different use of a panel of experts. First, a staff officer prepared a profile of the college and its supporting community. This was submitted to a panel of professors from off-campus, who were asked to indicate what courses and programs should be offered. The reasoning was that the experts, not affected by local community pressures, would be able to make a more objective appraisal of what really should comprise the curriculum.

Using a different sort of panel, W. W. Charters attempted to base the curriculum of Stephens College on the needs of college-educated women. He asked several hundred women to keep diaries of their activities. Then, he classified and codified these into nine clusters, which became the structure for the curriculum. The courses developed were intended to speak to the actual behaviors of women.

Similarly looking to the needs of people, the role and scope study[1] of the higher education system in Florida sought, with the aid

[1] Unpublished reports of the University of Florida, Florida State University, Florida A. and M., and the University of South Florida, 1962–63.

of economic and social analysis, to find what kinds of vocations the state of Florida needed. This information was then used to indicate the broad diversion of curricular responsibility for each of the state's public institutions. Each institution was supposed to develop its program and courses in the light of what the actual vocational needs of the various professions seemed to be. Many of the locally controlled junior colleges have developed their curricula in the same way. Courses or programs for whatever subjects the supporting community requests will be offered. The trick is to determine what a community actually does want, for it is obvious that any aggressive faculty member can generate some expression of interest in almost any subject. Further, the difference between a verbal expression of interest and actual utilization of programs is often quite remote. Thus, extension courses in engineering science are demanded by a local industry but not used by the people they were intended to help.

A more sophisticated approach to curriculum study is represented by a Columbia University study of general education. A faculty committee was appointed and a distinguished sociologist was granted released time to provide the staff work. He looked at general education as it was practiced in several similar institutions, the problems his own college had faced in the past, and the changed conditions of higher education throughout the nation. In the light of all of this, the committee made a series of recommendations, which then became the subject of faculty debate. Generally such monumental studies have provided more guidance for other institutions than for the campus that sponsored the study. The Harvard report, *General Education in a Free Society*,[2] made the concept of general education respectable but did not affect the Harvard curriculum substantially.

The history of the Harvard report underscores the most widely used device for curriculum construction, that is, what is being done elsewhere. A dean of a new college first collects catalogues of colleges that he regards as similar to his own and then constructs his curriculum based on normative averages. Or, a new course or program is described at a conference or in a journal article and immediately adopted by other similar and frequently dissimilar institutions. Within junior colleges, courses and programs on data processing, and within liberal arts colleges, honors programs seem to have evolved in this way. Although the United States does not maintain a ministry of education,

---

[2] *General Education in a Free Society* (Cambridge: Harvard University Press, 1947).

curricular practice is powerfully uniform, largely, one suspects, because of the propensity for colleges to emulate each other. David Riesman likens the collegiate enterprise to a snake with each portion of its body seeking to catch up with the portion in front. Snake-like movement frequently means that the head, middle, and tail are at approximately the same place at the same time, or that as a middle institution reaches the position of the head, the head has changed direction again. Riesman's worry is that the head usually doesn't know where it is going.[3]

Contemporary practice thus suggests that discussion, political activity, judgment of experts, emulation, and search for social needs are the prevailing methods of curricular analysis and development. There are, of course, refinements. St. Andrews College uses a panel of experts to talk with faculty about new courses. Faculty committees are taken to remote places to discuss seriously their curricular problems. The Danforth Workshop on Liberal Education is an effective agency in this regard. Teams from twenty-five colleges are brought to Colorado Springs each summer for three weeks of intensive shop talk. But such a workshop fosters further normative curriculum building. What is done at one place seems attractive to professors at other institutions.

Although generally not actually used as a basis for curriculum analysis, several significant attempts have been made to develop a theory of curriculum. Perhaps the most widely quoted are the insights of Alfred North Whitehead, who emphasizes the rhythm of education and its cyclic quality. He sees the stages of romance, precision and generalization following one another throughout life and setting the form and substance of each level of education. Thus, the infant first enjoys the romance of new objects for himself, then moves to precision as it clarifies perception of objects, and then to generalization in the form of language to classify objects. For those who continue beyond secondary school, the college or university course represents a period of generalization and the spirit of generalization should dominate the university. Courses should assume familiarity with details and should not bore students by forcing them to go over once-studied specifics. The function of the university is to enable one to shed details in favor of principles. But this does not suggest a prescribed curriculum for everyone. Whitehead sees at least three curricula—literary, scientific and technical—and by implication, subdivisions of these. But each

[3] David Riesman, *Constraint and Variety in American Education* (Lincoln: University of Nebraska Press, 1956).

should stress at the college level the generalizing function. Throughout *The Aims of Education,* Whitehead suggests approaches and even modes of teaching various subjects. Thus, he justifies, if one teaches Latin, reading of much Latin literature in translation. But at no time does he present justification for including one course over another.

John Henry Cardinal Newman also has things to say about the curriculum. But aside from arguing that theology has a key place in a curriculum, that a university should contain all branches of knowledge, and that students should not take too many subjects, his theories are of scant help to one who would build a curriculum. Indeed at one point he urges that if he had a choice between a university that stressed a wide range of subjects for all students and one that did absolutely nothing save tolerate students to live together, he would opt for the latter. He does, as did Whitehead, believe that a college subject should emphasize generalization, or in his terms, philosophy, and that one subject should relate to all others. He further saw a three-way division of subjects into God (Theology), Nature (Science), and Man (the Humanities or Literature). But as to which subjects within Science and the Humanities students should take, his theories provide no help. Really his lectures are more a guide to the structure of a university and a guide to teaching than a guide to the precise formulation of a curriculum.

A more recent formulation is that of Ralph W. Tyler, who argues that the objectives of education are value choices beyond which one can not go.[4] They are conditioned by such things as the needs of society, needs of individuals, and the laws of learning. But if a college develops a set of objectives that differ radically from those of another institution, there is really no way of validating one set against the other. But once objectives are stated there is a clear way of converting them into curricular form. First, they must be specified into descriptions of actual behavior, then realistic learning experiences must be found that produce the desired behavior, and then these experiences must be consolidated into patterns or courses. To Tyler there are appropriate and inappropriate ways of achieving objectives and the effective curriculum is the one that best achieves whatever objectives are set for it. By implication, Tyler would argue that the first and most difficult step in establishing a curriculum is deciding what goals should

[4] Ralph W. Tyler, *Basic Principles of Curriculum and Instruction* (Chicago: University of Chicago Press, 1950).

be sought. Once there is agreement on this score, the rest of curriculum construction is an engineering problem.

It is really in perfecting the engineering of the curriculum that several other contemporary theories address themselves. Paul L. Dressel, who stands in direct continuation of Tyler's emphasis on behavioral outcomes, sees ten problems that must be solved if a curriculum is to be viable. The gap between liberal and vocational education must be bridged; course and credit-hour structures must be loosened; common experiences must be provided; continuity, sequence, and integrity should be insured; fewer blocs of subjects should be the rule; courses should be more infused with psychologically sound learning devices; values should be considered; preoccupation with the West should be curtailed; better learning facilities should be created; and costs should be considered. As a tool to solve these problems, he uses a set of conservative limiting principles, such as a fixed proportion of work to be taken in common by all students, to establish curricular limits. Then, within those limits he would have the faculty, following a Tyler sort of analysis, decide what the content of courses should be.[5]

Earl McGrath ends up with a similar set of limiting principles through a somewhat different mode of analysis. McGrath, looking at commonly accepted desirable outcomes of undergraduate education, finds that achievement of those outcomes bears little relationship to the number of specific courses a department offers. But the number of courses is related to the cost of education. Hence, for economic reasons he arrives at a concept of a limited curriculum, the content of which can be changed as conditions change, but the size of which must remain constant.[6]

But there are other, less engineering styled, theories of curriculum. Father Robert J. Henle, S.J., identifies five different approaches to reality, each of which must be given curricular statement. The humanistic approach deals with concrete reality. The philosophical approach is an activity of pure reflective intelligence working upon actual experience. Science also is a descriptive of pure intelligence but it acts upon interrelationships of facts. Theology, of course, does not deal with the empirical world but with certain kinds of non-empirical data.

[5] Paul L. Dressel, *College and University Curriculum* (Berkeley: McCutchan, 1968).
   [6] Earl J. McGrath, *Memo to a College Faculty Member* (New York: Teachers College, 1961).

Mathematics is a discipline of pure intelligence, which develops a purely fictional world of intelligible entities related in certain ways to the physical world. To order these into a curriculum requires a theory of knowledge based upon personal experience with ways of knowing. To select from among the five and to balance the effort, Father Henle suggests several principles. Subjects should reveal the ultimate meaning and explanation of human life and reality. Courses should provide a personal experience for each approach to reality. Courses should relate the student to his own environment and prepare him to live in his own culture. Courses should be included because of the magnitude of their possible impact on students, and courses should be selected which produce personal insights at basic points.[7]

Father Henle's Roman Catholic orientation has a secular counterpart in that of Philip H. Phenix who seeks to provide meaning for people. The criterion for human nature is that human beings discover, create, and express meanings. And meanings possess various dimensions. First is that of experience, which refers to the inner life or life of the mind. Then there is rule, logic, or principle, which allows for categories of things. A third dimension is selective elaboration, which allows an unlimited combination of meanings. And the last dimension is expression or communication.[8]

Meanings can be divided into realms, which in turn become the structure of the formal curriculum. First is symbolics, which comprise language and mathematics. Second, empirics include natural science. Then, aesthetics contain the arts, synnoetics embrace personal knowledge, ethics includes more meanings, and the sixth realm, synoptics, refers to meanings that are comprehensively integrative. Since the available knowledge is so great in each of these realms of meaning, the prime task of the curriculum builder is to select from this richness that which should comprise the curricular content. Phenix suggests that all content should be drawn from recognized disciplines, exemplify representative ideas of disciplines, reflect and reveal characteristic methods of inquiry, and appeal to the imagination of the student.

But there are other, more casual but nevertheless supported, theories of curriculum building. The first really abdicates responsibility

[7] R. J. Henle, S.J., "Objectives of the Catholic Liberal Arts College," in J. Barry McGannon and others, *Christian Wisdom and Christian Formation* (New York: Sheed and Ward, 1964).

[8] Philip H. Phenix, *Realms of Meaning: A Philosophy of the Curriculum for General Education* (New York: McGraw-Hill, 1964).

for the content of the undergraduate curriculum by tailoring the courses to be offered to fit the requirements of the graduate school, or in the case of junior colleges to the demands of four-year institutions. This method assumes that the end of education is professional competence and that the responsibility for preparing people for such roles rests with specialized schools and departments. The undergraduate years simply provide students with those skills and that knowledge that will make work easier at the next stage. Were this rationale not so widely practiced to mention it seriously would almost be a caricature. But hundreds of liberal arts colleges are tempting financial ruin following just such a theory.

The second is a much more thoughtful approach, which is based upon Dewey's pragmatism. This holds that there is really no finite body of information. Rather, knowledge emerges and evolves as individuals seek to accommodate their conception of reality. Thus, there should be no formal curriculum. Rather, there should be students and faculty in close proximity. As students discover what they wish to study they find an appropriate teacher and chart a course of action. In the past the curricula of Bennington and Sarah Lawrence were based upon this conception. It was also reflected by James Madison Woods, who argued that Stephens College had no curriculum but rather 2,000 curricula—one for each young woman enrolled in school. The most eloquent contemporary spokesman is Harold Taylor and the most visible manifestation is the idea of the free university.

Now, any systematic theory of curriculum can likely result in a better educational program than can undirected growth not based on some theory. The very act of thinking through the content of education in terms of a set of presuppositions and premises forces conscious choice. Whether one translates abstract objectives into behavior, or selects from specified bodies of knowledge, or even tries to intuit what students really want when they express a desire for a given experience, the results will probably be a clearer, more effective education. Hence, in one respect one could argue that once a theory has been adopted, whether by chance or temperament, the biggest curricular problem has been solved.

But while a theory of the sort described can result in a logical theoretical curriculum, to put it into effect requires the solution to other theoretical problems and some quite serious practical ones. First among these is the criterion problem. How does a liberal arts college with limited resources decide, from among the enormous variety of subjects that could be taught, the ones that actually should be? The most generally encountered criteria may seem realistic, but also non-rational. To use the demands of a graduate school, the interests of individual faculty, the drawing power of courses, or the existence of attractive text material seems to deny that a curriculum can possess an internal logic and consistency. But each such element must be considered.

Allied with the criterion problem is the matter of setting limits on a curriculum in the face of the increase in knowledge. How does one decide what to drop when an infusion of non-Western material into the curriculum becomes necessary? Or how close to the frontiers of an expanding subject should undergraduate courses be kept? The significance of this problem can be judged by the fact that some argue that physics is moving so rapidly as a field that no college not a part of a graduate school should even teach physics. The professors are just not sufficiently abreast of new developments.

Then, there is the political problem. Given the premises of academic freedom, of professorial privilege, the pedagogical importance of a professor's enthusiasm for a subject, and departmental power over course offerings, how does a theoretical curriculum actually become a reality? In a few recently created institutions some effort was made to develop a theoretical curriculum before the faculty was appointed. But as quickly as the first professors arrived, the theoretical ideal was modified. Or, a group of division chairmen, working together for a summer in isolation from the campus, can create a structure, but once the faculty starts to discuss it, such matters as the possible displacement of individual faculty members, fears about budgetary hurts, and even alumni pressures become operative.

Related to the political problem is the administrative one. The two sources of official academic power are the central administration and the faculty. The central administration is in the position of being able to visualize a curricular total. But the faculty is generally given responsibility for curricular decisions. Thus, a central administration can know that an unbalanced curriculum is a serious financial drain on the entire institution. But the administrative trick is to manipulate the faculty into taking some action on the basis of this knowledge.

Just to arrange a system which utilizes departmental thinking, a college-wide committee structure, and the knowledge of administrators is a problem for which there has as yet been found no ideal solution.

While these and kindred problems cannot be solved in the absolute, a start can be made, as starts have been made for other, equally complicated human activities, by accumulating information. Just as the natural sciences rested upon detailed observation of nature, so should an educational theory derive out of an observation of specifics. Until the present, college faculties have not really possessed much real knowledge about the many factors that impinge on a curriculum. The idea of institutional research is really not very old. Now with this concept and with improved techniques of social research and with improved information systems, it would seem possible to obtain a great deal of information as to how the curriculum actually is working. Then, one must have faith that a faculty, faced with quantities of information, will be able to make more rational decisions about the curriculum it offers.

Consider how faculties might react if each year they were provided with such evidence as routine cost accounting of each course, department, and division, brief regularly written reports by lay advisory committees, yearly reports of alumni reactions to the various courses, periodic polls of student opinion taken throughout the year, yearly assessment of sophomores and seniors on standardized tests, and brief résumés of significant social and curricular developments. The argument here is that this is the stuff of which eventual curriculum theory must be molded. Information of this sort could approximate for the general faculty the insights that previously have been the province of the Whiteheads and Newmans.

CHAPTER 14

General Education

Ⓖeneral education, broadly defined as that portion of formal collegiate education specifically designed to affect the nonvocational life-style of the individual, is in a paradoxical situation. There is considerable evidence that it is decreasing in importance in the collegiate curriculum and that this tendency could continue to a point of extinction. This point of view is reflected in Jacques Barzun's observation of a half-dozen years ago that the liberal arts college (by which he meant the liberal or general components of the undergraduate college) was either dead or dying. He noted the spread of the advanced placement testing program and the enrichment of high school courses and speculated that secondary education would absorb the general education function. The downward drift of specialization in the undergraduate years would eventually result in the col-

lege serving in essence a professional or specialized preprofessional
mission.

Such a conviction is given validity by several developments.
Some institutions have reluctantly eliminated cores of general education courses and replaced them with introductory courses in disciplines
simply because of the staffing problem. Young professors have been so
thoroughly indoctrinated with the virtues of graduate work and disciplinary concentration, and the market has been so favorable, that
they will not accept a position in a college that expects them to teach
general or interdisciplinary courses. One university, which created a
separate college to offer general education courses to be taught by the
best minds on the campus, found that by the second year of full operation most of the courses were in fact being taught by part-time faculty,
faculty wives, or quite elderly professors, so near to retirement that
they no longer responded to the stimulation of the departmental jungle.

One way of accommodating lip service to general education
and pressures for specialization is the tendency to label so many courses
as satisfying general education requirements that no integrated educational experience even for a plurality of students is possible. To suggest
that Introduction to Business, Economics, Principles of Sociology, and
Social Psychology are of equal value in achieving social science outcomes of general education strains even the most flexible of logics.
This tendency seems especially characteristic of junior colleges, which
must accept many students with little or no success in academic type
courses, yet which must, because of state law, include general education in the experience of those who will receive an associate of arts
degree. It is also characteristic of state colleges and universities, which
prepare large numbers of teachers who need general education in their
records to obtain state certification. But it seems also to be true of such
institutions as private universities with long histories of concern for
undergraduate students. Each revision of general education requirements provides for more substitution of specialized courses in the name
of greater flexibility to accommodate individual differences.

During the 1950's, the general education movement generated
perhaps the most vital literature of any concerned with higher education. Journals such as the *Journal of General Education, Journal of
Higher Education,* and the *Basic College Quarterly* were filled with
discussions of new courses, approaches to teaching or the objectives of

general education. Conference proceedings, anthologies of course descriptions, and a number of monographs and research reports added volume, and frequently insight, to this literature. At present, however, the *Journal of General Education* seems more preoccupied with quite precious belles-lettres than with curricular problems and the renamed *University Quarterly* seems headed in the same direction. It has been seven years since the American Association for Higher Education has sponsored a book on general education; and annual workshop proceedings from such places as Catholic University or the University of California at Berkeley seemed preoccupied with governance, federal relationships, or freedom and order. It is true that a book about general education won the distinguished book award in 1966,[1] and Towson State did publish proceedings of a conference on general education.[2] But the frequently quoted materials are all a decade or more old.

Underlying this neglect, of course, is the growing preoccupation of higher education with graduate and professional work and research. Almost a third of all liberal arts colleges now offer graduate work, frequently as a ploy to aid in faculty recruitment. Within the university, professors assume that a standard load should be one advanced undergraduate course and a graduate seminar. Lower division work is left to teaching assistants or to a person of the same level called an *instructor*, one must assume for public relations purposes. The goal of undergraduate education, even in institutions for which it is inappropriate, is preparation for graduate school. This phrase has almost become the touchstone for curricular respectability and acceptance. Courses win approval if they are judged vital to a student who will go on to graduate school.

Most institutions are encouraged in this stance by the practices of prestige institutions, which, regardless of releases from public relations departments or speeches of their presidents, seem quite complacent with their specialized undergraduate programs, their 85 per cent of graduates who attend graduate school and the research orientation of their faculties. Their prestige is such now, although clearly this was not always true, that they can be so selective that their students could

[1] Daniel Bell, *The Reforming of General Education* (New York: Columbia University Press, 1966).
[2] Kenneth J. Hallam, *Innovations in Higher Education* (Baltimore: Towson State College, 1966).

and do either educate themselves or come already well along in such development. While in the wake of student unrest some major universities have begun to restudy the dimensions of undergraduate education, one is left with the impression that the forces of specialization and departmentalism emasculate ringing committee recommendations by the time faculty action is taken.

But there is another side to the question. Regardless of these regressive tendencies there is still a lively interest in general education and the outcomes of liberal education. Each year the Danforth Foundation conducts a workshop for representatives of twenty-five colleges. And each year at least half of these institutional teams elect to work on problems of general education at their institutions. Characteristic of many institutions is the statement of the delegates from San Jose State College for the 1967 workshop. This statement suggests both the interest and concern as well as some of the critical issues that must be resolved.

The problem we should like to explore at the Danforth Workshop is, simply put, "What should be the nature, scope, and function of general education at San Jose State College?"

Implicit in this simple statement is the fact that there is general dissatisfaction, on the part of the faculty and student body, with the general education curriculum as it currently exists. As presently constituted each student, by requirement of the California State Education Code, must complete 45 semester units distributed by formula among the areas of Natural Science, Social Science, Literature, Philosophy and Arts, Written and Oral Communications, Psychology, Physical Education, and electives.

To implement this legislative requirement the College has established lists of courses which meet each area requirement and the student, under advisement, selects courses from the several categories which combine to satisfy the State mandate. It should be noted that, due to dissatisfaction with this system, the College has in recent years embarked on two experimental programs in general education. A two-year integrated Humanities Program is made available to some students selected from the top ten per cent of the entering freshmen, and an even more selective group of students are eligible for participation in a Tutorials Program. Neither experimental program is available to the average student so, while these experimental activities seem to make a valuable contribution to the general education curriculum, the overall problem of improving an unimaginative, mechanical, and perhaps irrelevant general education program remains and it is to this overall problem we should like to address ourselves at the Workshop.

In its thought toward improving the general education program the faculty has not formulated specific criteria to guide the work of the Danforth Group. Even so, the tenor of the faculty seems clearly to be that:

It does want several patterns or routes by which students can meet the general education requirement, some if not all of which could involve interdisciplinary inquiry and activities;

It does want to provide continuity of educational experience, and therefore some depth as well as interdisciplinary breadth, in the general education programs;

It does want to use the general education programs to capture and involve the student in academic life, to put him in more intimate intellectual contact with at least some of his professors; all of which implies

It does *not* want "one" general education curriculum which, in effect, expresses an educational philosophy that the sum of X number of courses, selected from Y number of predetermined disciplines, yields an academically defensible approach to general education.

In this sense, and at this stage of our institutional thought, the Danforth Group from San Jose State College would welcome the opportunity to examine, with colleagues and consultants at the Workshop, alternative answers to the general question "What should be the nature, scope, and function of general education at San Jose State College?"

Then, too, when institutions make self-studies, as have several major universities following the eruption of student unrest, the discussion and reports typically stress the values of general education. Columbia, using a one-man committee, asserted its interest through Bell's *The Reforming of General Education*.[3] At the University of California, the Muscatine report urged the creation of new general education courses;[4] Harvard's Doty report reaffirmed belief in general education objectives and attempted to suggest ways by which they could be contrived.[5] Stanford's study of undergraduate education seems destined to

[3] *Op. cit.*
[4] Charles Muscatine and others, *Education at Berkeley* (Berkeley: University of California, 1966).
[5] Unpublished faculty report.

reassert the institution's concern with the liberal or general education
of students. While there can be considerable doubt that many recommendations will be enacted into academic legislation, the fact of the
interest is significant.

And relatedly, while the nature of general education requirements has changed, the amount has not. Indeed, Nelson-Jones gen-
eralizes that between 1955 and 1965 there has actually been an increase in the size of general education requirements.[6]

Much of this sustained interest in general education results
from student demands and expectations. Students, reared in an affluent and secular society, are asking that their education be relevant and
that it speak to their real concerns as human beings. When the university fails to make courses relevant, students have had recourse to
free university sorts of courses and have thus forced faculties to insti-
tutionalize more broadly conceived and integrated sorts of courses.
For example, consider the following courses, described in a free university catalogue:

> *All About the Draft*—An introduction to the workings of
> the Selective Service System. No prior knowledge about the draft
> is necessary, but any expertise will be welcome. Ideally we might
> all learn to be competent draft counselors; on a personal level
> we can at least learn new ways to relate to our own Draft Boards.
>
> *If You Want to Know the Taste of Water*—An extensive
> series of Zen meditations for the serious student. Each student is
> expected to do daily meditation on his own as well. Students are
> also expected to participate in whatever retreats and all-day med-
> itations that may be offered.
>
> *Sexual Morality Now*—Among the young these days most
> of the traditional moral questions are no longer even questions.
> Few, for example, would find anything worth discussing in the
> question of whether unmarried people should make love or
> whether teen-age girls should be provided with birth control pills
> if they want them.
>
> But the new climate of permissiveness raises as many ques-
> tions as it answers. For example, should (or can) a person love
> two people at the same time, and if one does, can one eliminate
> possessiveness and jealousy by sleeping with both at the same
> time (*i.e.*, in the same bed and at the same time)? The demand

---

[6] Richard Nelson-Jones, *General Education in American Higher Education, 1955–56 to 1964–65* (Stanford: Unpublished doctoral dissertation, 1967).

for exclusivity in love relations (*i.e.*, serial polygamy) has resulted in enormous problems, but is inclusivity a feasible alternative?

We will consider problems of tribal (group) "marriage," and the morality of orgies (e.g., should one know and/or love everyone in a group before making love with the group?). Is bisexuality where it's at? And perhaps the most interesting question of all, what do you do after you are married?

Suggested reading: Alexander Lowen, *Love and Orgasm,* Robert Rimmer, *Harrad Experiment,* Alan Watts, *Nature, Man and Woman.*

Compare the preceding course descriptions with the following.

Indeed we would recommend the immediate endowment of one or more ad hoc courses (with or without credit) in which professors might be able to supply the relevant scholarly and intellectual background to matters which had aroused the immediate interest of significant elements of the student body. In the last year, for example, courses on "The Idea and Uses of the University," on "Vietnam," or on "Literary Censorship" might have lent intellectual resonance to subjects of active student concern. Such courses might be given either by individuals or by groups.[7]

The general education implications of student concerns is well revealed in such statements as:

What I want is a world where people are free to make the decisions that affect their own lives, a world in which they're not trapped on a vast merry-go-round of concealed power, not forced into situations where the choice is already made for them. I want a "participating democracy" where I, for one, am involved in the working of the system I'm living in. I want a non-exploited system in which no one's making money off another man's work. I want people to be happy too. More than anything else I want a world where we're free to be human to each other.

I feel the university could be a fantastically exciting place in which to begin to create this kind of society. It's the only place that places a premium on skepticism, on questioning. But I'd like to see the university in the society, rather than be a function of society to come to grips with the problems we have to face today. I don't think the university does that but the potential is there.[8]

[7] Muscatine and others, *op. cit.*, p. 128.
[8] C. M. Katope and P. G. Zolbrod, *Beyond Berkeley* (Cleveland: World, 1966).

In a sense what that student is asking for could be translated into the goals for general education, lists of which were developed during the late 1940's and early 1950's.

T. R. McConnell, for example, writing in the *Encyclopedia of Educational Research*[9] held: "The purpose of general education is to enable men and women to live rich and satisfying lives and to undertake the responsibilities of citizenship in a free society. Although general education seeks to discover and nurture individual talent, it emphasizes preparation for activities in which men engage in common as citizens, workers, and members of family and community groups."

Ralph McDonald added another dimension with his argument that "the goals of the general education program must be realistic. They must be conceived in terms of the behavior of the individual student. They must focus clearly upon the attitudes, capacities, abilities, and values which are expected to be built into the lives of students. Furthermore, the goals must point directly to the elements in the heritage of free, Western, democratic society which are considered to be the common possession of college trained people. The ultimate test of the success of all general education can be had only in the evidences of constructive living on the part of those who have been reached by the program."[10]

The conventional wisdom of the profession regarding general education was well summarized in the report of President Truman's Commission on Higher Education with such goals as:

1. To develop for the regulation of one's personal and civic life a code of behavior based on ethical principles consistent with democratic ideals.

2. To participate actively as an informed and responsible citizen in solving the social, economic, and political problems of one's community, state and nation.

3. To recognize the interdependence of the different peoples of the world and one's personal responsibility for fostering international understanding and peace.

4. To understand the common phenomena in one's physical environment, to apply habits of scientific thought to both personal and

[9] Walter S. Monroe, *Encyclopedia of Educational Research* (New York: Macmillan, 1950).
[10] Ralph W. McDonald, "Fundamental Issues in General Education," *Journal of General Education,* October 1949.

civic problems, and to appreciate the implications of scientific discoveries for human welfare.

5. To understand the ideas of others and to express one's own effectively.

6. To attain a satisfactory emotional and social adjustment.

7. To maintain and improve his own health and to cooperate actively and intelligently in solving community health problems.

8. To understand and enjoy literature, art, music, and other cultural activities as expressions of personal and social experience, and to participate to some extent in some form of creative activity.

9. To acquire the knowledge and attitudes basic to a satisfying family life.

10. To choose a socially useful and personally satisfying vocation that will permit one to use to the full his particular interests and abilities.

11. To acquire and use the skills and habits involved in critical and constructive thinking.[11]

The paradox of course is clear. If students want something like what was called general education and if the colleges and universities could codify goals which were so similar to what students wanted, why then is there serious question as to the vitality and viability of general education? And the answers are equally clear although prescription is much more difficult. General education in the undergraduate college has lost respect and vitality for several reasons.

In spite of impressive purposes and goals stated for general education, the level of implementation has frequently been low. Poor teaching of arid materials, distant in idiom and substance from the concerns of students, alienate students regardless of the virtues claimed for courses. A History of Civilization course that attempts, chiefly through lecture and textbook reading, to cover the outstanding facts of the history of the West is not likely to be welcomed by students beguiled by the claim that the course seeks to explore man as a creative being. The student expecting to experience the thrill of participating in science is not likely to respond well to the young teacher of biological science drilling for taxonomic memory. In too many colleges and universities general education courses were viewed as just so many obstacles to be overcome on the road to a degree. And too many courses

[11] President's Commission on Higher Education Report, *Higher Education for American Democracy*, Vol. I, December 1947.

are taught as was one, in the Humanities, in which the professor lec-
tured so rapidly and dealt with such a range of materials that students
claimed that if they dropped a pencil they lost a full century.

In part this poor teaching is a result of the operation of the
reward system, at least in major universities. Since World War II the
availability of funds has allowed a research climate to develop in which
the greatest professional and financial rewards go to those who do research, consult, and of course publish. At one major university, when
full professors met to discuss who should be promoted, one professor
judged that while teaching excellence should not be held against a
candidate, certainly the school should never seek to justify promotion
on the grounds of teaching or counseling with students. A major staffing problem for general education is to persuade faculty members to
leave their departments, even for a year, to teach general education
courses. To do so jeopardizes continuity of research grants and consulting assignments, which have done so much to make college teaching
almost an affluent profession.

And the graduate school is in part to blame. Graduate education has become the acme of higher education and probably with some
good reasons. The American Ph.D. is well respected and has been
maintained generally at a high level of quality. But so great is the prestige of graduate work that individuals and institutions are tempted to
enter it at the expense of concern for undergraduate instruction. Currently institutions originally created as undergraduate teaching institutions are driving inexorably to become graduate centers of excellence.
Faculty members, many of whom have no real research talents, want
to teach graduate students, and one must suspect, enjoy the light (one
or two course) teaching load that graduate work seems to imply. And
of course the presumed nature of graduate study shapes the undergraduate curriculum. If graduate work is viewed as being highly specialized and with a research orientation, then it follows that students
should have acquired the basic tools of inquiry and the basic knowledge of a subject in the undergraduate years. Thus the undergraduate
curriculum must stress those disciplinary courses required by the graduate departments, rather than offering courses of indigenous worth to
students.

Since the majority of American college students receive their
collegiate education in large institutions they must experience bureaucracy in all of its impersonality. Thus far Western society has not in-

vented any better way of dealing with large-scale enterprise. And because the largest number of students must be accommodated during the years when general education is typically offered, bureaucracy operates in its most impressive way—and, to impressionable late adolescents, in its most oppressive way. In the minds of students and faculty, general education comes to be synonymous with the vast, impersonal bureaucracy. Courses listed in the time table or class schedule seldom mention the name of the person teaching sections. Indeed a student is a statistical aberration if in two successive terms or semesters of the same course, the lottery of registration grants him the same teacher. Thus the undergraduate sees general education courses as offering perhaps considerable service but precious little love. His resentment at the bureaucracy is displaced toward general education requirements. And professors feel the same way. Professors, although there are of course major differences among individuals, enter college teaching because they are individualistic, solitary workers who like ideas rather than people. Their experience in graduate school has suggested the ideal model of a professor, working on the frontiers of knowledge, who teaches his own course in his own style. Somehow teaching a staff-prepared course, with perhaps a stylized outline, from a cooperatively selected text, is repugnant to the faculty member and represents bureaucracy at its worst. Thus we are confronted with the situation of both faculty and students seeing in general education courses the worst excesses of a large-scale knowledge industry. The obvious distaste of course carries over into performance.

And such resentment is given plausibility if general education courses are subject to caricature. In the early 1950's, courses stressing personal adjustment were in vogue. In spite of commendable objectives, courses on effective living, personal and marital adjustment, and the like seemed to exemplify the worst of progressive education and to violate dreams of a college experience concerned with the good, the true, and the beautiful. The negative halo effect this created carried over to all required courses to such an extent that "man and" courses or "comp" courses were equated with Mickey Mouse or Rinky Dink —to use the idiom of students.

Although faculties would like to be more involved in governance—as would some students—the American experience assigns the most critical role to administration. And faculty administration must be blamed for some part of the low estate into which general education has frequently fallen. General education involves one of the most difficult tasks of education—that is, to motivate students to like something for which they have no natural inclination. Administration, not unlike parents, must contrive ways of involving students in forms of their cultural heritage that ultimately will be essential if the culture is to be preserved, but for which late adolescent students have at that time little taste. To do this demands a sense of purpose and a resolve that taxes the moral stamina of most deans and presidents. A dean may know that at least a fourth of student time should be spent on the fundamentals of his heritage, but in the face of student apathy and antagonism of faculty who would rather teach the narrow subject that interests its various members, it is just easier to give in. One of the most pathetic sights is to see a dean who has finally lost the battle to the forces of specialism and student resistance to what they need, who has rationalized the decision as in a way strengthening the general education program of the institution.

But even the most well-intentioned dean and faculty committee can err in how general education sequences are organized. Increasingly it is clear that late adolescents need quite specific sorts of experiences if they are to optimize their personal development. Very likely the seventeen- or eighteen-year-old needs experiences that will provide for expansion and enrichment of his impulse life through such courses as literature, philosophy, the fine arts, and even the philosophy of science. Yet this fact appears foreign to the logic of the mature person who feels that the tools of disciplined inquiry are of first importance. Thus the first year general education requirements consist of Rhetoric, Foreign Language, and perhaps Fundamentals of Mathematics or of Natural Science. To the student who wanted some chance to understand the forces in him which he could scarcely contain, such disciplinary courses are thin fare and he retreats from them either actually, or figuratively, by going through proper motions but without fundamental intent to assimilate what has been provided.

Then there is the invidious impact of science on the entire curriculum. Science is by its nature cumulative and persons must first acquire one level of understanding before moving on to the next. But other parts of the curriculum are not of this nature. It is quite possible to handle the first course in Shakespeare without having had a course in Elizabethan drama or the history of the English language. The history of the Old South can really be handled without broad surveys of American and English history. One does not really need American government before entering International Law. And courses on urban sociology, once one grasps the peculiar language of sociologists, can be taken before, after, or simultaneously with principles of sociology. Yet the power of the science model is so great that the entire curriculum is organized as though sequential treatment were mandated by natural law. Thus in general education courses students are expected to master some materials before getting to the big questions that perplex them.

Already implied is one of the great problems that general education has not overcome. That is, of course, the power of departmentalism. In a sense the way this operates is one more paradox. Departments, especially in larger universities, are research-oriented yet are composed of professors who really need, in a deep psychological sense, to teach. Departments want to be represented in general education requirements so that they will register their share of students. One can suspect that the inclusion of foreign language requirements in forms which can never bring about facility in a language are the best example of departmental desires affecting general education requirements. But other fields can be equally guilty. At present, in spite of an age of science, a good case could be made that science is less important than other subjects—say administrative law or economics—for the general education of students. But the faculty that would eliminate a science requirement would precipitate a veritable Verdun.

At least two other matters should also be mentioned. One is the economic fact of life that a budget confers power, status, and influence. In all save a few institutions, budgeting for general education is not treated separately but is assumed to be the responsibility of departments. Such a stance places too great a temptation in front of faculty members and so the lesser sums are made available to general education. One of the main reasons that general education in an institutionalized form has persisted at Michigan State University is that President Hannah wisely provided for a separate dean with a full budget and with definite staff position.

The second is the influence of accrediting agencies, which with sometimes misguided zeal have made the virtue of general education into a dogma. It is possible for some schools to serve society quite well just by developing specialized skills and talents. But because accreditation requires general education, institutions must at least make a gesture, whether or not they have the requisite resources. A half-hearted attempt is probably worse than no attempt and in the end serves only to discredit the entire concept.

Eventually these conflicting strands must be reconciled. There is need for something like general education. Yet there are major obstacles to providing it. Now one recourse is to accept the Barzun thesis as inevitable and turn the undergraduate college into a school of specialization. But the virtues of some form of general education are so persuasive that some other option might at least be considered. It probably is not proper that specific courses or materials should be prescribed for all institutions, although the temptation to do so is great. Rather a search should be made for some broad principles that will allow general education to flourish, if the will to have it flourish is present.

First, there should be a recognition that there are differences in types of institutions and that the substance of general education for one type would not be appropriate for another. The highly selective, developed private university faces different problems than the open-door junior college and these differences should be reflected in requirements.

Second, claims for the values of general education should be made more parsimoniously than has been customary. A good case could be made for the simple purpose of general education of developing in students the ability to read, write, and speak about the major domains of knowledge with a reasonable facility. This could be accomplished and without creating impossible hopes in the minds of students.

Third, it should be remembered that general education is intended to provide a common universe of discourse for people living in the last half of the twentieth century. The idiom of what is studied should be the idiom of that century. Too frequently the idiom of past generations has been stressed with a resultant rejection on the part of students. Eventually of course some of the major documents of the culture must become part of the individuals' intellectual equipment. But there is time for that to come, if motivation is first generated. And motivation requires acceptance of the idiom.

Fourth, it should be accepted that a college or university is a political organism and those in it should be willing to use political techniques to gain their goals. Indeed it is possible to organize colleges so that the powers of the faculty and administration are brought into tension so that creative energy can be released. Presidents especially should be encouraged to assume greater leadership and greater willingness to use political technique.

Lastly, and this may be impossible, while being the most critical, the power and influence of graduate study and research must somehow be reduced—at least in the large majority of institutions in which it is not really effective. It might almost be worth a retrenchment of federal support of research if the hundreds of junior colleges, liberal arts colleges, state colleges, and a number of state universities could operate free of the status system which says an institution is not of front rank unless it stresses graduate study and research. John Gardner tried to say this in his concept of excellence but failed. Perhaps the time has come to stress that excellence—real excellence in undergraduate education—is perhaps of greater worth to the society than even the excellence of university research.

PART FIVE

The Shore Dimly Seen

PART FIVE

CHAPTER 15

Preparing for
the 1980's

The future of American higher
education cannot escape the setting in which it will find itself. Barring
major war or severe economic recession, the outlines of American society for 1980 are reasonably clear. There will be upward of 230 million people as compared to the 180 million in 1960. More than half
of these will be under twenty-six years of age and over twenty-two million will be over age sixty-five. Nearly 80 to 85 per cent of that population will live in urban areas and a third of the nation's total population will live in ten such supercities as the continuous metropolitan belt
from Boston to Washington or from Gary, Indiana, well into Wisconsin, or from Mobile past New Orleans. Half of the total living in the
cities will live in complex suburban areas while the other half, including a disproportionate number of nonwhites, will occupy the central
city. Those people in the work force will average 30 or fewer hours

per week at work and will earn an average income after taxes of $8,724. This compares with the $6,285 which obtained in 1962.

And the broad educational context is also of relevance. Children enrolled in kindergarten through grade eight will number 31.5 million in 1975 over the 23.9 million in 1965. There will be 15 million high school students in 1975 compared with the 6.8 million in 1955. The 2.7 million fall enrollments in degree work in college for 1955 will reach 9 million by 1975 and perhaps 12 million by 1980. Graduate enrollment, which has become the fastest growing segment of higher education, will reach 1.1 million by 1975 and perhaps 2 million by 1980 (a number just over the total collegiate population in the mid-1950's). The large majority, perhaps 80 to 85 per cent of these students, will attend public higher education and a good three-fourths of them will attend institutions of over 20,000 students. Institutions of higher education will have increased annual expenditures from the 4 billion dollar 1955–56 figure through the 11.4 billion 1965–66 outlay to 22.5 billion in 1975–76; capital outlay over the period 1966–67 to 1976 will be over 30 billion dollars—this compares with the entire Gross National Product of 56 billion in 1933.

Such a vision of society can be frightening—especially to those of us who lived through childhood in small towns, sleepy suburbs, or farms, who attended college in the small liberal arts colleges of three to five hundred students that dotted—and for that matter still do dot—the American landscape. But we can no more escape this vision than we can escape the reality of atomic power, jet airliners, or automation. They are the facts that must govern the future development of higher education and they are the forces with which we must contend if we are to modify in any rational way the shape of higher education.

It is now quite possible, given the present observable tendencies, to predict reasonably well what higher education will look like in 1980—which is really just around the corner. But it should be remarked that such predictions are only extrapolations and could conceivably be invalidated if we the people wished to make the effort to change conditions or traditions. But, to the future. There are at least six domains about which safe predictions are possible. The first is the structure and organization. It seems quite clear now that the various states will create supra-institutional boards of control to insure more economical use of tax money and to insure that the full educational mission for the state is provided for. In 1958, only ten states had such boards; in 1968, only ten states did not have them. While a few states, especially in the Midwest, will drag their feet in the belief that state-wide control and coordination are detrimental to institutional crea-tivity, and at least one Southern state may perpetuate the sheer an-archy that characterizes the organization of higher education, most of the states will create some form of organization that will allow for dis-tribution of function. The prototype is, of course, California with its junior colleges, state colleges, and university. Just in the past three or four years this pattern has come to prevail in most state master plan-ning and it seems likely that the plans eventually will be put into effect. Even Minnesota, with its long tradition of maintaining only one uni-versity and some teachers colleges, now plans junior colleges, state col-leges that may come to offer the doctorate, and the university with at least several branches.

Generally these institutions comprising a state system will be of large size. The various campuses of the University of California, Illinois, and Missouri will average 25,000 to 27,000 students and such institutions as Michigan State, Minnesota, the City University of New York, and New York University will range between 45,000 to 65,000 students on a single campus. It is true that some junior colleges in out-lying places will remain small and the universities and state colleges in states having a stable, static, or declining population will not reach enormous size, yet even these may well double their present enrollments just because of the shifting complexion of the population to a condition in which the school-aged population is in the vast majority. The typical undergraduate students in 1980 will attend colleges or universities that average 20,000 students.

While the largest institutions will be publicly supported, even the private institutions seem likely to seek economies to scale by grow-ing in one way or another. Some will actually expand their own en-rollments, with much of this expansion done at the graduate level. These trends seem to be especially true of private universities located in dense urban areas now, as is Boston University. But smaller liberal arts colleges will also double their size, partly in order to obtain needed tuition money. Others, however, will grow through the process of merger. The once-discussed union of Vassar and Yale is only a little behind the actual merger of Case and Western Reserve and the possible mergers the growing number of associations of colleges make possible. Still others will grow by virtue of a change in mission coupled with the infusion of public funds. The University of Kansas City and Temple University each experienced pronounced growth once they became state affiliated.

Although definite evidence is not yet available, there is strong presumptive reason to expect a major expansion of the higher educational efforts of noneducational institutions. The recent mergers of publishers and large manufacturers indicate a belief on the part of corporation leaders that a large educational market is on the horizon. Federal funds for education are likely to become available for profit-making organizations. In 1962 some twenty-five million people were enrolled in some form of adult education with some 56 per cent involved in classes offered by noneducational institutions.[1] There are those who believe that private industry can offer some of the services required from higher education more effectively than can nonprofit schools and colleges.

Clearly the federal government is going to be increasingly influential in the support and even in the conduct of higher education. Universities fully expect the amount of research done by typical faculty members to increase to between a third to one-half of the work load and that this will be funded in large measure by federal funds. Responsible administrators of distinguished private universities see some form of sanitized direct federal support of institutions as being the only way private higher education can remain viable. Recently, ten private universities pooled previously confidential budget information for a composite report designed to show the Secretary of Health, Education, and Welfare just how critical was the plight of private higher education. At this moment it is impossible to predict the precise forms through which federal influence will be exercised, but the profession seems to be asking for direct institutional grants, some form of tuition relief, especially for graduate students, continuation of project contracts, and marked increases in funds for facilities. The idea of a national board of education or of elevating education to cabinet level is for the moment quiescent but one must assume a reconsideration of some such notion if the federal financial involvement increases at expected rates.

In 1965, partly in an effort to create a third force that would temper the centralization of effort that federal programs implied, con-

[1] John W. C. Johnstone and Ramon J. Rivera, *Volunteers for Learning* (Chicago: Aldine, 1965).

siderable attention was given to the compact of states. Although it is now a thing in being, there is no evidence that it, or similar structures are being seriously viewed as of much influence. When institutions mention external organizations that affect their planning and, of course, their growth, the state coordinating agencies and the federal government are the only two that appear relevant. And there is good reason why this is so. Major influence in such a complex undertaking as American higher education requires major financial resources. Presently any of several hundred universities have larger operating budgets than does the compact and it does not seem likely that states, pressed as they are with drastic demands for more building and expanded university budgets, will increase contributions to requisite levels for real power.

Secondly is the matter of programs and curricula. Clearly graduate work will become even more significant in the total higher education effort. As the bachelor's degree becomes more and more common, some other educational criterion for the purpose of ranking and sorting people is required. Presently the master's degree is emerging as that symbol. Virtually every developing institution anticipates rapid increases in master's level work in the arts and sciences and as well as the creation of new problems-centered master's for such issues as resources control, urban problems or museum curatorship. An emerging new mission is that of retraining people at a professional level and the master's degree is seen as an appropriate indicator of such retraining. A good example is a one- or two-year program leading to the Master of Business Administration for people whose bachelor's degree in engineering is five or ten years old. While doctoral work will clearly expand and many more institutions will offer the doctorate than do at present (the developing institutions all anticipate approval of doctoral education) the changes in the nature of the degree and its relative significance are not likely to be as profound as those related to the master's. Here it should be observed that while the press has given considerable attention to the ABD degree, graduate deans and faculties don't really expect this to materialize as an important symbol. Probably the automatic certificate of candidacy of the University of Minnesota will be around but it will signify little.

While doctoral work will be much as it is now, considerable change can be expected in several professional fields. Medical education, for example, is in for major reorientation, with perhaps two principal elements being stressed. The first of these will emphasize more and more precise diagnosis, using not only biochemical tests but computer-based diagnosis as well. At present in several university hospitals a more precise diagnosis can be made before a patient actually sees a doctor than if the doctor collected the medical history and made his own synopsis. As a counterforce to this dehumanization of practice, medical education will move clinical experience into the first year of medical school, probably having first-year medical students actually serving in community storefront sorts of clinics.

Administration, whether it be business, public, or educational, is coming to be viewed as essentially the same and as being rooted in the social and behavioral sciences. While it is not likely that vested interests of existing schools of education or business will yield their independence, newly created universities will develop schools of administration which will accommodate a variety of concentrations. And even in existing schools one can predict some form of rapprochement between educational, business, and public education.

Engineering has possibly been more self-critical of its educational effort than most professional schools and continues this stance with a new study of goals. But in spite of this it is less easy to predict trends for engineering than for other fields. Some institutions see engineering as a graduate program with the first professional degree being the master's; but others, responsive perhaps to practical demands from employers, insist on going back to a four-year bachelor's program with a considerable skills emphasis.

Education is generally viewed as a growth industry and will very likely expand several of its programs in response to clear statements of public policy. By 1980, schools of education will typically have major programs on preschool education, compensatory education, educational problems of the central city, and higher education. Since education looms so large in the future of the society, institutions that previously have refused to offer work in education are now planning to do so. A few existing schools of education are planning to become solely graduate schools concentrating on research and preparation of research workers, but the large majority, even those in comprehensive universities, anticipate a continuation of teacher and administrator preparation as being a major mission.

Other professional fields are also changing, but the big four suggest the dimensions of the sorts of things anticipated. The real enigma is the future nature of undergraduate education. Clearly there is unrest. Clearly there is study of the purposes and goals of undergraduate education, and clearly there are significant experiments with new sorts of programs, but no pattern seems to be emerging. In large universities the powers of departmental faculties seem undiminished and are exercised to tailor the undergraduate courses to fit the needs of intense specialization. And the departments in smaller schools follow the lead of scholars in major universities. But there is talk of and interest in new sorts of interdisciplinary courses—frequently influenced by the free university style of course. There is some feeling that specialization, especially in the professional fields, ought to await the graduate years. There is some awareness that some kinds of remedial or compensatory education may be required within four-year colleges and universities if they are to serve an even more heterogeneous student body. At this point, however, the only responsible prediction must be that there wil be less change in undergraduate education than in other sectors. This is so partly because generally students and faculty are reasonably happy with what they are doing and getting. This notion may shock in view of the vast literature about student unrest. But a careful perusal of that literature reveals that students are really not protesting about teaching or the curriculum. It is their private lives and some of the moral dilemmas of the entire society that have them upset.

Although one cannot be sure of the undergraduate program, one can see now with reasonable assurance the nature and mission of several types of institutions. It seems clear that the large majority of students who receive the bachelor's degree will do so in comprehensive universities. These may be the older established universities, the newly created ones such as one finds in Florida or New York, or the former normal schools turned state colleges or state universities. The mix of graduate and undergraduate students in some of these may shift toward an ideal of 60 per cent upper division and graduate to 40 per cent lower division, but the number of universities that will reach this by 1980 is limited. Junior colleges, in spite of claims of apologists that they will provide the lower division work for the majority of those seeking a bachelor's degree, seem destined to serve another mission. In Arizona, for example, the creation of junior colleges scarcely affected the expected increases in freshman applications for four-year institutions. Arizona seems an especially good state in which to study this, for 97 per cent of its students are in public higher education. Junior colleges by 1980 will probably have concentrated down on the three

functions of providing some higher education for that segment of the
population that previously never aspired to any higher education, of
providing considerable technical-vocational training, leading to immediate employment, and of providing a great deal of adult education
for what is really becoming an educating society. Whether such a
mission is accepted in theory, in practice it is almost a certainty.

The future shape of private liberal arts colleges is much less
clear although some trends do seem to be emerging. Of those which survive, most will double in size during the next decade. The two hundred
some odd institutions that presently offer master's programs will be
joined by an equal number that see master's work as a means of satisfying faculty and meeting such emerging social needs as the preparation of junior college teachers. Some of the weaker colleges that previously served a junior college function for students from a limited
geographic region will be forced to close as soon as they begin to compete with public junior colleges. But by 1980 this number does not
appear to be large. After 1980, when the building programs of state
systems of higher education have been completed and when the effects
of the presently declining birthrate become operative on higher education, a different story may be told. It also seems likely that the single
sex institutions will for the most part have gone co-educational in one
form or another. There will be some, especially Roman Catholic wom-
en's colleges, that will serve only one sex, but the trend illustrated by
the Vassar-Yale conversations, the Colgate plans, the projected mergers of such pairs of colleges as St. John's and St. Benedict's, and the
Princeton announcement seem reasonably clear and inexorable.

The third domain is that of students and while these words may
return to haunt, several clear-cut tendencies seem to be appearing.
The first is an increase in the discontinuities of college attendance.
There was a time when, in popular stereotype at least, attending college was a four-consecutive-year experience. The high and steady 50
per cent dropout rate was assumed to be normal. Now it appears that
in many of the large state universities a graduating class of 30 to 35
per cent is typical but that by a decade later 65 to 70 per cent of that
freshman class have graduated with a bachelor's degree from some
place. There also seems to be emerging a pattern of students changing
types of institutions for financial or other personal reasons. A family
finds four years of high cost private education too expensive so allows
a child two years at a public and two years at a private institution

with the election of which two years are spent at what type of institution quite optional. Then, too, the Peace Corps, Vista, overseas experience, and, of course, military service provide an increasing number of options that allow students to discontinue their formal education for a period of time.

A second trend is implied by the very real concern of students over the private sectors of their lives. Much of the protest literature and many if not most of the complaints one hears on campuses have to do with institutional infringement on activities that students regard as private. Except in the most custodial institutions, then, one can expect a gradual reduction of institutional regulation of student hours, eating and sleeping arrangements, inter-room visitation, and regulation of personal conduct. So marked is this trend that institutions building residence halls now should plan them so that coeducational or even cohabitational residence living would be possible by the closing decades of this century. Private apartments near campuses already make this a de facto arrangement. The matter of making such arrangements *de jure* is merely a question of time. The conditions of urban living for which most students will have experienced a taste, personal freedom during periods of interruption of formal education which will be increasingly the rule, and a fundamental shift in social notions of standards of personal conduct—all combine to force a new ethic. The only conjectural point is how long individual institutions will resist embracing it.

A third and related facet of the domain of students concerns the role of students in governance of the academic or professional functioning of higher education. Again, at the risk of running counter to the prevailing conventional wisdom, there is little evidence that the vast majority of students want or would accept responsibility for the governance of higher education. A few somewhat older militant students demand a voice in all manner of things from the selection of a president to acting on the curriculum. But by and large students are not protesting how the educational part of the college is being run. The students at Berkeley were reasonably well satisfied with the education they were receiving. And even those who do criticize the educational part of their collegiate experience seem to be asking for instant insight rather than the chance to do the hard grubby work of contriving a curriculum. One also gets the impression that a number of students who have been quite demanding for a voice in governance are not really students in the sense of carrying full course loads. Rather a new breed of professional student has emerged who is somewhat older than average and who spends most of his time as a quasi-administration person. All of this leads to the conviction that student significance in actual governance is not likely to be greater than it presently is.

Finance is a problem that, were it not so significant, should better be left until comprehensive basic research has been done. But a few observations may even now be made. First, it seems clear that unless new sources of funding are found, virtually every private institution in the country will be doing deficit financing every year from now on. Some of the major institutions with large endowments will be able to maintain this rate for a number of years. But other less well-backed institutions could follow the pattern of the University of Pittsburgh before 1980. Tax-supported institutions, while in considerably better condition for the future, also can expect serious financial problems, especially as they seek to construct the new facilities needed to accommodate the anticipated increases in enrollment. State and local tax sources are beginning to weaken and one can anticipate a number of failures of bond elections and legislative curtailment of spending rather than increased sales, income, and property taxes. The state of New Hampshire, for example, recently placed the university in a serious situation when the legislature refused to pass either a sales tax or an income tax. Now currently a great many schemes have been proposed to solve the financial riddle. The tax rebate plan has the support of some of the small private colleges as well as considerable support in Congress. The full tuition payback through income tax deductions seems to be attracting a good bit of favorable attention. Institutional grants are favored by a number of universities but the scheme runs into difficulty when institutional quality becomes involved. Extrapolation from the recent past suggests that the most likely massive form of federal aid will be in some form of direct assistance to students thus allowing tuition to rise to the level of full cost of instruction. This belief is supported by the fact that direct aid was made possible for some undergraduate students a good six or seven years earlier than theorists believed possible in the light of the congressional ethic regarding character debilitation of undergraduates if they were paid to go to school. Although a number of theorists have urged some Americanized version of a University Grants Committee to allocate support of institutions, present evidence does not support a contention that such a transplant would work.

The fifth domain is as sensitive as the financial one and once again the evidence and speculation are unclear. There have been the National Education Association reports, which indicated acute shortages of faculty in the future. And there is Allan Cartter's speculation[2] that the shortages, although somewhat real in the past, will soon be rectified, and by 1980 there could even be a surplus of Ph.D.'s. If present expectations of institutions are realized, there must be acute shortages well into the 1980's because university leaders expect a fairly steady decrease in teaching loads to a point where a three-hour load is regarded as normal. Further, if junior colleges should attempt to upgrade their faculties to as much as 20–25 per cent Ph.D., the shortages could well become much more severe. Quite possibly after 1980 the newly developed Ph.D. granting institutions and a stabilized enrollment will result in a balance between supply and demand. But until then one must expect the market for college teachers to be reasonably tight. That administrators believe this to be true is evidenced by the general anticipation that faculty salaries will continue to rise at rates of 5–7 per cent a year through at least the early part of the 1970's and possibly beyond.

The sixth domain is that of teaching and it is in this area that utopian thinking seems farthest from emerging reality. Utopians see computer-based instruction, multimedia classrooms, automated learning carrels, computerized information retrieval systems all an essential part of campus 1980. And there is considerable experimentation going on, especially in some of the professional schools. But the typical faculty member in 1969 who is in his middle forties gives not the slightest impression of entering the wonderful world of new media. It has been twenty years since television burst on the cultural scene and one does find more television being used than in the 1940's. But if such a simple device to adapt to educational purposes has taken that long to move into not the main but the side educational stream, it does not seem likely that more complicated technology will find any readier acceptance.

This is the vision that is now coming into focus. The implications are clear. Higher education can take a determinist position and

[2] Allan M. Cartter, *An Assessment of Quality in Graduate Education* (Washington, D.C.: American Council on Education, 1966).

assume that since these developments seem inexorable, they must be accepted. Or, it can accept that the major strands are fixed but some modifications are possible. Or, it can take predictions for what they are, that is, extrapolations from an existing set of circumstances that can be invalidated if it cares. Clearly, this last is the more healthy and creative option. If it is accepted, several immediate steps are indicated.

1. Higher education must examine every technique of education from the traditional concepts of what work is academic to the values of the doctorate in the preparation of college teachers and be willing to reject those which cannot be warranted.

2. Higher education must invent new ways by which private and public institutions can relate to each other and still preserve the pluralism that has been the glory of American higher education, and this includes finance.

3. Higher education must become more specific than ever before as to why the society should support it and utilize its services. If it does this and acts on the findings, the future pattern could be much more different than present trends suggest it will be.

CHAPTER 16

The Future of Higher Education

The future shape and substance of higher education to at least 1980 can be reasonably predicted in broad outline by examining its recent past and by observing developments that are presently taking place. Such an exercise is occasion for both faith and despair—faith in the pragmatic quality of the institution which has enabled it to solve so many vexing problems, and despair that on a few critical matters, emerging responses are so far from the ideals of its spokesmen. At this point it is difficult to determine which sentiment will ultimately prevail.

No analysis of higher education should ever be made, especially analyses leading to extrapolation into the future, without the perspective of the unprecedented successes of higher education in solving the enormous problems the supporting society has presented it since the end of World War II. Indeed it can well be argued that higher education has been too successful. This has led people to expect too much

from it. At the root of much student protest is frustration that colleges
and universities do not serve well as a church, clinic, sanctuary, or
arbiter of all social values. But these successes are of significance not
only for the achievements they signify but also as indications of what
is to come. Social institutions function in many ways like biological
organisms. Successful experiences are perpetuated and unsuccessful
ones extinguished.

Consider what has been accomplished during the last two
decades:

The veteran enrollments were accepted and accommodated
and a new conception of financial aid added to the culture. Current
efforts to find ways to channel even more massive amounts of federal
funds into higher education are made in the shadow of P.L. 346 and
P.L. 16 (G.I. Bill of Rights).

Those born during the post-World-War-II baby boom have
been and are being provided collegiate experience on a scale and at a
cost undreamed of in any other society, including the Russian, indeed
undreamed of in the United States until the veteran experience suggested what could be done. College enrollments have jumped from
1.7 million in 1940 to 3.2 million in 1958 to almost 7 million in
1967–68.

Faculty salaries, once it was recognized how seriously under-
paid college teachers were, have increased by almost 100 per cent since
1958. Professional salaries are now competitive with almost all other
professions and the end of increases is not yet in sight.

The Sputnik-inspired demand for academic rigor has been met
with increasingly stringent admissions standards and an increasingly
demanding undergraduate curriculum. The two-century tradition of
extension of curricular material downward into lower levels of education has been accelerated through such techniques as the Advanced
Placement Programs, the new high school curricula in sciences and
mathematics, and the paperback book.

Much to the chagrin of some, the apathetic generation gave
way to a quite unsilent one, whose concerns for values are so acute
that the present student generation could set a new stance for the entire society. Student activism was sparked by the civil rights movement
and its present expression is a search for a value system, capable of
rejecting war as an instrument of politics. Young protesters were taught

in American schools and colleges that may have succeeded too well in inculcating liberal beliefs.

The public policy statement of President Truman's Commission that at least 50 per cent of all high school graduates could handle and should have some collegiate education has been achieved and a goal of almost universal higher education (for all youth save the severely mentally retarded) became a foreseeable possibility.

The temporary dilution of the training of college teachers, occasioned through the effort to meet demand, is being rectified and during the decade of expansion the proportion holding the doctorate increased from 41 to 51 per cent.

The strong vein of Know-Nothingism in the American character finally gave way, in part, of course, due to the precepts of Pope John; and ways have been found for the religiously related and secular institutions to cooperate and eventually to receive some kind of support from tax sources. The future, of course, will not be all smooth, but it is by now clear that church-related colleges must and will have tax support.

Higher education, once the luxury of the upper and the intellectual middle classes, has now achieved the status of a major—perhaps the major—instrument of national policy to be used in solving the most critical of domestic issues.

The one-time almost complete lack of information about higher education as a social institution has given way to the flood of research-spawned evidence. Most institutions either have or are planning to have offices for institutional research or institutional planning. And the publication of books about higher education is increasing enormously.

The Manhattan Project and other war-inspired liaisons between the federal government and the intellectual community provided the prototypes for such intense research cooperation that some even fear a new power elite has been created consisting of government-military-industry and the university.

These things have taken place and must constitute elements of any picture of the future we draw here. But there have also been some failures. An ideal of a democratic society is diversity of institutions to accommodate pluralism of belief. And while this value is proclaimed, in reality institutions seem to move toward a mean, becoming more like one another. The increase in the proportion of students educated in public institutions is at rates of about 2 per cent a year, and it is possible to anticipate a time when not over 10 per cent of all students will attend private colleges or universities. Thirty per cent of liberal arts colleges now offer graduate work and the teacher's college is almost a thing of the past, and this is the fate, too, of separate men's and women's campuses.

Colleges have attempted to solve the riddle of a general or liberal education for undergraduate students, but the forces of parental desire that students be trained for a vocation, the specialism of even liberal arts departments, and the lack of appeal general education really has for students have been too powerful. The general education movement of the forties and fifties has faltered and attempts to reform the movement have generally not been widely adopted. The free university sort of course now seems to have been a momentary phenomenon and undergraduate faculties are in search of a new mission. While Barzun's thesis may not yet be validated, that is, that the undergraduate college is either dead or dying, the interesting experiments to revive or perhaps recreate a viable undergraduate mission have as yet not been sufficiently accepted to make prognosis hopeful.

Colleges have heard the argument that other professions have innovated and been able to extend better service to more people at less cost. But as yet higher education has either not found the proper innovative devices, been reluctant to use them if available, or been too insensitive to opportunities for innovation. Cost of education has tripled while enrollments have doubled. Typically those institutions, with a few notable exceptions, which have emphasized new patterns of instruction have been regarded by the pacesetting institutions as not being quite respectable. And for various reasons, some of which are not quite compelling, the most visible of the experimenting colleges, Parsons, was exiled. That experiment was contaminated, but there can be real question as to whether it was in poorer condition than other colleges re-accredited that same year.

Higher education is evolving, as do all social institutions, in response to both internal and external forces. The following pressures seem to be the operative in the expansion of graduate and professional education:

Society demands highly trained manpower. In one way or another every institution hopes to produce its share of leaders in fields significant to the society. Thus, interest is declining in theology but increasing in education and urban planning. Moreover, expansion of scholarly disciplines creates a dynamic for growth. As scholarly fields emerge, new subspecialties are created and institutions wishing to remain in the forefront of intellectual life must develop these new fields regardless of the cost. Faculty recruitment is another force toward increased specialization. In order to attract recent products of graduate schools, new specialties must be offered, especially graduate specialties, whether a balanced curriculum needs them or not. In addition, in many institutions there is a tendency for faculty pressure to mount for more doctoral work, even when such an effort would jeopardize the undergraduate mission. Presidential aspirations must also be considered. In spite of the growth of faculty power and Clark Kerr's mediator-type president, institutions still project the shadow of the president and his interests do find their way into the curriculum. Beyond the president, statewide master plans or role-and-scope studies have some impact on institutional mission and not always a healthy one. It may, of course, be that these studies simply codify accomplished fact but administrators do seem to look to such studies for guidance. Beyond the impact from the state, there is federal influence. One can agree that there has really been little overt federal control of higher education, but still see considerable federal influence. Just the availablility of funds for some purposes but not for others is enough to shape an institution's character. Then, too, political pressures intrude. The present shape of higher education in California results in part at least from the belief that political pressures have been applied. And, of course, idiosyncratic forces operate. A vigorous department head, an institution's traditions, or just proximity to an intellectually vibrant urban area help shape evolving futures.

He who would scan the horizon of the future with any degree of clarity must examine how these forces operate and understand characteristic responses. But he must also search for the more fundamental elements within the society that will ultimately be reflected in the activities of colleges and universities. In one sense the period since the end of World War II can be judged the period of the most profound combinations of revolutions of any comparable period in human history. It probably is the combination which makes their impact so powerful. These are well known and may be quickly summarized:

The information explosion has created more knowledge than

any person or institution can assimilate. The curriculum has become
so dislocated that unity becomes almost impossible. How can administrative law, computer science, Negro history, non-Western art, African
studies and economics be added to an already overcrowded list of curricular imperatives?

The fact of affluence poses several different sorts of problems.
First, how to develop people who can accept affluence when their
ethics, psychology, sociology, and economics are predicated on the uni-
versality of poverty and scarcity? Second, how reconcile the fact of
affluence with the fact of extreme poverty and then to correct the im-
balance which emerges? One could argue that the crises of Hunters
Point, Detroit, and Newark were at least in part caused by color television, two-car living, and a hedonism which a majority of a society
could afford.

The revolt of colonial peoples is, of course, related. For American education this most clearly means a search for ways of educating
segments of the society previously judged ineducable. Much of the research interest of the U. S. Office of Education seems designed to do
just that.

The technological revolution provides frequently unwanted
leisure. It has been argued that if the defense-related economy were to
falter the productive power of the technology is so great that the needs
of the society for goods could be satiated and still not need a major
portion of the work force. An extension of this notion holds that unless
people are taught to handle leisure, half of the population will have
to be kept under sedation by the mid-1970's.

The last of these critical revolutions is, of course, the weapons
revolution, which in a sense has made total war as an instrument of
national policy intolerable. Theology, demography, law, ethics, and
even the arts seem to be struggling to adjust to this one fact. And, in
a minor way, student protests about Viet Nam are not unrelated.

Such pressures and forces provide bases for inference about the
future. But the future may also be predicted by extrapolation from
observable developments and by attending to plans for the future
which responsible officials are making. These extend from the most
casual assumption that an institution will keep on doing what it has
been doing to elaborate almost utopian schemes involving automated
colleges and narco-education. Indeed the last half of the decade of the
sixties could be categorized as the time of planning. State master plans,

institutional self-analyses, commissioned studies of the future and even
conferences and speeches such as this are endemic. Now, much of
what is being discussed will not come about in any appreciable way by
1980 or even 2000. The force of cultural lag nowhere operates more
effectively than in higher education. But some things will come about:

It seems clear that by 1980 every state will have a state master
plan for higher education and some form of statewide coordination
and control. Higher education has simply become too expensive and
too significant for state government to allow it to function in the laissez-
faire manner of the past. A few voices will be raised against this with
the claim that such systems have not proved their worth. A few states
may resist, at least to the extent of having a formal structure, but without real power. But the days of institutional autonomy for at least
public higher education are numbered. And the same is very likely
true for the private sector.

It is also clear that federal involvement in higher education
must intensify. Few private universities or major state universities could
even survive in their present form if federal support were withdrawn.
And states are approaching limits of their own existing taxing powers
while the costs of higher education continue to mount. The federal
government then is the last recourse with its non-regressive powerful
tax base. The form this support will take is more difficult to predict
for higher education is divided on the matter. At this point it seems
most likely that it will involve continuation of categorical aid with
some reduction in research contracts especially for big science.

To this will be added some form of scholarship and guaranteed
loans to students but with a cost-of-education allowance for the institutions. And federal support for construction of facilities will probably
be increased. These seem more likely than any massive direct institutional grants or the creation of an American version of a University
Grants Committee. But more centralized federal policy will be needed
and by 1980 the cabinet rank for education should have become a
reality.

Whether the society needs the products or not there will be
major expansion of graduate work so that by 1980 graduate enrollments should be larger than were all college enrollments in 1952. This
is explainable by the fact that as the bachelor's degree becomes more
common, some other symbol is needed to screen people, by the fact
that retraining professional workers will be the rule rather than the

exception, by the fact that new jobs seem to require more advanced training than just a bachelor's degree, and by the fact that the society just cannot use all of the bachelor's degrees it produces. Graduate study is a socially acceptable and personally not too destructive substitute for work. And more and more institutions will be offering graduate study whether or not they have the requisite resources. Teachers colleges, turned state colleges, seriously plan on entering doctoral work. Liberal arts colleges will offer master's work, partly as a bribe for new faculty and a few in response to local pressures will enter the doctoral field. While a very few institutions will be exclusively graduate, that dream of Harper and Jordan does not seem likely to come true. Undergraduates are too sound a financial investment—almost an endowment—for universities to give them up. It is this fact alone that will negate the claims of junior college theorists that junior colleges will provide the lower division work for a majority of those who will receive a bachelor's degree. In only one state has there been a substantial drop in the proportion of university enrollment in the lower division.

Unless some form of sanitized state or federal aid is provided private institutions, the days of many are numbered and the viability of others is threatened. The major private universities have begun to encounter serious financial problems and are responding by deficit spending, using gain from investments, curtailment of programs, and intensifying search for more funds. Private universities which previously served a local clientele have now priced themselves out of the market and are attempting to find a new one. While in public their leaders sound sanguine, in private many feel that within five to ten years their institutions must join a state system. The examples of Kansas City, Buffalo, Temple, and Pittsburgh are so clear. Private liberal arts colleges are an even more serious situation. Between 1957–58 and 1967 many of these have enjoyed their most prosperous years. Salaries have increased, new building started and new programs launched. But the cost has been high and was met by doubling enrollment and tuition at a time when demand was so great as to allow this to happen. But to maintain progress, the same thing must be done in the next decade. Conditions, however, have changed. Now states have begun to assume responsibility for higher education and have or will have enough spaces so as to restrict seriously demand. Already in the fall of 1967 private colleges were reporting difficulty in filling residence halls. Now the first step which will be taken will be a reduction of standards for admission. And this won't be all bad. In a number of institutions, the accidents of demand produced a student body brighter than the faculty. But after that the future is bleak. Some will merge in a search for economies to scale, some will diversify (although this is dangerous), some will affiliate, and others will continue but by offering a less than adequate program.

Because of its uniqueness and because it is so politically desirable—and powerful—some mention must be made of the junior or community college. This, when first conceived, was to be the locus of lower division undergraduate education. Such a development did not transpire and for years the junior college served as an extension of secondary education. Since World War II, however, it has become more comprehensive in nature and claims to offer lower division bachelor's work, general education, technical-vocational education, adult education, and to serve as a center for community cultural interests. Enrollments have grown and states, in an effort to extend relatively inexpensive higher education to all youth, have all created one or more. When one examines what in fact happens in junior colleges, their future form comes clear. While two-thirds to three-fourths of all freshmen who matriculate in a junior college say they intend to transfer, not over 15 per cent actually do. Those who do seem to succeed reasonably well in a four-year institution. When one examines enrollment, a typical pattern is for the evening, adult enrollment to be larger (frequently twice as large) as the day enrollment. When one examines attrition rates one finds as much as two-thirds dropout rate between the freshman and sophomore years. All of this leads to the conclusion that the junior college will likely make its biggest contribution to the society by extending some limited higher education to those segments of the population that never before expected any, by providing vocational training for one or two years leading immediately to employment, by providing adult education as one way of helping people cope with leisure. This is what is happening. It is a commendable set of purposes. Some theorists or apologists have just not yet made it de jure.

Higher education in 1980 will be for the most part conducted in large institutions located in large metropolitan areas. While some isolated junior colleges will remain small, even they will likely be parts of a larger district, as will liberal arts colleges be part of a university created from existing consortia. The typical undergraduate, however, will attend a university of 20,000 students or more located in a city of 100,000 people or more. In some of these there will be attempts to subdivide into cluster colleges or other units designed to provide small-group experience. But one can't predict too many of these partly because the problem of departmentalism has not been solved. How command faculty loyalties from a cluster college and at the same time allow them to develop as research scholars in a department? Experience thus far suggests that departmental loyalties win and that the cluster college receives either part-time allegiance or a different sort of faculty from the university proper.

As to the shape of the curriculum, the future is unclear. Both undergraduate and graduate institutions are planning major interdisciplinary efforts but actual achievement is so limited as to make hazardous a prediction that such work will be in the mainstream by 1980. There is currently considerable interest in new problems-centered courses, programs, and even degrees. But the powers of departmentalism may prevent these from expanding because of the threat they pose to disciplines. The argument is widely heard that one cannot study urban problems, one can only be an urban historian, economist, or sociologist. The new hardware—television, computer, multimedia classrooms, and automated information retrieval systems—are all available and touted by their exponents. But the walls of academe are thick and 1980 will probably come and go with such devices still classified as experimental.

Students and student life also present an enigma. Clearly students will be made more and more responsible for their private lives. Institutions will gradually relinquish supervision over such matters as the relationship between the sexes, the use of alcohol, and student living arrangements. Indeed some institutions will not only condone co-educational or cohabitational living, as they now do, but actually provide university facilities, in the form of apartment-style residence halls to facilitate it. Students will have the potential political power to concern themselves directly in the governance of higher education. Whether they will use it is not so clear or if they use it, whether it will be done wisely and creatively. There is some evidence that the large majority of students are not really concerned and the minority that is concerned is either worried about the moral dilemmas of the society or views the university as an impossible institution which must be destroyed along with the rest of society before utopia can be achieved.

Many other things could be said. Faculty salaries will continue to rise into the early 1970's. Faculty research will become more and more attractive. Strong graduate schools will become more and more selective in the limited dimensions of academic aptitude. The college teaching profession may well be unionized in all save a few elite institutions. Large-scale testing will be even larger and more significant in the lives of students. But enough has been stated to indicate the broad directions in which higher education is moving.

Higher education will do these things and will succeed reasonably well. However, that success will be hollow and in the end lethal if it does not transcend its own past, its own evolutionary process, and its own mission by attempting to solve several imperatives. Thus far it has not, and to the extent that higher education does not modify its stance, it opens the way for destructive forces to grind colleges and universities—indeed the entire society—to a halt. This is no idle alarm. There is already evidence of the results of ignoring these cultural imperatives. When a handful of students can disrupt a major university, when frustrated humans turn cities into battlefields, and when youth can reject the fundamental values of a culture, a crisis is at hand.

Higher education will have to meet that crisis on three fronts. First, the Negro community must be helped into the mainstream of the national intellectual life. Further, national leadership from the Negro community at least proportionate to Negroes in the total population must be identified and cultivated. Similar claims could be made for other minority groups but the Negro community is so qualitatively significant as to deserve special attention.

At this point one cannot be sanguine that higher education will respond. While a few places, such as the University of California at Berkeley, have honestly called for an effort to increase the proportion of Negro students, regardless of the cost, most have done nothing. Graduate schools will accept all qualified Negro students but will not modify admissions policies to enable Negro students to become qualified. Junior colleges will not reject Negro students but will move to locations which by the sheer fact of distance deny students from the ghetto. Selective four-year colleges wish for more Negro students but use their scholarship resources for students with the best chance of survival, that is, white, Anglo-Saxon children from middle-class intellectual homes.

What is called for is a major revision of what is proper for higher education. The major universities must be willing to support Negro graduate students for a year or two years of pre-graduate work. The states must be prepared to offer massive scholarships of $2000 to $3000 for Negro youth regardless of past academic achievement and regardless of whether or not they appreciate it. The entire enterprise of higher education must be prepared to expand capacity to handle 700,000 to a million more students, for this is the enrollment which would come if proportional enrollment were to be accomplished. This effort incidentally could be financed for a year with the funds used for just one month to continue the war in Viet Nam.

Making such efforts will be no nine days' wonder. One obvious reason is that the white, middle-class, political power establishment may still be reluctant and base their arguments on the myth of who is and is not educable. This seems especially clear in the institutional stance of an unwillingness to modify admissions standards. But another, perhaps even more serious obstacle is beginning to be apparent. For a host of reasons, many in the Negro community are becoming suspicious of what might be called *white liberals*. Illustrative is the negative reaction of the Urban League to a desire on the part of one junior college president to extend branches of a college campus into lower-class areas, including some predominantly Negro and some predominantly white. The liberal leadership has been in effect told, "We can no longer trust your motivations or your sentiments." The only way such reluctance and distrust are likely to be overcome is for the predominantly white community to begin to take drastic steps, all without coercion. To name a few quite simple ones: If every predominantly white institution throughout the United States set as an immediate institutional policy the recruitment of 10 per cent of its total student body from the Negro community, without respect to formal admissions requirements, this might signify an interest in reform. If every college administrator would cause his service and social groups to extend immediate invitations to leaders of the Negro community, without respect to whether leadership was professional or not, the message might be communicated.

The research and service power of higher education must be brought to bear in a sustained way on the problems of contemporary society in magnitude similar to the nineteenth-century effort in agriculture. Thus far efforts regarding urban problems, resources, air and water pollution have been episodic, shifting emphases as the availability of project research funds dictated. As a result, no cumulative effort has been possible. In some way continuous tenured support must be provided so that men can devote their entire careers to problems-centered research and teaching.

Increasingly Americans live in urban areas and increasingly these urban areas are becoming uninhabitable for human beings. It is in the urban areas that the most critical domestic problems are more visibly manifest. It is just possible that higher education does have the talent, the potential insight and skills of inquiry that could help solve the riddle of urbanism. The solution will come only with the same sort of long-term sustained and supported efforts that made the land-grant colleges viable. This clearly requires a different conception of funding and it clearly implies a different way in which colleges organize their efforts. Presently professors are given their organizational security from the department. To do what is suggested here will require that departmental bands be loosened and new structures capable of maintaining tenured professors created. As a mild corollary, this whole concern for the urban area suggests that other cities should follow the recent lead of New York City and create new, attractive, and well-staffed colleges and junior colleges in deteriorating parts of the city. Such a decision has the potentiality of changing the character of a neighborhood if the institution will extend itself into the community.

In some way higher education must realize the fact of the upward extension of childhood into the late twenties or early thirties and make adjustments in the curriculum in custodial relationships and in the entire private sector of student life. In a very real sense some of the more militant student protests have come from students in their mid-twenties who are physically and emotionally adult but who find themselves without the full identity that comes from being economically self-sufficient. In a way they demonstrate some of the attributes of adolescence and for similar reasons. It now seems clear that students will be expected to mature earlier, as part of the emphasis on academic rigor, but to continue dependency longer. This phenomenon will require that colleges and universities must regard students with new eyes. Unless they do, these older children, adolescents or alienated, whichever term suits, can destroy and have already demonstrated the power to do so.

There must be a sense of urgency about this matter. Students who have been denied complete role fulfillment can move quickly into a philosophy of nihilism and complete despair. On a number of college campuses the leadership of some of the more militant student groups seems at present convinced that the society in its present form cannot be repaired. Some of these young people are quite ready to bring the university to a halt as well as the entire society. This fact must be coupled with the fact that the age group currently demonstrating such feelings will within the decade come close to holding the balance of political power. This will come when the majority of the nation will be below twenty-five years of age. The responsibility of higher education is clear but the techniques for assuming this responsibility far from certain. Just the first step, however, seems critical and that is for each responsible educator to test every single assumption he makes about the nature of student demands and the relevance of programs for the needs of youth.

The evolving form and substance of American higher education seem remarkably clear, but this evolution will justify faith only if these imperatives are considered the most serious of educational and social problems. And we in the academy must be sufficiently flexible to modify in major ways existing and evolving practices.

Bibliographic Note

No attempt is made to provide an exhaustive bibliography supporting the points of view expressed in this book. However, there are some works that seem so germane to the central thrust of this volume that readers might wish to examine them in greater detail.

The broad social and economic background factors against which the contemporary college scene might be viewed are at least generally indicated in three anthologies: Seymour E. Harris, *Education and Public Policy*, 1965; Seymour E. Harris, *Challenge and Change in American Education*, 1965; and Lewis B. Mayhew, *Higher Education in the Revolutionary Decades*, 1967 (all three published by McCutchan Publishing Corporation, Berkeley, California).

Analyses of college student characteristics and the concerns of college students have become, since 1964, many and varied. However, five volumes seem to have captured the essence of such matters:

243

Nevitt Sanford (Ed.), *The American College* (New York: Wiley, 1962), is a monumental collection of research and polemical reports that seem to support the developmental concept of college students. Lawrence E. Dennis and Joseph Kauffman (Eds.), *The College and the Student* (Washington, D.C.: American Council on Education, 1966), has codified what might be called the liberal conventional wisdom regarding the interaction between college students and the collegiate environment. Kaoru Yamamoto (Ed.), *The College Student and His Culture* (Boston: Houghton Mifflin, 1968), serves somewhat the same function. However, it does not duplicate the materials edited by Dennis and Kauffman. More recent empirically-based insights are contained in Joseph Katz and Associates, *No Time for Youth,* 1968, and Paul Heist (Ed.), *The Creative College Student: An Unmet Challenge,* 1968 (both published by Jossey-Bass, San Francisco). The Katz volume summarizes four years of research on students at Stanford University and the University of California at Berkeley, and the Heist volume brings together a number of research efforts dealing with creativity and the creative college student. Both books produce highly consistent findings suggestive of a need radically to reform undergraduate education.

Of histories of higher education there are many; however, John S. Brubacher and Willis Rudy, *Higher Education in Transition* (New York: Harper, 1968), seems to provide as broad a portrayal and is as insightful as is available. The contemporary permutations of the evolution of higher education are indicated in Samuel Baskin, *Higher Education: Some Newer Developments* (New York: McGraw-Hill, 1965). It describes in some detail and makes some assessments of such recent innovations as independent study, uses of the new media, and utilizing the community as a resource for learning. The fact that higher education has emerged as one of the major forces in American life is well established in Christopher Jencks and David Riesman, *The Academic Revolution* (New York: Doubleday, 1968). The book argues that the revolution consists of the success of American higher education in capturing the interests, affection, and financial support of the entire society but on terms established by the professionals within higher education.

Ideas concerning the future of the society and of higher education are codified in two volumes: the Summer 1967 edition of *Daedalus,* entitled "Toward the Year 2000: Work in Progress," and

Alvin C. Eurich (Ed.), *Campus 1980: The Shape of the Future in American Higher Education* (New York: Delacorte Press, 1968), bring together in two volumes about as much concerning the future as can be safely extrapolated. Three major issues or developments that run throughout this volume are changing concepts of student rights, the need for undergraduate curricular reform, and the emergence of graduate education as a determining force in higher education. These issues are explored in considerable detail in E. G. Williamson and John L. Cowan, *The American Student's Freedom of Expression* (Minneapolis: University of Minnesota Press, 1966); Daniel Bell, *The Reforming of General Education* (New York: Columbia University Press, 1966); and Everett Walters (Ed.), *Graduate Education Today* (Washington, D.C.: American Council on Education, 1965). There are, of course, other treatments of these matters, but these three seem to serve as the most efficient entrée into each problem.

For a year-by-year summary of monographic literature dealing with higher education, Lewis B. Mayhew, *The Literature of Higher Education* (Washington, D.C.: American Association for Higher Education), seems the most complete source containing as it does reasonably long critical comments about each book cited.

Acknowledgments

A number of the chapters in this book are based on material published elsewhere. I thank the following for permission to use portions of my previously copyrighted work:

McCutchan Publishing Corporation for material from "Campus Conflict and Confluence," in *Higher Education in the Revolutionary Decades* (Berkeley: McCutchan, 1967).

The Southern Regional Education Board for material from my essay, "The Stimulus Response," in *The College Campus 1968* (Atlanta: Southern Regional Education Board, 1967).

The American Council on Education for material from "Institutional Factors and the Learning Environment," in Lawrence E. Dennis and Joseph F. Kauffman (Eds.), *The College and the Student* (Washington, D.C.: American Council on Education, 1968).

The American Association of Colleges for Teacher Education

for material from "Curriculum Innovation," in *Frontiers in Teacher Education,* Nineteenth Yearbook of the Association (Washington, D.C.: American Association of Colleges for Teacher Education, 1966).

Improving University and College Teaching (Summer 1966) for my essay, "Contriving a Hawthorne Effect."

The White House Conference on Education for material from "Innovation in Higher Education," in *Consultants' Papers* (Washington, D.C.: White House Conference on Education, 1965).

Northeast Missouri State College for material from *General Education: A Reassessment* (Kirksville, Mo.: Northeast Missouri State College, 1968).

The Southern Regional Education Board for material from *The Collegiate Curriculum: An Approach to Analysis* (Atlanta: Southern Regional Education Board, 1967).

The State University of New York for material from "The Future of American Higher Education," in *Innovation in Higher Education* (Albany: State University of New York, 1967).

Index